S0-ACB-952

CITY AND COUNTRY IN THE THIRD WORLD

Issues in the Modernization of Latin America

City and Country In the Third World

Issues in the Modernization of Latin America

Edited by
ARTHUR J. FIELD

SCHENKMAN PUBLISHING COMPANY, INC.
Cambridge, Massachusetts, U. S. A.
London, England

The conference for which these papers were prepared was supported, in part, by grant RD-2483-G from the Social and Rehabilitation Service, Department of Health, Education, and Welfare, Washington, D.C.

The support of the A. Cohen Foundation (of New York) is also gratefully acknowledged.

Library of Congress Catalog Card #72-79679

by Schenkman Publishing Company, Inc.

Cambridge, Mass. 02138

DEDICATION

To my father, Irving H. Feinfeld,
who has made so many good things possible

ACKNOWLEDGEMENTS

The essays in this volume are somewhat revised versions of papers originally prepared for the International Symposium on Work and Urbanization in Modernizing Societies which took place November, 1967 in St. Thomas, Virgin Islands, under the auspices of the Caribbean Research Institute, College of the Virgin Islands. The meeting was funded by the Social and Rehabilitation Service (formerly the Vocational Rehabilitation Administration), U.S. Department of Health, Education, and Welfare, and by a grant from the A. Cohen Foundation (of New York).

The advice and assistance of the following is gratefully acknowledged: Edward Towle, Director of the Caribbean Research Institute; C. J. Austermiller and Stanford Gerber, formerly of the College of the Virgin Islands faculty; Sonya and David Hough, of St. Croix; Roger R. Ricketts, gentle flower child now a medic in Viet Nam; secretaries Gudy Fiondo, Florence Rivera, Sharon Gibbs, and Carol Ruhl.

CONTENTS

PREFACE

The stream of writings about the development problem facing the hundred or more modernizing nations around the world has begun to reach flood proportions, and as a desperate effort to make up for centuries of scholarly neglect, this is certainly as it should be. Another, and to some extent welcome, problem has now arisen, and that is one of finding ideas and programs which are, at the same time, useful and persuasive. The most valuable and certainly the most interesting writings in any field are the controversial ones bearing the flavor of competition and conflict among ideas, lines of analysis, and personalities. We remember such works and are drawn to them again and again because the author shows a commitment, a personal stake in the outcome of the debate and in the impact of his ideas on the world beyond academic circles.

There is always the danger, of course, that conflict will force an argument downward into the defense of dogma, rather than upward toward more convincing evidence and more powerful models and theories; but, in the broad and complex field of social issues, clearly little can be accomplished without taking such risks. What is needed least of all in the current literature explosion in the social sciences is more work by authors writing consciously or otherwise within the frameworks and "definitions of the situation" of reigning establishments. In the 20th Century, the best scholarly writing must inevitably be radical.

All this is by way of introduction to the issues presented and discussed in this book. In our time, few topics have aroused as much controversy or received as much commitment among social scientists and planners as the revolutionary changes taking place in the "have-not" nations of the world, most of which have only recently attained statehood and independence. On questions of national development or (to avoid the ethnocentric implications of calling centuries-old civilizations "under-developed") national modernization, few authors are "value-free" and many hold in actual contempt those who claim to write with absolute impartiality and dispassionateness. In brief, if the papers collected in this volume have a fault, it is not lack of commitment.

The reader will have a better understanding of the issues raised here if he knows some of the background to the conference for which these papers were written. In 1966, I directed an interdisciplinary meeting on the subject of urbanization and work in modernizing societies.* There were no formal papers, and the entire time was devoted to raising and fighting out many of the questions confronting efforts to plan for urbanization and economic development. To say the least, the arguments were furious, but they were also instructive. First of all, sociologists, anthropologists, economists, and others discovered how little they know about each other's fields, and how much of what they consider basic and self-evident is held to be doubtful and even nonsensical by others. Revelations of that kind are, unfortunately, much too rare. Secondly, the participants disagreed about almost everything, from questions of fact about the proportion of rural-to-urban migrants in Latin America who had previously had urban living experience to such broader questions as whether peasants lack achievement motivation. The debate was so provocative that, in 1967, I organized another conference, this time with formal papers, and asked the participants to present their research with attention, wherever possible, to three of the most difficult questions suggested by the earlier meetings: What are the REAL obstacles, internal and external, to national development, as opposed to popular but perhaps mythical notions about the obstacles to development? What is the relative importance of the different obstacles as measured by their consequences and the difficulties of attacking them? What are the probable and actual consequences of different solutions? The success or failure of the present volume will depend on the skill with which the authors face these questions.

The papers assembled here have all the virtues and vices of work by men with varying personal commitments to the social, political, and economic development of the world's modernizing nations and, indeed, the call to the conference which produced them deliberately asked the authors to take positions and make judgments. In the interest of fruitfully challenging the participants to consider both the theoretical and in-the-field implications of the questions raised, the group assembled included some who are primarily teachers and researchers and others whose work is more directly in project planning, organization, and execution. Somewhat to my surprise, it was not this division which provoked serious disagreement, but rather the division between those who treated the countries they studied as closed systems and those who find much of their analysis of national development problems in inter-national relationships. Most of the papers here are based on

*Arthur J. Field (Ed.), *Urbanization and Work in Modernizing Societies,* Detroit: Glengary Press, 1967.

research and work experience in Latin America, and the inter-national relations discussed are largely with the United States. As American foreign policy comes to take Latin America more and more seriously, its impact on modernization processes will grow, and it is useful, indeed, to study the planned and the unintended consequences of that policy. In many ways, of course, the problems discussed here are generic to the "third world of development," to use Horowitz's phrase, and it is hoped that scholars, planners, and "change-agents" throughout that world will find value in this book.

ARTHUR J. FIELD
Troy, New York
March, 1970

I

ISSUES IN THE USES OF RESEARCH

In a volume of essays, all of them the products of research into the politics, economics, and culture of the Latin American part of the Third World of poor and problem-ridden nations, it is important to consider the impact of the explosive growth of empirical research and critical analysis (including this book) on the issues and problems they treat. In Part I, then, we consider the question, "What happens to all that research?" As Field notes, there has been no shortage of writings about research, but most of it has focused on methods of conducting scientific studies, problems of data-processing and relating data to social theory, and, particularly in the past few years, the influence of the sponsor on the product. Despite the increasing importance of social research as a profession and an industry and its increasing acceptance as a basis for policy and action, the consumption side of the picture has been curiously neglected.

In his essay, Field develops a set of propositions (designed to be treated as hypotheses) about the determinants of research consumption. Recognizing that research may be used and misused in innumerable ways, he defines "consumption" broadly, saying that "to consume research is to be influenced by it," and allows, immediately, that much research, published and unpublished, is never consumed at all. His framework considers the stock of available research as given, and takes the consumption of research as the dependent variable, that which must be explained; the causal variables are identified as the membership and organizational characteristics of the potential consumer (limited here to governments and their agencies) and the environment–political and cultural–within which the potential consumer is found.

Field's analysis has several interesting implications. One is that much research that now appears in scholarly journals and texts appealing largely to narrow audiences of specialists could be of great value, for example, to government agencies in Third World countries, but instead goes unknown and unused because techniques for converting it into forms intelligible and palatable to agency staffs and applicable to concrete problems are lacking. This does not mean that all research should be of the applied variety (which would certainly hinder the growth of the social sciences AS SCIENCES), but rather that a new breed of professional–of the sort now being recruited and trained by the specialized agencies of the United Nations–is needed to bridge the gap between the workings of social science and the needs of city and countryside in the underdeveloped majority of the world. Another implication of equal importance is that available research (and specially commissioned studies) are most efficiently used to attack national problems where the public, particularly through its pressure groups and voluntary associations, is educated to the level at which its awareness of current social studies makes it a potent influence on the policies and practices of government officials and agencies.

In short, accepting the importance of social research in the solution of problems of modernization and development, Field suggests some of the relationships which must be examined and understood in the task of bringing the potential consumer and the libraries and data banks of information together in the attack on poverty, disease, misery, and ignorance.

APPLYING SOCIAL RESEARCH IN THE THIRD WORLD: WHAT DETERMINES THE CONSUMPTION OF RESEARCH?

Arthur J. Field

> *. . . to tell the truth is not merely a good intention. It's a damned difficult thing to do. It's a skill, to be practiced. It's a technique. It's an effort. It takes brains. It takes watching. It takes humility and self-examination. It's a science and an art.* (Armstrong, 1951)

INTRODUCTION

It was almost thirty years ago that Wendell Wilkie challenged an isolationist America with the advice that we wake up to the fact that there is only One World. In his sense, of course, there IS only one world, and a crisis anywhere sooner or later reverberates everywhere. In another sense, however, there are still three worlds, loosely distinguishable as the Capitalist World, the Communist World, and the Third World of poor and struggling countries making up most of Latin America, Africa, the Middle East, and Southern Asia (Horowitz, 1966). This essay is concerned with that Third World, the one that contains the majority of the Earth's population and land area.

Not so long ago, Americans and Europeans were unbelievably ignorant about the Third World, but this is becoming less and less true both for the man in the street who cannot avoid seeing the daily headlines of war, revolution, and hunger and for the social scientist whose universe has also been forced to expand. Two developments, in particular, have fostered an explosive growth of research activity and information. The first of these was the break-up of colonial empires leading to the freeing of ancient nations and the creation of new political states. This meant that people whose economy and government had for centuries been controlled by a handful of European powers or, as in the case of Latin America, had essentially been isolated from the modern and developed nations, found themselves facing the challenges of political independence, economic development, and social modernization with little of the organization, knowledge, and equipment necessary for these enormous tasks.[1] Their poverty and instability demanded action on political and economic and, no less, on humanitarian grounds.

The second major change followed from the first. Not only did the Third World need data and technical assistance, but they needed it quickly. They found themselves calling more and more on the experienced social research and social action professionals of the developed nations, sometimes through such international agencies as the United Nations, sometimes through contracts directly with research personnel and consultants in the United States and other developed nations. The increasing demand and the lucrative market for research and planning not only brought scholars into the international development field under a variety of sponsorships–the Third World governments themselves, European and North American governments, international agencies, and private foundations–but it also stimulated the creation and proliferation of such large-scale private research organizations as Arthur D. Little and Constantinos Doxiadis which work on problems of corporate investment as well as on social issues. These organizations began aggressively to "sell" research services in two ways, first, by propagandizing for the idea that formal, scientific research is necessarily basic to action, and, secondly, by offering to carry out the research that more and more economic aid programs are demanding.

Among the leaders of the change toward the acceptance of research as a serious and persistent need have been the newly-created research centers–university-based and autonomous. These centers carry out studies and perform the equally important task of training large numbers of research scholars, administrators, and technicians from Third World countries. Through cooperative arrangements training is also made available in those countries themselves. This program has been accompanied by a rapid increase in the number of professional and scholarly journals disseminating research findings, conferences and symposia for the exchange of ideas, and data banks, libraries, and information retrieval services.

In brief, research in the Third World is a growth industry. But as the information explosion spreads, so does the need to ask what happens to all the research, all the papers, books, print-outs, and microfilm. How much of it is ever used? How much is seen at all? What distinguishes the research that is used from that which is forgotten? There is ample evidence that much of it is applied successfully or makes its contribution in other ways, but there is also evidence that much of this research is wasted and misused. The present paper is an exploratory move toward a better understanding of the determinants of research use.

Basically, there are two sides to research: production and consumption. Of the two, the production side has received much more attention, particularly in terms of sponsorship, research theory, and methodology.[2] My focus, therefore, will be on the consumption side, taking the stock of research product as given, and considering the complex factors determining its use.

This is indeed a broad topic and I shall limit my treatment largely to the determinants of the use of research by governments, leaving the important question of private uses for another time. This seems an appropriate distinction because, in the underdeveloped countries, at least, the major development and modernization decisions are in fact going to be made by governments.

STATEMENT OF THE PROBLEM

The first broad question has already been asked, "What determines the uses of social research in the Third World?" The second general question being asked is, "How to increase the efficiency with which research is used?" In this frankly exploratory approach I shall use the method of an inventory of propositions, hoping that they will prove to be useful guides to the empirical research which has yet to be done. Before proceeding, however, some of the basic terms require definition.

I shall consider ***research*** to be any systematic and deliberate gathering of information, by reasonably scientific methods, leading to a formal, usually published, final report. There are obviously many types of research differing with respect to the scope of the questions asked, the research methods, the size of population studied, the extent to which a particular study uses other research as background, the kinds of conclusions reached, and the form of the final report. It is therefore difficult and, perhaps, unnecessary to develop a more specific definition; for my purposes, the most important distinction is between social research, broadly defined, and all other ways of gathering information and insights–consulting friends, reading horoscopes, seeking divine inspiration. Further, I am concerned largely with formal attempts to answer specific questions, rather than with such undigested masses of statistics as are routinely collected by government agencies–numbers of tourists arriving by ship, numbers of automobiles licensed, numbers of persons receiving welfare assistance–although they may form the raw material of scientific studies. In other words, my interest here is in exploring what happens to formal social research in the Third World.

Research is *consumed* if it influences thinking and behavior in any way. Specifically, research is consumed (1) if it influences other research, (2) if it influences individual behavior, (3) if it influences planning and organized action, whether or not it contains specific recommendations, and (4) if it influences the development of policy and strategy. This set of categories requires elaboration.

(1) Much research is used directly only in other research, and this is especially true of the material published in journals and books appealing

entirely to scholarly audiences. Indirectly, of course, some of this material will come to influence planning and programming, especially as it is summarized and made available in popular forms. My hypothesis here would be that most scientific research influences only other scientific research, particularly if it is intentionally directed toward theory-building.

(2) Some research will influence individual behavior directly as it is reported and summarized. For example, the publicity given to relations between cigarette smoking and cancer has led many people to stop smoking.

(3) A certain amount of research is used in planning solutions to human problems and organizational problems; e.g., research on the social effects of public housing may lead planners to change the design of housing projects. Research on the effects of red tape on public welfare services may lead agency directors to simplify intake procedures. Further, research which contains recommendations and detailed plans is consumed when it is implemented or when it influences decisions about action programs.

(4) Research may also be consumed if it influences the development of policy and the general approach agencies take to problems within their sphere. In any society, there will be considerably more debate about policy alternatives than social action, and also more attention to describing and interpreting social events. Some research catches on because it meets the needs of the moment for concepts (culture of poverty, community power structure, alienation) and innovative action (guaranteed annual incomes, ombudsmen, cooperative marketing).

Obviously, some research is consumed in multiple ways. For example, a study whose recommendations are put into practice may also contain data which will be used in other research, and policy implications which will change the practical interpretation of current ideologies. Other questions are also raised by this definition of consumption. It seems clear that there are no necessary connections between an investigator's intentions and the ways in which his work is used. Often, in fact, research will be used in ways contrary to his intentions; studies showing poor academic achievement among Negro children may be used by racists to support their belief in innate Negro inferiority. Some research contracts asking for specific recommendations will be commissioned with the covert objective of postponing action. Some research will be misunderstood, and it may be difficult to decide whether action based on a misreading of research can legitimately be said to constitute consumption. To some extent we shall be concerned with all of these uses of research, but at the moment, my point is simply that they all represent forms of consumption. In brief, to *consume* research is to be influenced by it. It is not sufficient to have reports available nor to read research without being influenced by it, although availability and contact are obviously necessary for consumption.

Although all four types of consumption are important, in the present paper I shall be concerned largely with types 3 and 4, that is, the direct influence of research on organized groups in the solution and prevention of social (including political and economic) problems. In other words, we shall be looking for answers to the question of what determines these forms of research consumption.

THE DETERMINANTS OF RESEARCH CONSUMPTION

Disregarding the suggestion of some cynics that the function of most research is simply to be published, most producers of research hope that it will be consumed, that is, influence thinking and behavior in at least one of the ways previously described. Nevertheless, much research—there is no way of measuring how much—is never consumed at all; it may never be published and, if published, may never be read. In addition, and more important, much research is never used where it is needed and, if used at all, is misused and misunderstood. What makes the difference between use, non-use, and misuse?

There are several points of view from which the determinants of research consumption may be analyzed, specifically, of the sponsor, the producer, and the potential consumer, and it will be obvious that each of these has its influence. The reputation of the sponsor may predispose a government official for or against a piece of research. The producer may have the knack of couching his conclusions in terms that are readily summarized and adopted. The staff of a particular agency may be well trained in searching bodies of literature for usable research. In addition, some research will be particularly timely and receive publicity and mass media coverage it otherwise might not; where a study appears may be a crucial determinant of its use.

In the present paper, I shall take the viewpoint of the potential consumer, reasoning that it is, in fact, the consumer's characteristics which ultimately determine research consumption. There is the implication here that the consumer is usually separated from the sponsor and producer, which is probably the general case. Sometimes, of course, all three functions are combined in a single agency, which raises interesting questions about whether an agency's policy and implementation are significantly more affected by "in-house" research than by research on similar questions carried out by investigators having no ties to the agency. The vast bulk of research, however, is not carried out by the potential consumer, and the agency with its own research staff is the exception to what is generally found. In any case, in the inventory of propositions which follow it is on the potential consumer, rather than on the sponsor or the producer, that we shall focus.

INVENTORY OF PROPOSITIONS

In this exploratory inventory of propositions, the dependent variable will be the consumption of research and the causal variables (1) demographic (referring to the characteristics of the staffs of governmental and quasi-governmental agencies), (2) organizational (referring to the characteristics of the agencies themselves), and (3) environmental (referring to the political, social, and cultural climates within which agencies function). In analyzing the relationships between these variables, the emphasis will be on the forms they typically take in Third World countries, although in some propositions the relationships are very likely to be universal.[3]

I. THE CONSUMPTION OF RESEARCH IS A SPECIFIC ORGANIZATIONAL CHARACTERISTIC WITH NO NECESSARY RELATIONSHIP TO ANY OTHER CHARACTERISTIC. High consumption of research (as well as high propensity to conduct research) will appear largely as the result of deliberate administrative efforts to foster it through the creation of research staffs, the recruitment of professionally trained personnel, and the development of a climate in which familiarity with research literature is specifically rewarded, materials are made available through an agency library, staff are expected to be active in professional societies, and so forth. It is not necessarily related to the political and economic power of the organization, the problem areas within which the agency works, and similar variables.

a. *However, THE AMOUNT OF RESEARCH CONSUMED WILL VARY DIRECTLY WITH THE EXTENT TO WHICH AN AGENCY IS A BUREAUCRACY (IN WEBER'S SENSE OF LEGAL-RATIONAL AUTHORITY) AND INVERSELY WITH THE DEGREE TO WHICH IT IS GOVERNED BY TRADITIONAL AND CHARISMATIC AUTHORITY. One reason for this is that the departments of a bureaucratic agency are more likely to be required to keep detailed records and to put the evidence and reasoning justifying their plans and operations into writing. This practice is conducive to seeking out available research materials, if only to find useful models for presenting reports and defending actions.*

This proposition is true only within limits because agencies will inevitably deviate from Weber's ideal-type of bureaucracy. The more rigid the bureaucracy becomes, the less likely is its staff to be knowledgeable about current research because it will avoid knowing about (and therefore perhaps inadvertently giving others access to) evidence which challenges existing rules and policies. The exception to this rule occurs where the agency is following a specific model, for example, the British legal system, in which case there will be some prestige attached to knowing the literature about that system.

II. A special set of propositions concerns agencies with their own research staffs. WHERE AN AGENCY HAS ITS OWN RESEARCH STAFF, WHETHER THE RESEARCH PRODUCED BY THAT STAFF WILL INFLUENCE THE AGENCY'S BEHAVIOR WILL DEPEND UPON (1) WHO INITIATES THE STUDY, (2) THE EXTENT TO WHICH IT TAKES POLITICAL CONSIDERATIONS INTO ACCOUNT, (3) THE SOCIAL DISTANCE BETWEEN THE STAFF AND THE ADMINISTRATION, AND (4) THE AUTHORITY OF THE RESEARCH STAFF WITHIN THE AGENCY. The research produced by an operating agency's own staff is most likely to be consumed if (1) its findings validate decisions already made by agency officials, (2) its findings and recommendations are limited to the specific political environment in which the agency operates, (3) its research on the local setting is supported by research findings about areas which serve as "reference areas," that is, countries, regions, systems of government which the agency administration takes as representing desirable models, and (4) if the agency culture is dominated by professionalism and nationalism, rather than by traditional colonial thinking.

a. *THE HIGHER THE EDUCATIONAL LEVEL OF RESEARCH AND PLANNING STAFFS RELATIVE TO ADMINISTRATORS IN THE SAME AGENCY, THE LESS LIKELY ARE ACTUAL PLANS AND PROGRAMS TO BE BASED ON STAFF RESEARCH. This is the type of situation in which administrators, particularly political appointees, will define themselves as "practical" men as compared with the "ivory tower idealists" of the research staff, and assume that scientific research (and ideas gathered from foreign studies) must be contrary to political realities and an "instinctive understanding about our people." This will be somewhat less true where the agency has no operating responsibilities; that is, it plans and researches, but does not execute, programs and projects. Such planning agencies may define their role as one of presenting the complete picture to political decision-makers, much depending upon the level of democracy and leadership prevailing in the society.*

b. *However, THE CLOSER THE EDUCATIONAL LEVELS OF RESEARCH AND PLANNING PERSONNEL AND ADMINISTRATORS IN THE SAME AGENCY, THE GREATER THE*

CONSUMPTION OF RESEARCH BECAUSE (1) RESEARCHERS WILL HAVE GREATER EXPECTATIONS THAT ADMINISTRATORS WILL BE INFLUENCED BY SUMMARIES OF RESEARCH CONDUCTED BY OTHERS AND RESEARCH FINDINGS OF THE STAFF MEMBERS THEMSELVES, (2) MORE KNOWLEDGEABLE ADMINISTRATORS WILL EXPECT STAFF MEMBERS TO KNOW THE RESEARCH LITERATURE, AND (3) BECAUSE THE ADMINISTRATOR IS MORE LIKELY TO HAVE ACHIEVED HIS APPOINTMENT BY MERIT THAN BY FAVORITISM. This proposition is based on considerable experience, but it would not surprise me if it failed the test of empirical research or showed only a weak correlation. The difficulty is that personality enters as an important variable; where one official will enjoy dealing with his research staff as peers, another with equal years of schooling may be frightened and threatened by the implied challenge.

III. The educational and professional levels of the entire agency staff are important, also. THE HIGHER THE EDUCATIONAL LEVEL OF AGENCY STAFFS, THE GREATER WILL BE ITS CONSUMPTION OF RESEARCH. Higher education suggests greater familiarity with the research process and the available literature, greater facility at understanding and applying it, and greater respect for scientific research as a basis of policy and action. The more educated staff members are also more likely to have other researchers as their reference group and, therefore, to be under greater pressure to keep abreast of current work.

The converse is also true, and the lower the educational level, the less research consumed. This is so because (1) staffs have not been trained to see the relations between scientific research and decision-making, (2) most of the research material in professional and scholarly sources will be unintelligible to them, and (3) because Third World countries have by and large not developed techniques and media for providing simplified but accurate summaries of research. In addition, they are less likely to attempt to conduct their own research (which requires familiarity with the ways in which others have asked the same questions) or to belong to professional associations.

The relation between staff educational level and research consumption will be influenced by the type of education received; in particular, a classical education is likely to produce attitudes which deny the usefulness of social research and consider empirical research as a low prestige occupation. Many Third World countries have yet to overcome the prejudice against "practical" higher education which was inherited from the imperial powers, and where the most prestigious college degree is in Law, engineering and social research are likely to rank low.

IV. THE AMOUNT OF RESEARCH CONSUMED WILL CORRELATE POSITIVELY WITH (1) THE PROFESSIONALIZATION OF THE STAFF, (2) THE STRENGTH OF TIES BETWEEN RESEARCH AND OPERATING AGENCIES AND LOCAL AND FOREIGN ACADEMIC COMMUNITIES, AND (3) WITH THE AMOUNT OF COMMUNICATION BETWEEN BRANCHES OF THE SAME AGENCY WITHIN THE COUNTRY AND WITH SIMILAR AGENCIES IN OTHER COUNTRIES. For example, if the staff members of an organization see themselves as city planners and, therefore, as part of an "invisible college," rather than as civil servants and government workers in general, they are more likely to be aware of and influenced by city planning literature.[4] In many Third World countries, one is more likely to receive research literature as a member of an international professional society than as a faculty member of the local university.

What is crucial here is that, in countries with very small numbers of social scientists and trained planners, there is little opportunity for the cross-fertilization of ideas gained from familiarity with (and participation in) available research. In addition, it is not so much familiarity with research which determines its effective consumption, as familiarity combined with an understanding of how research conducted elsewhere can be converted into programs reasonably suited to one's own setting. Very often, those conversion techniques will not be published as part of formal research, and can be gotten only from personal conversations with "opposite numbers" at conferences and symposia.[5] It is in such personal relationships that one also learns about useful sources of research, that is, the relatively isolated researcher or administrator in a small country in Africa or Latin America receives advice and exchanges experiences about particular journal articles and books (among the for-practical-purposes infinity of available materials) which have proved to be valuable. "Word-of-mouth" and simple availability probably stand side-by-side as the most important determinants of the consumption of any given piece of research.

The extent to which the staff of operating agencies, e.g., social workers, teachers, health aides, community organizers, etc., will be aware of research in the areas in which they work will vary with their degree of professionalization as measured by their amount of training, their membership in professional associations, their image of their work as a career, their image of their occupation as a profession, and the relation between advanced education and salaries and promotions. The relationships here are unclear, and it would be interesting to see empirical research on the question. One difficulty is that the professional self-image requires familiarity with the critical literature and research only to the extent that the self-image has a "scientific" component; failing that, there is no more reason why a Latin American social worker should know about current developments in small group research than that an American public school teacher will know about experiments in learning theory. Another difficulty is that interest in keeping up with a profession will vary with the participation in decision-making and the autonomy of the worker; workers involved in decision-making are more likely to do their "homework."

> a. *Operating agencies only rarely conduct research evaluating their own effectiveness voluntarily, nor are they likely to be influenced by (that is, to consume) research on similar programs elsewhere. In short, OPERATING AGENCIES, THOSE WHICH RUN PROGRAMS, CONSUME VERY LITTLE RESEARCH OF ANY KIND UNLESS THEY HAVE THEIR OWN PLANNING AND RESEARCH STAFFS. A measure of this is the extent to which agency administrators everywhere tend to be ignorant of the scientific research literature and the activities of their counterparts elsewhere, but enormously alert to political currents. The greatest ignorance will concern scholarly research, particularly if it appears only in academic journals, and there will be more awareness of findings appearing in the "trade magazines" of a profession. The problem, of course, is not that scholarly research is necessarily irrelevant to social action, but that it needs to be converted into usable terms and made readily available. If it is easier to conduct one's own study than to find the information one needs in the mass of published data in the United States, it must be infinitely easier to do so in countries without elaborate information retrieval systems.*
>
> *In this context, one of the greatest values to the research carried out by such international agencies as the United Nations is their ability to persuade member nations to order their governmental units to gather data and provide evaluations of programs. The quality of the given nation's social welfare report to the UN may not be high, but doing the research at all will contribute to improving the climate for all research in the country, for having it both conducted and consumed.*

V. The consumption of research as a concept says little about its actual effects, and a proposition about this relationship is necessary. THERE IS NO NECESSARY RELATIONSHIP BETWEEN THE CONSUMPTION OF RESEARCH AND THE DECISIONS MADE BY AN AGENCY. The amount of research information from all sources moving into an organization, that is, made available to the staff, tells us little about how it is used. There are several reasons for this. First of all, much social research concerns public preferences and priorities, each with an implied political and economic price tag; rationality in such cases will be defined as maximizing movement toward agency objectives while minimizing costs, rather than acting on the highest public priorities or the greatest need. Secondly, social research may have a prominent place in the decision-making process but, by its nature, its findings will rarely be conclusive enough to dictate specific actions in the sense that discovering a shipment of canned fish creating botulism will dictate that it be destroyed.

One of the obstacles to systematically studying what happens to research is that research is inevitably involved in a cumulative process from which it is difficult to extract its influence. This is particularly important because most of the studies bearing on particular problems do so only indirectly; they were conducted in other settings, perhaps for other purposes. Even an agency thoroughly committed to knowing the research evidence and the theoretical developments in its field will have to adapt available materials to its specific environment and, unfortunately, little is known empirically about the points at which agency staff members use information published outside of the agency and usually outside of the country to influence complex planning and programming operations, or how. Research, it must be emphasized, has its direct influence on staff, and only through them on the organization itself.

The application of formal research will often increase the rationality of organizational decisions, but it cannot, of course, guarantee their effectiveness in application. First of all, even where there is a strong commitment to using research, as noted above, the evidence bearing on a specific local problem may simply not be available, and the use of studies based on analogous situations and comparative research may be misleading. Secondly, although available evidence may seem to dictate certain lines of action, the agency may simply not have the resources in money and personnel or the ability to duplicate the conditions under which the research conclusions held true where they were developed. In other words, an administrator may actively seek to apply the latest information to the problems he faces, but conclude accurately that it cannot be done because he cannot duplicate the necessary assumptions. His consumption of research may lead him to the frustrating awareness of what could be done if conditions allowed it, and its greatest value may be in leading him to work toward developing those conditions. On the other hand, this frustration may turn him against efforts to adapt the vast amount of research available to his specific situation because there is no reliable way to do it, and because, in a poor country, his staff is likely to be even less qualified to try it than he is. He will often pay more attention to a few rules of thumb that have worked for him in the past than to the entire literature of social science, and fortunately for the people he serves, his decisions will often be none the worse for it.

To put the matter baldly, one of the major determinants of the use of research is the success an agency staff has had in using it in the past. There are any number of agencies which produce a great deal of their own research and absorb more from outside, but use very little of it, either because they don't know how or because they (and perhaps the whole country) lack the resources necessary for converting information and plans into buildings and programs. In addition, the broader the scope of the particular study, in terms, for example, of national land or tax reform, the less likely is an agency to have the power to implement it.

VI. THE TRAINING FUNCTION OF RESEARCH ACTIVITY IS OFTEN MORE SIGNIFICANT THAN THE INFORMATION GATHERING FUNCTION. This point is usually overlooked because of an overly narrow definition of research, but it is particularly true of studies cast in the form of demonstrations, that is, tests or trial runs of actual programs. In such cases, although efforts may be made to keep records and test hypotheses and alternate approaches, unless the research personnel are clearly separated from the field workers in the program, it is very likely that the only benefit will be in the training the latter receive. In the typical demonstration program, the final project report is rarely treated as serious research literature, but it may be usefully summarized in the course of other research and make a useful contribution in that way. In addition, the trained personnel will carry the results of the program as part of their own personal experience and disseminate it informally in their contacts with other workers in the field.

It would certainly be desirable to have administrators and staff qualified in both research and program operation, but this combination is rare even in developed countries. Experience in demonstration projects suggests that it requires considerable skill to induce researchers and program staff to cooperate in a project's objectives, and there has been little success in training personnel to play both roles well. One token of a project's success is the respect it gives field workers for the research process and its uses and problems.

VII. The political environment within which agencies operate will vitally affect their use of research. THE MORE DEMOCRATIC THE SOCIETY,

THE GREATER THE AMOUNT OF RESEARCH CONSUMED BY GOVERNMENT AGENCIES. Where the society is characterized by open controversy among government agencies and political parties, and where non-governmental groups actively lobby and attempt to influence legislation and administrative decisions, more research will be consumed (1) to strengthen plans and proposals, and (2) to support and justify actions. In other words, the importance of knowing the available literature–critical and empirical–increases where the actions of agencies are subject to continuing evaluation and criticism. It will be noted that the proposition does not specify how research will be used, and unquestionably much of the time spent reading and reviewing studies and data is little more than a hunt for justification for decisions made on non-scientific grounds.

a. *THE GREATER THE POLITICAL RESTRAINTS ON OPEN DISCUSSION OF ALTERNATIVES, THE SMALLER THE AMOUNT OF RESEARCH CONSUMED. All government agencies have unofficial but well-understood lists of "politically-unthinkable" ideas. Individual staff members may consume such research privately, that is, read materials containing ideas unacceptable to their employers, and sometimes such ideas may be smuggled into plans and proposals. Such attempts are not likely to succeed, however. In an authoritarian setting, administrators develop a nose for subversive ideas or they don't survive; in a more open, but highly political setting, officials develop a mental trash can into which they throw the radical proposals unavoidably churned up by research staffs.*

More likely, such material will be unknown to research staffs because it is simply not available, their education has not trained them to understand it, and their careers may be endangered if they are suspected of being sympathetic to it. It will be noted that this is much more true of the social research with which we are concerned here than it would be of research in physics or engineering. Two additional points are relevant here.

The more an agency's decisions are subject to political pressures, the more likely its staff is to misuse, misinterpret, and neglect available research. This response is not limited to Third World countries and, regardless of where the agency is located, is correlated with the agency's political power in contradictory ways. On the one hand, an agency with great political power (or strong backing from political authorities) may feel that it has a free hand to consume large amounts of research even where the findings reflect upon it unfavorably; on the other, given great political power, it may choose not to do so because it is relatively safe from public criticism. Government agencies in the Soviet Union and the United States, particularly those in the social and economic (as opposed to the engineering, physical science, and military) spheres, are not noted for their interest in foreign research even where their political position makes it feasible and, equally important, their record of failures in the Cold War suggests that even when they do read foreign research, they misunderstand it.

Secondly, a restrictive climate for the consumption of research implies a political orthodoxy with overtones especially strong in the area of social action. Where, for example, as was true in the Soviet Union until recently, the only acceptable Sociology was based on historical materialism, one is unlikely to find useful social research conducted or reviewed except as the "mistakes of the politically benighted."

b. *Most consumption of research is indirect, that is, through summaries and conversations with persons who may have seen the original sources or, themselves, received indirect summaries. THE AMOUNT OF RESEARCH CONSUMED IN A COUNTRY WILL VARY DIRECTLY WITH THE NUMBER AND STRENGTH OF NON-GOVERNMENTAL ORGANIZATIONS ATTEMPTING TO INFLUENCE GOVERNMENT POLICY. As a correlate, the amount of social research conducted will vary in the same way. Non-governmental organizations consume research to provide analyses of current issues, critiques of current programs, and summaries of research findings in forms useful to government officials. Such organizations may be political (including political parties), academic (for example, university research centers), or professional and industrial (producing trade magazines and studies directed for and against proposed legislation). The proposition is somewhat self-evident because there is likely to be a close relationship between the number of organizations with research functions in a country and the number of college graduates, and this is obviously related to the amount and kinds of research which will move into governmental decision-making in the country. It is nevertheless extremely important because it describes the infrastructure conducive to high research consumption, that is, it concerns the organized activities which "process" available research into forms which can be applied to plans and programs.*

c. *MASS MEDIA WILL ORDINARILY PLAY ONLY A MINOR ROLE IN DISSEMINATING RESEARCH IN GENERAL, BUT MAY BE IMPORTANT IN LEADING THE ADOPTION OF SPECIFIC LINES OF ANALYSIS DERIVED FROM RESEARCH. Only rarely do the media anywhere provide systematic coverage of current social research; most such research is simply not considered news, but there are exceptions particularly where the study—on worker morale, educational reform, agricultural productivity, or political dissent—bears on issues which have come to be defined as national problems. The mass media are important in at least two ways. They may provide the most important source of information about current research which government officials are likely to see, because their reports are condensed and highly selective and are also likely to be seen by others, and, to the extent that government agencies are sensitive to public pressure, they may provide most of the information the man in the street has about current research, and thereby form the basis of his evaluation of government performance.*

CONCLUSIONS

This inventory of propositions is intended to indicate the kinds of empirical research required to gain us a better understanding of what works for and against the large-scale and constructive use of the growing wealth of information, interpretation, and theory being produced around the world. It suggests that future studies in that direction will have to attend to the characteristics of agency personnel, the agencies themselves, and the environment within which they operate. My purpose has been to call attention to the importance not only of studying the problems of the Third World, but also of maximizing the usefulness and the use of such research; in this process, the burden must be shared by the sponsors, the producers, and the potential consumers, and it need hardly be said that the task must be cooperative.

NOTES

1. This is not to say that no research was done in the Third World prior to 1945, but rather that the largest part of it was conducted from the point of view of the imperial power's needs in administering colonies and possessions, and is of limited use to independent governments seeking to chart an autonomous course.

2. Until recently, materials on the research process (other than on scientific research methods) were also fairly rare, but this lack has somewhat been made up in several recent volumes presenting behind-the-scenes critiques of actual research projects, cf. Vidich, Bensman, and Stein (1964); Hammond (1964); Sjoberg (1967). These works also devote some attention to the relations between researchers and sponsors. The fact that more has been written on research production than on consumption has, of course, been recognized by others. As Donald Schon has noted with reference to prediction studies,

> there is a tendency among those interested in forecasting to concentrate on methodology rather than its use. Our approach should be to begin with potential use and user requirements, and to move from there to relevant methodology. (1969:138)

3. It may be of interest to those considering further research on the propositions presented here that my initial attempt to divide them into the three categories of causal variables was unsuccessful because my search for significant propositions required the use of more than one type of variable in most cases, either in the proposition itself or its interpretation.

4. The concept of the "invisible college" has been developed recently to suggest the persisting relationship–informal, voluntary, intermittent–among scientists working on similar problems. As Diana Crane suggests (1969:349), researchers working in a particular field develop different kinds of groupings, from those in which scientists are "divided into small groups, sharing the same interests, speaking only to each other, and reading and citing only each other's work" to those in which they work by themselves and with a few others whom they accidentally discover. At the latter extreme, much of the literature on a subject is so scattered that it is impossible for scientists to build on each other's work, and there is no accumulation of core scientific knowledge. I would suggest that this is what seems to characterize most governmental agencies (and perhaps private organizations and businesses, as well), certainly across national and, especially, language barriers. The mechanisms for coordinating large numbers of research projects have yet to be developed, although much work is being done on information exchanges and retrieval systems.

5. This can quickly reach a point of diminishing returns (or negative returns) if the handful of trained persons in a country comes to occupy several

administrative positions, teach at the university, engage in private consulting practice, and spend the remainder of their time flying to and from conferences. They may indeed know more and more about current research, but it will be of doubtful benefit to the researchers and operating personnel under them.

BIBLIOGRAPHY

Armstrong, Charlotte

1951 "The Enemy," reprinted in *Ellery Queen's Mystery Magazine* 54, 1 (July, 1969), 67-86.

Crane, Diana

1969 "Social Structure in a Group of Scientists: A Test of the 'Invisible College' Hypothesis," *American Sociological Review* 34, 3: 335-52.

Hammond, Philip E.

1964 (Editor), *Sociologists at Work.* New York: Basic Books.

Horowitz, Irving Louis

1966 *Three Worlds of Development: The Theory and Practice of International Stratification.* New York: Oxford University Press.

Schon, Donald A.

1969 "Forecasting and Technological Forecasting," in Daniel Bell (Editor), *Toward the Year 2000.* Boston: Beacon Press, 127-38.

Sjoberg, Gideon

1967 (Editor), *Ethics, Politics and Social Research.* Cambridge, Mass.: Schenkman Publishing Co.

Vidich, Arthur J., Joseph B. Bensman, and Maurice R. Stein

1964 (Editors), *Reflections on Community Studies.* New York: John Wiley & Sons.

II

ISSUES IN POLITICAL CHANGE

Some of the most vexing questions in the study of modernization and development concern the roles of governments, political parties, and elites. The difficulty lies essentially in the fact that where an entire nation is in flux and significant movement toward national goals almost certainly requires the drastic redistribution of power, there are, first of all, no clear starting points to the analysis, and, secondly, no universally determinate relationships among the parts of the social system. For example, leadership is an essential ingredient in mobilizing a population, that is, in preparing it for action that breaks with established political, economic, and cultural patterns. But the search for rules and theories for predicting whether a movement will generate successful leadership, the class from which such leadership will come, or the appeals that will succeed founders on the enormous variability of national and regional settings, as well as on the state of a country's international ties. Again, the liberal dilemma–whether major changes can or will be accomplished peacefully within existing institutional arrangements–constantly reappears in studies of the Third World, with no end to the evidence and arguments from a dozen equally scholarly points of view. In Part II, we consider some of these questions.

The essay by Horowitz focuses on the functions and consequences of political instability, arguing that in Latin America, at least, the long history of revolution and internal war not only bears no necessary relation to social and economic development, but often serves largely to maintain quasi-feudal social orders. He suggests that political turmoil often exists side-by-side with static social systems, and that such turmoil is used (if not always deliberately fostered) for just such purposes. As he puts it, "in order for a political system to 'survive' in Latin America, it must perennially change its policies and generate instability as a survival pattern." What is particularly important in the Horowitz analysis is his attempt to trace the historical roots of what he calls "the norm of illegitimacy," and to show the advantages of the concept for developing a theory of politics for Latin America as a whole, a macro-theory, as it were, as compared with theories stressing, for example, salvation through the middle classes, the military, or the peasants.

Horowitz also launches a frontal attack on the idea of the nation (and the importance of nationalism) as the best level of analysis for understanding Latin America. What is most important, rather, is "the common subordinate positions which the nations of Latin America occupy with respect to the United States," which may be reflected, economically, in the fluctuating prices of coffee and other basic export crops, or, militarily, in a dependence upon foreign arms and money. "The norm of illegitimacy is . . . guaranteed by an imperial system that sees the constant circulation of local elites as beneficial to its own interests."

Finally, Horowitz makes another contribution in his insistence upon distinguishing between modernization and development as processes which may operate almost independently of one another. This leads him to suggest that "the ideology behind the 'revolution in rising expectations' is anchored to the modernization process, while the ideology of 'revolution from below' is clearly anchored to the industrialization process." The point becomes especially important as an argument against the simplistic view that economic development of any type and regardless of sponsorship inevitably leads to social modernization—literacy, high social mobility, and greater respect for individual rights.

One of the basic controversies among researchers, planners, policy makers, and revolutionaries concerns action priorities. This is true not only because every decision about investment in industry, agrarian reform, education, or regional development benefits some sectors of the society at the expense of others, but also because many of the problems are too pressing to wait until the next Five Year Plan or the one after that. For example, as Barraclough and Domike indicate in Part III, it cannot safely be assumed that rural problems will stand still while Third World nations gamble on rapid urban industrialization. Further, as recent history shows, the lesson suggested by the Soviet Union and China is that only repression and terror can enforce extremely discriminatory practices in which one sector of the nation is sacrificed in the interest of rapid growth in other sectors.

The dilemma of modernization (including social welfare) OR economic development—a fundamental example of the problem of action priorities—is posed by Huizer's essay which takes the pressing need for agrarian reform as given, and stresses the belief that only the organized pressure of agriculturists—peasants, plantation workers, and others—can lead to the enactment and enforcement of the reforms necessary for a stable rural economy which at the same time improves the lot of the average farmer. The dilemma lies in the probability that improving the lot of the farmer, by itself, will work against national economic development because, for most poor countries, the surplus that can be wrung from the land and the rural worker is the major, perhaps the only, source of capital for autonomous economic growth.

It is universally agreed that agriculture must be made more productive to feed growing populations and provide a source of development capital, and also that making it more efficient will require (1) radical political changes reflected in genuine land reform, (2) major social and cultural changes in terms of education and social class relations, and (3) attention to the problems of unemployment and underemployment which can only be aggravated by the rationalization and mechanization of farming. What disagreement there is lies in how agrarian reform is to be defined and the relative shares of public funds which should go into agricultural development as compared with manufacturing and overhead capital (roads, railroads, schools, etc.)

The definition of agrarian reform is complex and subject to very large amounts of ideological bias. Huizer, for example, defines it as the measures necessary to increase the security and level of living of the rural population; what is not clear is whether these goals are compatible with increasing productivity, that is, whether they can be achieved without the concentration of land ownership which many economists feel necessary for maximum production, but which is often precisely what now keeps rural populations in poverty. Regardless of the economic consequences, however, Huizer's analysis of the importance of rural political organizations in the national development process, and the conditions favoring successful organization, are a valuable contribution to the argument.

The articles by Horowitz and Huizer mesh in at least one important respect; both stress the political mobilization of the masses as conducive to genuine (as opposed to illusory, symbolic) change and vital to the growth of national autonomy. They also agree that economic growth will be slow, uneven, and unlikely to benefit the vast lower classes in Latin America unless it is largely autonomous, that is, under national rather than foreign control. They differ in that Horowitz takes the macroscopic view, implying that only a large measure of continental unity can shake off the dominance of the metropolitan, imperial powers (if it can be done at all), while Huizer suggests the extent of constructive changes possible through the redistribution of power at the national and local levels. The two approaches complement one another.

In contrast to the first two articles in this section, Whiteford focuses on a single country, Colombia, and uses it as a model in calling for "political realism" in the analysis of the role of aristocracies. His attempt at realism leads him to attack the view commonly held by scholars and social critics that traditional aristocracies are by their nature reactionary obstacles to modernization and development. He supports his argument in several ways. First, he suggests that the aristocracy, by their virtual monopoly on education and administrative experience, are indispensable to the formulation of national policy and the directing of government agencies and programs. Secondly, he offers evidence that they are not a monolithic clique, but may be found in all political parties and on all sides of current issues. Finally, he suggests that progress has in fact been made under aristocratic and oligarchic rule, and that more progress will be made as other sectors of the society become politically mobilized. As an alternative to the unpredictable consequences of revolution, he holds, it is better to retain and reform the aristocracy. As he put it during the Conference discussion, his view is very much like the sign in the Western saloon that read, "Don't shoot the piano player. He's doing the best he can."

Between them, the three essays in this section sharply illuminate the knotty problems of political change. Each of them has its followers at home and abroad, and the next century will see the playing out of these themes, perhaps in peace through continental unity and cooperation, more likely in revolutionary violence with large measures of foreign intervention.

THE NORM OF ILLEGITIMACY: TOWARD A GENERAL THEORY OF LATIN AMERICAN POLITICAL DEVELOPMENT*

Irving Louis Horowitz

Contrary to academic mythology and sociological folklore, we are faced not with inadequate data in the area of Latin American studies, but rather conflicts between severely circumscribed and limited theories that work well enough for national units, and a collection of data about Latin American societies having little correlational significance at the hemispheric level. Macroanalysis has been especially weak in the area of Latin America for various reasons, primary of which is that almost every kind of theory about a developing nation has a contradictory outcome when applied to different nations within the Hemisphere.

The dilemma of forging an adequate theory is not restricted to the practical side. There is also the broader confusion surrounding the concept of legitimacy. As in so many other areas, Weber turned Marx upside down. For Marx, the State represents a monopoly of illegitimate power because politics is merely the organized machinery of one class for oppressing the others. For Weber, on the other hand, the State is organized primarily as a service agency, not a power dispenser. The State is thus an administrative staff having a monopoly on the legitimate use of force in order to enforce order in society.[1] It is evident, then, that for Marx the essence of the State is power; while for Weber the core of the State is authority.

Without wishing to resolve such a pervasive dualism in the sociological literature by fiat, for the purpose of this study, I consider it quite feasible that certain societies do operate in Weberian terms, while others operate in terms of the Marxian conception. More specifically, those societies which over a long period of time display norms sanctioned in law and made viable through mass participation can be considered legitimate; while those societies that rest visibly and demonstrably on unaccepted or barely tolerated power structures and relations can be considered illegitimate. One might declare that nations as different as Great Britain and the Soviet Union illustrate forms of legitimated authority; while most nations of Latin America illustrate forms of illegitimacy.

It is important to distinguish between illegitimacy and violence. Latin American societies operating in terms of the norm of illegitimacy, while often prone to greater outbursts of mass violence, just as often display an institutionalization of illegitimacy which drastically reduces the amount (and certainly the quality) of violence manifest in them. Illegitimacy may function as a Paratan device to circulate elites in the absence of laws sanctioned at the top or recognized as valid guidelines at the bottom end of society. The definition herein used is that legitimacy is the perception of the State as a service agency rather than an oppressive mechanism, and that this perception is cemented by a common adhesion to either legality or mass mobilization. The norm of illegitimacy, however, perceives the State as primarily a power agency, which relies on illegal means to rotate either the holders of power or the rules under which power is exercised.

I. The Internal Dynamics of Illegitimacy

Consider the relationship of the middle classes and militarism. During the fifties the most popular theory advanced by scholars and policy-makers alike held that to the extent to which the size of the middle class is increasing, there is a decrease in the extent of military involvement in political and social life. United States policy between 1957 and 1962 was largely based on the premise of this middle class salvation theory of Latin America.

The data do show (as far as Uruguay and Costa Rica are concerned) that with an increase in the size of the middle class there has taken place a parallel decrease in the size of the military. Yet even this is dubious, given the election of a military leader as President of Uruguay and the increased participation of Costa Rica in Central American regional defense schemes. But in turning to countries like Argentina and Brazil, which also have large and growing middle classes–as a matter of fact the Argentine middle class is the largest of all Latin America–we find the reverse situation. Instead of showing an inverse correlation between middle-class growth and militarism, there are parallel growth lines of militarism and the middle class. The same is true for Brazil. And the steady promotion of "civic action" programs, with their direct appeals to middle-class military cooperation, only serves to stimulate such outcomes. In fact, a coalition between the urban bourgeoisie in Rio de Janeiro and Sao Paulo and the military served to oust the Joao Goulart regime in 1964. The middle sectors, far from weakening military dominion, had the reverse effect. The situation in Peru and Argentina, while showing national idiosyncracies, is analogous in that there too, military interaction with the middle classes provides stability with legitimacy. Clearly, *prima facie* theorizing is inadequate as a guide to the understanding of Latin American social structure. Unfortunately, when the myth of middle class salvation broke down, it was replaced by an even less tenable myth, that of military salvation.

Old myths about the military die hard. There is a school of thought which attributes to the military a unique developmental orientation. We are told: if this generation wants to attain a rapid rate of development, social science must stop treating the military as pariahs. It is claimed that given the unique organizational efficiency of the military, the degree of their mobilization, the degree to which they have constant labor available for social purposes, and the degree to which they are a national force and symbol, they are not only a force for development, but may turn out to be a unique force.[2] An empirical look at the data does not drive us to any such optimistic prospects for military rule. They fail to show that the military are especially good at promoting a developmental pattern, at least in Latin America.[3]

The military have simply failed to act as an autonomous or unified group. Oftentimes they act as agents of other social classes or powerful government alignments. The view of the military as leaders in civic action, with respect to Latin America, ignores one of the gravest difficulties of all, namely, the exorbitant cost factor in their maintenance. The military establishment is expensive and wasteful. When a country like Chile buys twenty subsonic jet fighters, that portion of the federal budget intended for agrarian reform or industrial modernization is seriously impaired. The developmental *ideology* of the military, even when present, is thus undermined by their feudalistic *organization*. The so-called modernizing military phenomenon does not stem from a sober appraisal of the complex social stratification system so much as from a profound search for the key to hemispheric stability.

It is not exclusively the contradictory aspects of Latin American development that make a general theory an elusive goal, but the degrees of variation found in the social structure of the Hemisphere. Recently, for example, one writer has distinguished six different types of working-class organizations that can be found and correlated with different nations. They are the following: (1) countries with little urban or industrial concentration and with a small middle class; (2) countries with isolated mass situations, without a large urban industrial concentration and with a small middle class; (3) countries with isolated mass situations, without large urban concentrations, and with a large middle class in their urban sector; (4) countries with little urban and industrial concentration, but with a large middle class;

(5) countries with large urban-industrial concentrations, and a large middle class in their urban sectors; (6) countries with isolated mass situations, but without large urban-industrial concentrations and a large middle class.[4] While, formally speaking, such tabular compilations are useful, and can be transformed into elements of an operational appraisal, listing differences is no more a theory of Latin America than noting the existence of different regions can be said to comprise a theory of United States development. Nor will simplified attempts at correlational analysis take us very far, since the Bolivian working class exhibits political influence well beyond their economic level of existence, and likewise, the organizational strength of the Chilean working class exhibits a marked superiority with respect to that of Argentinian workers who, in turn, have a higher economic life style.

For many years, between 1945 and 1965, the nation-by-nation accounting system has served to overcome traditional obstructions placed in the path of intelligent theory construction by the *pensadores* and *historiadores*. But compensation has led to over-compensation–to the idealization of the nation as a unique unit of analysis. The limits of the nation-building model of analysis have not been accounted for. The needs of constructing a usable theory for the continental complex have not been explored. Although a significant start in overcoming a reliance on linear models has been made by Rodolfo Stavenhagen (1966/67, pp. 25-37), the debris of nonsensical, but widely held notions of Latin America, persists. It is now imperative to elaborate upon generalizations that help us to comprehend the level at which Latin America does exist as a unit.

We should first consider certain assumptions about the nature of Latin American politics that may appear outrageous at first glance. Above all, we must take a critical look at the doctrine that survival requires the stable maintenance of a democratic, libertarian, or parliamentarian order. The likelihood is that the reverse is more nearly the case. In order for a political system to "survive" in Latin America, it must perennially change its policies and generate instability as a survival pattern. This is not to say that instability must be attributed to a deliberate plan. Rather, that the political-military complex can respond to latent structural sources of instability, such as population explosion, crop failures, transportation and communication breakdowns, etc., in such a way as to manipulate these structural deformities for the purpose of maintaining political illegitimacy.

The maintenance of political illegitimacy had deep roots in the colonial history of Latin America. Under the Spanish legal and political organization the king held a position above the law. But this formula also involved an acceptance rather than an imposition upon the masses. The basic juridical formula of the crown being above the law had as its corresponding political formula the idea of acceptance rather than violence. The nonviolent character of illegitimacy makes possible its continuance even at present. As one scholar recently noted, "the rule of the Spanish king was authoritarian in the sense that it was not bound by legal enactments and regulations. Under the Spanish conception of law, the king was acting within the system of *derecho* but without being subject, in practice, to the *ley*. The term *derecho* refers to the system of law in general, including its philosophical and idealistic aspects. The word *ley* applies to enacted legislation. Although it might sound redundant, the Spanish monarch was in possession of an 'authoritarian' authority." (Moreno, 1967, pp. 308-320) This trans-legal status of rulers, combined as it was with incredibly detailed laws binding the ruled to the State, is therefore a longstanding condition.

Let us then start with what might be termed the norm of illegitimacy, or the norm of conflict, and consider those norms based on a consensualist apparatus to be largely inoperative. This kind of approach provides something valid and valuable in the study of Latin American society, namely the comprehension of illegitimacy as a style of "doing business." Such an approach allows us to ask an entirely different set of questions than is generally asked by nation-building approaches to Latin America: In effect, how has the area engendered an "institutionalization of crisis" as a *normative* pattern of politics?

The methodological component in this dilemma is that we have sound treatises on each nation *in* Latin America, but correspondingly, unsound doctrines *on* Latin America. The sociology of international stratification is roughly equivalent to where the formal study of social stratification was a quarter of a century ago. The units of measure are different, but the problems are roughly analogous. The work of the thirties convinced many that crude measures of social class needed refinement. This led to a series of doctrines that treated every sub-class as a unique entity that was qualitatively distinct from other sub-classes. Now, in the study of Latin America, and as a reaction to the totalistic approaches of the "big thinkers" of the classical tradition, the nation or even parts of nations have come to be defined as unique entities that are qualitatively distinct from other nations in the Hemisphere. Mexico, Brazil, and Argentina have produced their "exceptionalist" theorists in good number. At a time when some researchers have given up the quest for a unified theory of the Hemisphere, they have pointedly produced a sophisticated body of literature that is qualitatively superior to what previously existed. Yet, even in the results achieved, a certain parallelism with social stratification doctrines of yesteryear can be detected. While there are sophisticated studies available of every nation in Latin America–Cassanova on Mexico (1965), Germani on Argentina (1962), Furtado on Brazil (1965), Fals Borda on Colombia (1963, 1967), to name but a few–there is no significant study of Latin America as a whole which can serve as an explanatory theory about the continent. The position can now be taken that available nation-by-nation accounts have a fragmentizing effect on theoretical generalizations of a hemispheric dimension, and hence result in the general acceptance of static models of Latin American social structure.

To accept the idea of nation-building as fundamental is no less unsatisfactory than to accept the idea that class uniqueness defines all aspects of stratification. To begin with, it is hard to prove that the idea of nationality is any more powerful than that of religion, ethnicity, urbanism, industrialism, or any other organizing principle of social life. Indeed, in many nations, the idea of nationhood is a referent only for the urban middle classes. But beyond the formalistic objections that might be raised by a pluralistic framework is the empirical objection to nation-building approaches that would deny the reality of Latin America.[5] There *are* commonalities: in social history, in class composition, in political organization, in language cluster, and above all, in the common subordinate positions the nations of Latin America occupy with respect to the United States.

In dealing with Latin America as a real entity we are no longer confined to nation-building concepts. It is the line, perhaps the chain, between the United States center and the Latin American peripheries that becomes the organizing link for understanding what constitutes Latin America. The relations between nearly every nation of Latin America and the United States are more direct (at the technological, political, and military levels) than the relations between any two nations within Latin America. This is particularly plain in the military sphere, where the United States is the organizing element which fuses the various hemispheric Defense Pacts, and which unabashedly provides an ideological cement to such operations (cf. Porter, 1967). This is not to deny the relevance of civil or military arrangements among Latin American nations, but only to indicate that such relations are derivative rather than originative, secondary rather than primary (cf. Saxe-Fernandez, 1967, pp. 39-57). Therefore, in explaining the absence of legitimation in both its political and military aspects, we are compelled to introduce the external factor, the role of imperialism.

Latin American elites, while neither impotent nor unified, are not legitimized by a pluralist ideology, nor are they formed primarily through social demands from the masses. Therefore, such elites often lack valued skills of public administration or civic expertise on one side, and the sure knowledge of popular support on the other. These elites often acquire power by unstructured methods. They breed counter-elites with a similar dismissal of technical standards of competence and a like contempt for the popular classes. What evolves are neo-Falangist systems. There is no elite in Latin America which simply legitimizes itself by legal succession of its power. Rather, there are class columns of particularistic power, each a pillar supporting a weak public government, and each cancelling the potential for total power of the other classes or sectors. Falangism is basically a system where multiple elites have a mutual cancellation effect in order to support a public government structure. But, also, each has the power to prevent any other class or group from ruling for any extensive length of time. What each lacks is the power to maintain, establish, and legitimize that rule for a long period of time. In this way, Falangism promotes the personalist style, the *Caudillo* system. But since Falangism is a model for maintaining delicate balances between groups of equal weight by a strong central leader, any displacement of weight creates a crisis in the system as a whole. That is why the area has been run more by Machiavellian foxes than by Platonic lions.

Revolution, or the *coup d'etat,* is often greeted with a sigh of relief by participating social sectors, no matter what the political coloration of the regime or the class involved in the *golpe.* The constancy of such revolutions remains a means to alleviate the tension of groups pulling with equal strength in all directions at once. The *golpe* is a *politically* distributive mechanism without being a *socially* disruptive mechanism. It is a means of changing established policy. No government is thereby ever able to fully legitimize itself by electoral procedures alone, thus producing what I call the "norm of illegitimacy." Long-range periods of constitutional, or at any rate, tranquil government rule become a heavy price to pay for many elite groups whose bases of power remain insecure—or never were secure. They must act quickly, decisively, since candidates who fill office for a legally prescribed period become a threat. If national office is legitimized in electoral procedures, many traditionalistic pillars of society would collapse. It is precisely to prevent their own collapse that such elite groupings of Latin America institute a norm of illegitimacy. This situation has been appreciated by Charles Anderson (1964) when he noted that "with the possible exception of Peron, political intervention by the military in Latin America does not seem to have the effect of overhauling the power system of the society. Rather, under military governments in Latin America, holders of important power capabilities in the society are assured that their position in the society will not be endangered, and are permitted some participation in the political process."

Why are elite groupings of Latin America unable to develop legitimizing models, and why are working classes unable to develop revolutionary models? In part, it is because the management of their affairs is often not in their own hands. For example, although the working class of Brazil may be well organized into unions, and even constitute a "labor aristocracy," the fact is that the unions themselves are often dependent on the whims of the political organization of the State apparatus. This was particularly true from Vargas to Goulart. The State apparatus, for its part, is contingent for its support upon coffee growers and the profits that they bring in from Parana. In turn, the coffee growers in the south are dependent on the international monetary system which regulates the price of coffee, and even regulates the supply of, and demand for, coffee. In other words, elite formations lack a leadership base to press their members' claims and are not free to bargain, to negotiate a public policy. These elites have status without corresponding power. They have enough status to counteract the pressure of other groups, but not enough power to rule. Only the military can act freely to establish new balances and relieve the strain of equal pull in all directions. This it may do by permitting new elite groups to penetrate the political processes, but this mediating role only makes the army the backbone of illegitimacy. The military are too tied into foreign interests themselves and too involved with commercial activities to do anything more than underwrite the norm of illegitimacy throughout the Hemisphere.

The most sophisticated stage of the internal dynamics of illegitimacy is when military structures are overturned by other portions of the military elite. This serves to circulate elites without running even the small risks in "civilianization" of the nation. This sort of military rule is clearly indicated by the fact that not long after the Ecuadorian National Congress was dissolved by the Military Junta, it allowed a constitutent Assembly to be elected on October 16, 1966, to write a new Constitution. More realistically, the three-man army junta was overthrown by an air force group, who in turn underwrote the Conservative Party rule and appointed Otto Arosemena Gomez as interim President (Mallory, 1967). This indicates how extensive the norm of illegitimacy is in Latin American politics—a form of politics that the military are largely responsible for, and yet a form of rule clearly unsuited to long-range mass political mobilization. For this reason, among others, civilian parties continue to prevail in the formal political infrastructure. Thus, the most advanced form of the norm of illegitimacy is when a ruling military junta so much as threatens to civilianize itself, *i.e.*, liberalize its conditions of rule; other portions of the military rapidly move into the political arena to sustain the norm of illegitimacy.

How are nation-building and revolution-making related to one another? How do such interconnections fit into any known facts about Latin America?

To establish such a connection we have to appreciate the role of Latin American *Samurai*—the free floating nineteenth century *caudillo* turned professional twentieth century officer in a situation that demanded nationalism, but disallowed populism.

Since the armed forces of Latin America are interest armies, the analysis of military phenomena cannot be based on one structural type of armed force, such as the federal army sponsored by the national State, but must take into account those military groupings representing other elite (or would-be elite) interests: regional armies and gendarmeries sponsored by local sub-governmental units; feudal and private armies sponsored by the superordinate class, race, or ethnic groups. This classification illustrates not simply the divisions within the military, but how the norm of illegitimacy finds organizational representation and ideological expression in the military sector no less than the political sector.

Militarism is not simply a professional activity in Latin America. Because of its internal control character, it seeps into the life styles of Latin American society in a way which is uncharacteristic of other regions of the world. The military ethic is far more extensive and more potent than the simple numerical count of the size of the armed forces and general staff would reveal. Precisely because the military underwrites the militarization of civil administration, it reinforces illegitimacy, and becomes the key source of Right-wing nationalism. Given its domination by international powers, its nationalism is more rhetorical than real.

It might be objected that this view tends to consider the military a foreign body in the structure of social classes. In point of fact, the military are clearly integrated into most Latin American societies. However, it is important to recognize that the military are not a social class in themselves, but rather function as extensions of certain classes, *i.e.*, they are attached to the landed aristocracy or to the urban middle classes. They only rarely act as a class for themselves, even if they sometimes seem to act as a group in themselves. This marginal role in the social structure accentuates the instability of overt military rule. They are compelled to solicit support from one or another sector of the class network; this then creates the basis for further *golpes* and illicit politics.

This satellitic role of the military is particularly apparent in Latin America, while particularly well hidden in the Middle East, because of the well-defined and long-standing class network existing in Latin America. The "Nasserist option" does not really obtain. Nasserism depends for its strength on an ill-formed, misshapen "classlessness" which exists primarily in many parts of the Middle East. The role of the military as a force for national development, such as the monumental achievement made by Ataturk and the Kemalist forces in Turkey, simply cannot be replicated in Latin America because of the well-established sophistication of class organization in Latin America. Therefore, if the military are not a "foreign body" in Latin America, neither are they a unique force chosen by history to determine the destiny of Latin America.

II. The Imperial Dynamics of Illegitimacy

Take three terms like "modernization," "industrialization," and "development," which in the social science literature are used with such remarkable interchangeability that one begins to wonder why three words are required at all. From my perspective, however, these words not only mean entirely different things, but are often at odds with one another (Horowitz, 1966). Consequently, we have a linguistic barrier to a unified theory of Latin America. The indicators which we have of the Latin continent used in connection with modernization, when employed with any degree of precision, seem to refer to things extending from electrification, creature comforts, highways, and the construction of supermarkets to the unfolding of innovative cultural forms.

Many indicators of modernization–life expectancy, literacy of the masses, sophisticated communication and transportation networks–seem to link up with the urban process. Indeed, modernization is oftentimes used as a surrogate for the urban process. On the other hand, the concept of development is often spoken of as a surrogate for industrialization. The measures used in defining economic development are intimately linked to industry–per capita national production, the consumption of energy, the population employed in business, commerce, and service industries. This distinction between modernization and industrialization is not simply academic. Even if we confine ourselves to the above measures, it is plain that the degree of modernization can diverge radically from that of industrialization. Argentina is as "modern" a society as West Germany, while both Brazil and Mexico are much closer to the big three of the United States, England, and Germany than they are to the Afro-Asian new nations. However, if we substitute measures of industrial potency, developmental levels reveal themselves to be radically different from modernization scales. At the industrial level, Argentina and Brazil come up as being more akin to the Congo and Haiti than to the big three western powers (cf. Germani, 1962). Seen in this light, the ideology behind the "revolution in rising expectations" is anchored to the modernization process, while the ideology of "revolution from below" is clearly anchored to the industrialization process. Thus, development might be said to encompass a double interchange–the interaction of modernization and industrialization forming the core problems of developmental processes and strategies alike.

Economic theory has been adopted to clarify these differences between modernization and industrialization. However, it cannot go beyond its own limits as a science; it can ably *translate* into a more precise language the dilemmas of development but it is no more in a position to *resolve* these dilemmas than phrenology was able to settle problems of mental disorder. Monetarism has been used, especially in present-day Brazil and Argentina, as a device for moving beyond the import-substitution bottleneck into the modern economic sector without revolution. Structuralism has been used, especially in Mexico in the thirties, Cuba in the sixties, and now to a lesser extent in Chile, to overcome import-substitution bottlenecks by creating a more potent national heavy industrial and mining pattern. The link of structuralism is to industrialization what the link of monetarism is to modernization (cf. Felix, 1965, pp. 137-153).

Each strategy of economic growth has its own strains, and each creates political spin-offs. The monetaristic solutions create internal colonial stress by sharpening the conflict between have and have-not sectors, between the largely urban sectors and the largely rural sectors. Thus modernization creates the seeds of social disequilibrium by sharpening the strain between sectors. The structuralistic solutions, in an effort to escape the control by foreign imperial economies of their national economy, face a different set of problems, but a set no less harsh in its implications. In order to lay the basis of an industrial society, a considerable amount of sacrifice is required of the lower classes, the rural classes, and even the middle classes. But what is sacrificed is precisely what monetarism can buy: creature comforts and high standards of personal living, nothing short of the most visible results of "modernization." Thus, structuralism too creates a strain toward disequilibrium within the underdeveloped societies of Latin America.

In short, monetarism and structuralism, which both start out with great expectations to alleviate the material conditions which create revolutions, seem to terminate as economic ideologies inadvertently inducing that which is most dreaded in the other—further dependence on the external economic sector.[7]

Modernization and developmental orientations do not exclude revolutionary alternatives and may parallel an increase rather than a decrease in revolutionary sentiment. The problem of this paradoxical convergence is this: Latin Americans perceive the most modern results of technology; but rarely do they acquire the industrial means for creating such results on an autonomous basis. Attempts to emulate and replicate specific national models oftentimes end in frustration and puzzlement. Frustration of mass goals, which is produced as much by the awareness of cases of advancement as by failure to reach it, makes for revolutionary types of people and for revolutionary types of situations. Revolutionary sentiments are not simply a consequence of underdevelopment, but more properly a result of polarization between developed and underdeveloped sectors. And these polarities confront each other in Latin America not exclusively as a class question, but as a question in international stratification. The large-scale foreign corporation, along with the large-scale penetration of foreign military-bureaucratic forces, produces the same effect in the "periphery" as it does at the "cosmopolitan center": it serves to absorb foreign wealth and soak up foreign labor power.

The factor of illegitimacy is enhanced by the simple device of removing basic strategy decisions from the Latin American orbit and centering them in the imperial concentration points. To execute such control successfully, however, a portion of the Latin American decision-making elites, whether military or civilian in background or occupation, becomes intimately involved in the satisfactory conduct of the local groupings. Thus, instead of being linked to the developmental process, a portion of the local elites become tied to the security of foreign investments. Since these imperial dynamics have the deeper effect of placing the legitimating agencies in foreign control, the actions of the nation-State system in Latin America tend heavily to become repressive. The norm of illegitimacy is therefore guaranteed by an imperial system that sees the constant circulation of local elites as beneficial to its own interests.

The power of the imperial center to determine the forms of Latin American societies is perhaps best illustrated by the case of Bolivia. This country exhibited many tendencies present in Mexico and Cuba: an authentic popular revolution (of the MNR in 1952), a powerful trade union organization, and wide-spread political mobilization, conditions which are clearly necessary ingredients in any model based on legitimation from below. However, the economic fortunes of the nation, while emancipated from "internal colonialists" remained linked (more firmly than ever) to the foreign purchasers of Bolivian natural resources. The radical labor movement, which had the power to cancel a national bourgeoisie, found itself overmatched in competition with the international bourgeoisie. Bolivia became the most heavily subsidized nation per man in the entire world (including all the Near Eastern nations). The United States became the effective underwriter of what was supposedly the most radical political structure in South America. But if the Bolivian miner found his wages improved over pre-revolutionary times, the Bolivian political structure found itself even more dependent on foreign capital than in the pre-revolutionary era. Thus, far from guaranteeing legitimacy from below, such foreign imperial dominion only returned the situation to a *status quo ante* in which the military sector performed its classic function of guaranteeing survival through illegitimacy.

Although it is readily admitted that United States policy, at both the diplomatic and defense levels, is a contributory factor to Latin American militarism, such an admission still perceives of such intervention as a response to, or a product of, local circumstances. I would advance the proposition that what has taken place in increasing degrees is the foreign management of internal conflicts in Latin America. This raises the possibility of a new United States imperialism based on political rather than economic considerations, and therefore, tactically dedicated to indirect management of Latin American military establishments rather than direct interventionism. With the rise of overall strategies on a grand scale, with the assertion that the basic purpose of American national policy is to promote and secure a structure of hemispheric relationships compatible with the values of the United States, local control, idiosyncratic regimes, and classical Latin American strongmen must themselves be bridled—so that the local military no less than the local political administration are plunged into the norm of illegitimacy as a way of maintaining stability by virtue of the requirements of *Pax Americana.*

The new imperialism is conducted largely through political policy whose principal instrument is military assistance with increasing emphasis on the preparation of the armed forces for counterinsurgency operations. As General Porter made perfectly plain in Congressional testimony, the aims of security must take priority over national development. "The Military has frequently proven to be the most cohesive force available to assure public order and support of resolute governments attempting to maintain internal security. Latin American armed forces, acting in conjunction with the police and other security forces, have helped to control disorders and riots, contained or eliminated terrorists and guerrillas, and discouraged those elements which are tempted to resort to violence to overthrow the government."[8] It will be observed that illegitimacy of rule is markedly different from the uses of violence as an agency of mass political mobilization. For what the imperial center requires is a continuation of illegitimacy, but not a continuation of violence. Hence, the classic function of the *coup d'etat* is aborted. It becomes an instrument to prevent, rather than stimulate, rapid, unchallenged social change.

The norm of illegitimacy is underwritten by military assistance programs that transform disparate peripheral and regional military *caciques* representing indigenous factors into a highly coordinated and unified grouping representing an international commitment against communist penetration of the Hemisphere. Joint military operations between the nations of Latin and North America, standardization of equipment, arranging central command structures, increasing conferences and meetings at regional as well as continental levels, all of these serve to transform randomized types of illegitimate rule into a normative pattern of illegitimacy, or at the least a search for order in trans-national terms, *i.e.*, in terms of the interests of the cosmopolitan center.

Such programs, however, circumscribe the level and form of the political activity of Latin American military establishments. They are faced with the choice of supporting United States policy for developing counterinsurgency capabilities (and hence undermining any sort of legitimation that would be derived from mass participatory revolution), or supporting nationalistic factions and jeopardizing their foreign assistance pacts (and hence negating the military elite as a factor in policy-making in Latin America). Whatever the particular decisions taken now, United States policies of military globalism tend to make obsolete earlier efforts at a standard typology of Latin American military styles and forms based exclusively on internal political affairs.

There are severe limits placed upon any autonomous developmental pattern in Latin America. To be sure, these are old nations which have long histories. They are also far more developed than most Asian countries and most African countries in terms of the size of their respective modernized sectors. But the most important point is that Latin America shows the face of the future to other sectors of the Third World. It reveals plainly that liberation from colonialism is radically different than liberation from imperialism. Indeed, the positive termination of the colonial phase may, as a matter of fact, stimulate imperial investment—both in terms of money and manpower. Furtado has expressed the special characteristics of economic instability which made possible the current imperial stage of illegitimacy:

> In Latin America, development induced by the industrial revolution in Europe and the United States was enough to transform part of the economic systems inherited from the colonial epoch, but not enough to create autonomous systems able to generate further growth. Hence, Latin America remained on the 'periphery' of advanced industrial economies at a time when markets for primary products were far from able to generate the dynamism required. (1966, pp. 375-85)

The norm of illegitimacy can arise only in a context where structural requisites for legitimate authority are absent. Legitimate authority can be institutionalized either through mechanisms of law or through mechanisms of class. But if mechanisms of law are inadequate to meet the demands of the society, and mechanisms of class are too underdeveloped to come to the fore, and if both the legal machinery of the State and the class potency of the State are blocked by imperial factors, then the whole discussion of the nature of the legitimation process involves an examination of imperialism.[9] Modernization and industrialization express the contradiction in developmental terms, just as imperialism and nationalism express the contradiction in geo-political terms. For this reason, the connections between these dual processes must be understood if a theory of legitimation is to be forged.

It might be asked: Why doesn't a similar imperialism lead to similar results the world over? If there is an imperialist factor, should it not show up as roughly equivalent in its inputs and consequences the world over? One response that presents itself is that the United States has differential commitments the world over; hence radically different consequences flow from its involvement. When one speaks of the "overextension of the United States commitment," it is hard to imagine that Africa can be viewed in the same way as Latin America. Although a similar set of "interests" may obtain, there are widely varying "obligations." The basic problem for the United States in the second half of the twentieth century is its "security." In determining this security, the place of Latin America is far more central than that of Africa. In Latin America, development induced by the industrial revolution was enough to transform part of the economic system inherited from the colonial epoch, but not enough to create an autonomous system capable of generating autonomous growth. In this, Latin America, precisely because of its profound *modernization,* is more directly linked to the cosmopolitan centers of industrialism than are the nations of Africa and Asia. The latter remain traditional but also politically far more mobile and free-wheeling. Thus, the special relationship of Latin America to North America, and vice versa, creates a special set of results.

In the nineteenth century imperialism was a less weighty phenomenon than now. However, if we take the relationship of the British Empire to the growth of Brazil, or if we examine the history of British colonial overseas relationships in Argentina in the nineteenth century, we will see everything from the organization of the cattle industry to the organization of the railroads directly related to the impact of the overseas factor. Whether we consider Spanish colonial rule in the eighteenth century, British colonial rule in the nineteenth century, or United States colonial rule in the twentieth century, one of the essential constants in Latin American—however shifting in form—has been the presence of an imperial factor. And it is the interpenetration of traditionalistic classes with highly sophisticated international monetary elites that provides the material bases for the norm of illegitimacy.

What becomes clear is that the norm of illegitimacy is serviceable both to the internal needs of the political-military order which gives visible direction to Latin American policies, and to the international needs of the economic order which limits the directions that the indigenous elements may chance upon. Thus, nationalism from within and imperialism from without, far from being at loggerheads over the management of Latin America, serve more often than not to complement each other. The touching faith in nationalist solutions as a means for transcending imperial domination simply ignores the character of the nationalisms manifested in Latin America. The nationalism of the Right, which has prevailed in nearly every country of the Southern Hemisphere, offers scant optimism for avoiding imperial control. Indeed, such "nationalist" leaders of the "whole people" as Juan Peron, Getulio Vargas, and Rojas Pinilla were compelled to abandon their optimal plans for a countervailing imperialism of the Southern Hemisphere and settle for a "partnership" with foreign corporate wealth. They were trapped in the supreme contradiction of satisfying the requirements of the neo-Falangist elite arrangement, and hence having to finance their nationalistic ambitions through outside sources, the much maligned foreign capital.

Given this set of circumstances, a theory of Latin America cannot avoid being incorporated into a larger framework of the interplay of nationalism and colonialism. The definition of Latin America is itself a consequence of this interplay. If this formulation strikes the observer as crude, lacking in sophistication, so be it! The objective situation is itself crude and lacking in sophistication. The norm of illegitimacy is informally sanctioned from the lowest petty official living off of bribes in some remote customs house in Asuncion or Sao Paulo to the highest official living off the mineral produce of Latin America in some highly visible counting house in New York or London. To break the cycle of crisis and collapse, to eliminate the norm of illegitimacy as an operational code for Latin America, means to break the organizational impasse created by both local bureaucrats and imported businessmen.

Appendix: Some Qualifying Aspects to the Norm of Illegitimacy

As I indicated at the outset, we do not have any adequate general social theory of Latin America. And although I would maintain that the kind of approach outlined here, focusing on the interpenetration of national elites and imperial investors, is the main pivot in a system of survival through illegitimacy, this by no means explains the actual behavior of *all* Latin American nations. While it might be quite serviceable for sixteen of them, there are at least four cases where the norm of illegitimacy does not obtain—certainly not in "ideal-typical" form. They are Chile, Cuba, Mexico, and Uruguay (and perhaps Costa Rica). But rather than resort to a mobilization-integration model (Germani, 1964, pp. 391-408) which indeed was a first serviceable attempt at a general theory, I would rather like to explain why, at least in two cases—those of Mexico and Uruguay—the norm of illegitimacy does not presently obtain.[10]

The first fact to take into consideration about Uruguay is that from its inception there existed a relatively strong parallel dualism: a rural political party representing landholding economic interests and an urban party representing middle class and organized working class interests. The stability of its political system was therefore more a result of the neatness in the division of power, in the stability of the equilibrium, than in any perfectly meshed network of mass mobilization and integration.[11]

The neatness of class and elite divisions is itself a consequence of the second major fact about Uruguay. It evolved as a buffer State separating the two titans of the Southern Hemisphere, Brazil and Argentina. Thus, it comes into existence without the myriad of sub-class pressure groups and shadow elites which pervade nearly every other nation in the Hemisphere. Uruguay has no need to call upon the military to expand or contract civil power, since the balancing act was achieved by administrative fiat at the start of its national independence period. At the same time, Uruguay is in a position to function in terms of legitimate authority, since such small-nation legitimacy itself provides essential security to the large nations with which it borders. Whatever the nature of Brazilian and Argentine politics, they nonetheless retain a shared interest in seeing to it that Uruguay is run on at least semi-democratic principles.

At the same time, the satellitic aspects of Uruguay are also reinforced by the fact that, like Denmark and Finland in Europe, Uruguay is a modernized nation and not a developmental nation. It has been moved to evolve satellitic economic relations without sacrificing its political autonomy. Indeed, Uruguay has engaged in an historic trade-off characteristic of a number of more advanced small nations: it performs a willing (or at least a knowing) satellitic economic role in exchange for a guarantee of political sovereignty.

The exceptional circumstances in Uruguay's historical evolution–its parity of class cleavage and absence of parasitic sectors and its trade-off of economic independence for political sovereignty–serves to explain why this small "Switzerland of the Western Hemisphere" is able to escape the hard fate of its more powerful neighbors. Yet it would not be quite accurate to say that Uruguay is a legitimate polity in the classical sense, since what one finds is a peculiar "withering away of State power." The political system in Uruguay serves to allocate bureaucratic functions and to adjudicate the claims of various social factions; however it does not have real autonomous powers to act. This situation could thus be described as semi-legitimacy.

In a country like Mexico one might inquire: Does not legitimate authority obtain? Do you not have the orderly transfer of power? Have you had any revolutionary upheavals since the Revolution of 1920? Is there any evidence of a military *coup d'etat* coming? Surely, if the question of legitimacy is linked to the satisfactory management of succession crises, Mexico would be the direct opposite of Argentina or Peru. But is such a criterion of formalistic succession on much better footing than personal charisma? Several kinds of answers can be fashioned.

Mexico did have a twentieth century national revolution which at the very least gives to it a degree of autonomy absent in most other countries in the Hemisphere. But Mexico is now undergoing a crisis of a very profound sort. Mexico is a single-party State. It has one major party which regularly receives between eighty-five and ninety percent of the vote; two minor parties, one Left and one Right, share the remaining ballots. The choice of officialdom is increasingly becoming internal through the party mechanism. The party mechanism of PRI is becoming a political IBM system: balancing out the needs, requests, and demands of different sectors. The Mexican polity has been properly characterized as "a complicated system of exchanges between interest groups and an oligarchy that provides decisive and sometimes rather ruthless leadership." (Anderson and Cockroft, 1966, pp. 11-28). The pillars of power are becoming increasingly uneven, and the possibility of tumultuous change is pressing.

The crisis has not been made manifest in Mexico precisely because the public sector of the economy has become so powerful, bureaucratic, and entrenched that it is even hard for a class such as the private industrial class to exercise any autonomous power. The Mexican military budget has been considerably enlarged in the last three years. The growth of sporadic guerrilla insurgency which has been widely reported and the recent student riots at the National University of Mexico have each indicated the growth of illegitimate forms of political behavior. The steady investment in domestic rather than foreign industry taking place in Mexico has exacted a great toll from the national working classes. The high growth rate of Mexico's economy prevents any outbreak of mass violence. But what would take place if there were a growth rate decline, or a weakening of Mexico's economy as a result of a concerted boycott by the Central American Trade Association, is difficult to ascertain.

In a country like Mexico, the abortive character of the 1910-20 Revolution is beginning to have its effects. Nonetheless, it should be kept in mind that Mexico remains one of the most *stable* regimes in the Hemisphere. Yet even a background in revolution does not exempt Mexico from the legitimacy crisis. For although Mexico achieved its legitimacy through mass revolution, it was able to guarantee its polity only in the thirties, when it successfully carried through an oil nationalization plan that met with the hearty disapprobation of the United States. The Mexican problem is how to maintain this network of legitimacy in a period when its economic resources are now large enough to compete with the United States at least on a regional basis, but not powerful enough to cancel United States interests as a whole. How Mexico can manage the dynamics of imperialism will thus become a critical factor in evaluating its long run chances for legitimate rule.

Therefore, as in the case of Uruguay, Mexico too reveals a peculiar deterioration of State power, or at least its inability to define its power in any context other than that provided by the ruling political party. The Mexican State does not have powers to act; the PRI does have such powers. In this situation, where the party rather than the polity is endowed with legitimacy, this situation could be described as *quasi-legitimacy.*

In the two negative cases introduced – Uruguay and Mexico – what one finds on inspection is not simply a generalized confrontation of legitimate versus illegitimate forms of polity, but rather some sophisticated shadings that reveal elements of both, and virtues (or vices) of neither.

NOTES

*This paper is one of two studies attempting to work out a general theory of political participation in Latin America. The other study, entitled "Political Legitimacy and the Norm of Conflict," appeared in *Comparative Political Studies,* Vol. 1, No. 1 (1968).

1. Compare and contrast Karl Marx and Friedrich Engels (1932, pp. 31-32), with Max Weber (1947, p. 154).

2. The best example of this kind of approach is in United States Department of Defense (1964). For a more recent example along similar lines, see Willard F. Barber (1966).

3. I have attempted to summarize the position of the Latin American military in my study of "the Military Elites " in Lipset and Solari, (1967, pp. 146-89).

4. Torcuato Di Tella (1964, 1967) has pointed out key differences related to the above and provided a useful typology for examining working-class organization.

5. One scholar who has come to appreciate the reality of Latin America and use it as an organizing principle in his work is Donald Marquand Dozer, (1962).

6. I have tried to express the nature of such terminological differences in *Three Worlds of Development* (Horowitz, 1966C).

7. This dovetailing of outcomes between monetarism and structuralism is made painfully, if inadvertently, clear in the set of papers on *Inflation and Growth in Latin America,* edited by Werner Baer and Isaac Kerstenetzky (1964).

8. Robert W. Porter, Jr., *op. cit.* For confirmation that Porter represents the dominant U.S. policy, and not simply an idiosyncratic viewpoint, see the testimony of Lincoln Gordon on the "Foreign Assistance Act of 1966." (Gordon, 1966), and Richard R. Clark (1966, pp. 18-19).

9. Whatever the evidential shortcomings, this response to the logic of the situation is well appreciated by Andre Gunder Frank (1967).

10. My reasons for omitting Cuba and Chile from consideration here are that in the case of Cuba, I have attempted to provide some sort of accounting elsewhere, (Horowitz, 1966a, b) and in the case of Chile, my knowledge is far too limited to make an attempt at even an educated guess.

11. See, on this, my study "La politica urbana en Latinoamerica," (1967b). I might add in this connection that the discussion on Uruguay was omitted from the English language version of this paper.

BIBLIOGRAPHY

Anderson, Bo and James D. Cockcroft

1966 "Cooptation in Mexican Politics," *International Journal of Comparative Sociology*, Vol. 7, No. 1.

Anderson, Charles W.

1964 "Toward a Theory of Latin American Politics," in Occasional Paper No. 2 in *The Graduate Center for Latin American Studies,* Nashville: Vanderbilt University.

Baer, Werner and Isaac Kerstenetsky, editors

1964 *Inflation and Growth in Latin America,* A publication of the Economic Growth Center, Yale University. Homewood, Illinois: Richard D. Irwin, Inc.

Barber, Willard F.

1966 "The American Concept of Counterinsurgency: Some Latin American Applications," Presented at the American Association for the Advancement of Science, Washington, D.C. (mimeographed).

Clark, Richard R.

1966 "U.S. Military Assistance in Latin America," *Army Digest.*

DiTella, Torcuato

1964 *El sistema politico argentino y la clase obrera.* Buenos Aires: Editorial Universitaria de Buenos Aires.

1967 "Populism and the Working Class in Latin America," *in Government and Politics in Latin America* (tentative title), New York: Frederick A. Praeger.

Dozer, Donald Marquand

1962 *Latin America: An Interpretive History.* New York: McGraw-Hill Book Company.

Fals-Borda, Orlando

1963 *La violencia on Colombia: Estudio de un procese social* (with Herman Guzman Compos and Eduardo Umana Luna). Bogota: Ediciones Tercer Mundo (second edition).

1967 *La subversion en Colombia: el cambio social on la historia.* Bogota: Ediciones Tercer Mundo.

Felix, David

1965 "Monetarists, Structuralists, and Import-Substituting Industrialization," *Studies in Comparative International Development,* Vol. I, No. 10.

Frank, Andre Gunder

1967 *Capitalism and Underdevelopment in Latin America: Historical Studies of Chile and Brazil.* New York and London: Monthly Review Press.

Furtado, Celso

1963 *The Economic Growth of Brazil.* Berkeley and Los Angeles: University of California Press.

1965 *Diagnosis of the Brazilian Crisis.* Berkeley and Los Angeles: University of California Press.

1966 "U.S. Hegmony and the Future of Latin America," *The World Today: The Royal Institute of International Affairs.* Vol. 22, No. 9.

Germani, Gino

1955 *Estructura Social de la Argentina.* Buenos Aires: Editorial Raigal.

1962 *Politica y Sociedad en una Epoca de Transicion: De la sociedad tradicional a la sociedad de masas.* Buenos Aires: Editorial Paidos.

1964 "Social Change and Intergroup Conflicts," *The New Sociology*, edited by Irving Louis Horowitz. New York and London: Oxford University Press.

Gordon, Lincoln

1966 Testimony on "Foreign Assistance Act or 1966," *Hearings Before the House Committee on Foreign Affairs,* Washington: USGPO.

Horowitz, Irving Louis

1966a "The Stalinization of Castro," *New Politics,* Vol. IV No. 4.

1966b "Cuban Communism," *Trans-Action,* Vol. 4, No. 10.

1966c *Three Worlds of Development: The Theory and Practice of International Stratification.* New York and London: Oxford University Press.

1967a "The Military Elites," in *Elites in Latin America,* edited by Seymour Martin Lipset and Aldo Solari. New York: Oxford University Press.

1967b "La Politica Urbana en Latinoamerica," *Revista Mexicana de Sociologia,* Vol. XXVIII, No. 1.

Mallory, Water H., editor

1967 *Political Handbook and Atlas of the World: 1967.* New York and Evanston: Harper & Row.

Marx, Karl and Friedrich Engels

1932 *Manifesto of the Communist Party.* New York: International Publishers.

Moreno, Frank Jay

1967 "The Spanish Colonial System: A Functional Approach," *The Western Political Quarterly,* Vol. 1 XX, No. 2, Pt. 1.

Porter, Robert W.

1967 Statement before the House Foreign Affairs Committee on the FY 1968 Military Assistance Program.

Saxe-Fernández, Juan

1967 "El Consejo de defensa Centroamericano y la *Pax Americana,*" *Cuadernos Americanos,* Vol. CLII, No. 3.

Stavenhagen, Rodolfo

1966/67 "Seven Erroneous Theses About Latin America," *New University Thought,* Vol. 4, No. 4.

United States Department of Defense

1964 "Civic Action: The Military Role in Nation-Building," *Armed Forces Information and Education,* Vol. III, No. 14.

Weber, Max

1947 *The Theory of Social and Economic Organization.* New York: Oxford University Press.

PEASANT ORGANIZATIONS IN THE PROCESS OF POLITICAL MODERNIZATION: THE LATIN AMERICAN EXPERIENCE

Gerrit Huizer

I

The need for agrarian reform in Latin America to promote economic improvement and political integration will be taken for granted in this paper. The aim is to sympathetically examine the experience of peasant organizations in the region, and particularly the role they play in gaining the political objectives of the peasantry. Peasant organizations are not only important as pressure groups bargaining for agrarian reform, but also as they help their members to achieve the fuller participation in the social and political life of the nation which "modernization" implies.

Because of the strength of the economic and political interests opposing agrarian reform, the development of community and peasant organizations has been difficult in most of Latin America. These interests likewise oppose other forms of political participation by the peasantry. I must, at the outset, frankly state my predisposition in favor of peasants' political activities, and the orientation of my studies toward finding ways to accelerate the growth of political participation and structural reforms. Three related issues will be explored here: the political aims of the peasant organizations, the factors affecting peasant "organizability," and the processes by which the organizations have developed. The experience of Mexico, Bolivia, Venezuela, Peru, and Colombia provide the major examples (Huizer, 1967, 1968; Huizer and Hewitt, 1969).

It appears from historical examples that serious changes in the peasants' power position are not a consequence of well-intentioned planning or legislation, but result from increasing the bargaining power and organized pressure of the peasants themselves. This pressure is requisite to gaining needed legislation and even more essential to effective implementation of reform laws.

An interesting and important example of the ups and downs in peasant influence on legislation and implementation is found in Mexico. Sustained and militant peasant pressure by the movement lead by Zapata could only be appeased by the land reform legislation of 1915. Later, strongly organized and armed peasant organizations won large-scale and drastic implementation of the early legislation during the period of the Cárdenas presidency (1934-1940), after the process had been stagnant for many years. The same kind of pressure was again effective in 1958 when symbolic invasions of lands, after many years of legal petitions by the peasants had failed, were staged by a "popular socialist" peasant movement in the Northwestern states of Mexico. Several *latifundios* which existed in circumvention of the law were expropriated and distributed among the petitioners after these invasions. The most spectacular case was the 300,000 hectare estate of the Cananea Cattle Company in Cananea, Sonora, owned by United States citizens. The movement was led by Jacinto Lopez and owed much of its success to his able and determined leadership. The fact that the Lopez Mateos government in Mexico (1958-1964) stepped up the agrarian reform efforts was partly due to the impact of this movement, which covered the states of Sinaloa, Sonora, and Baja California with many simultaneously organized peaceful invasions.[1]

In Bolivia, the armed peasant organization around Cochabamba, which spread to most of the country in 1952-1953, was the most important factor in the promulgation of agrarian reform legislation and in the actual take-over of most of the *latifundios* even before proper implementation of the law was possible (Patch, 1960).

The Convención Valley in the Department of Cuzco in Peru obtained special land reform legislation in 1963 after the peasant organizations in the area headed by Hugo Blanco had created a movement which threatened to spread across the whole nation (Huizer, 1967, pp. 167-173; Craig, 1969). In Venezuela, unrest and turmoil created by the peasants who were organized mainly by Acción Democrática militants in spite of adverse political conditions were institutionalized and controlled only after agrarian reform was well under way. After the Pérez Jiménez government was overthrown in 1958, an estimated 500 occupations of land took place, particularly in the more densely populated parts of the country where the Federación Campesina de Venezuela was strong. Those lands which the peasants expected to obtain through the agrarian reform program which had been announced were taken by them to speed up the program (Huizer, 1967, pp. 203-208; Powell, 1969).

There are exceptions to this rule, of course. In the early 1950's in Guatemala, a land reform law was promulgated, and the peasants were organized at the initiative of political forces which were favorable to the peasant cause, but this program was undone within two years. Chile may be on its way to becoming another exception.

As peasant organizations gain strength, they typically become involved in a growing network of interest groups – cooperatives, credit societies, and development committees. The most important groups to which these organizations link themselves are generally political, and political groups often have a radicalizing influence, leading to the setting of goals beyond those originally expressed by the peasants. Thus, the movement in La Convención as well as that of Cochabamba started to pressure for full-fledged agrarian reform on a regional and even national scale after they had received no satisfaction of their earlier, more moderate demands.

There are also political groups which try to mobilize peasant movements and, once they are in full control, turn them to political purposes not primarily in the interests of the peasantry and, sometimes, contrary to those interests. Some of these politically-dominated organizations try to soothe the peasants rather than encourage their demands for strong reform measures. In the same way, some political forces seek simply to buy off or corrupt the peasant movement and its leaders. In Mexico, Zapata, who was sought out with such aims, did not give in; others, however, have. In Venezuela, the peasant organization was led by politicians from its beginning, and they eventually expelled the radical peasant leaders from the movement. In Bolivia, the strongly organized peasants were able to influence the main political party, which needed their support, to the benefit of the agrarian cause, and today, the achievements appear practically irreversible.

II

The considerable impact – in both active and passive ways – of peasant organizations in the modernization process justifies special attention to the "why" and "how" of the formation of such organizations and movements. What are the conditions which make it easy or difficult for them to be organized, to grow, and to become influential? A number of preliminary hypotheses, based on the literature and my own experience in the field, will be offered here.

About the "organizability" of the peasants, much can be learned through comparing the different areas in which important regional or nation-wide peasant movements started. It then comes out clearly that they are among the less poor and less "marginal" agricultural areas in Latin America. This was the situation in the sugar plantation area in Morelos where the Zapata movement started. The Department of Cochabamba, where the reform movement was strongest, is one of the richest agricultural areas of Bolivia. La Convención valley in Peru, the sugar cane areas in Pernambuco in northeast Brazil, the State of Veracruz, in Mexico, the densely populated states of Aragua and Carabobo in Venezuela, are all economically above-average areas in which important peasant organizations came into being. Another characteristic which these areas share appears to be that they are relatively densely populated, less isolated and/or less rigidly traditional and feudal. Some of these areas have easy access to major cities; in others, the "modernizing" influence of industries, such as mining, can be clearly seen.

There is evidence that organizations originate more easily among peasants who are working or have worked independently, and whose expectations regarding welfare are at least somewhat above the subsistence level. In plantation areas, such as Morelos, the peasants led by Zapata experienced independence shortly before they were all "proletarianized" and transformed into wage workers for the sugar estates.

More important, however, than the actual situation of relative well-being, (compared with most other peasants in Latin America), is the fact that changes occurred in this situation which tended to diminish the security of the peasants. The condition of the peasants under the traditional order does not, by itself, provoke them into organizing. Organizations have sprung up where there has been an important "erosion of the *status quo*." A *change for the worse* can awaken them to defend the little they have, and this may occur in many ways. For example, in the area where the Brazilian Ligas Camponesas were started in Pernambuco the landowner of the Galileia estate sought to introduce sugar cane production on lands where for years subsistence and commercial crops had been cultivated on a tenancy basis. His efforts, including the use of violence to impose the new system, provoked the peasants to organize in their own defense.

Generalizing, it appears that a strong sense of frustration will often induce peasants to take the risks inherent in joining together. A secure, benevolent, paternalistic *status quo* is not a favorable climate for such activities. But, once the situation erodes so as to create acute frustration, people become restless and "organizable." In Mexico, the indigenous communities had very low levels of living, but were relatively quiescent until the feudal *latifundios* sought to usurp the little they had, taking over much of their traditionally-held lands. This set off what, by some accounts, was one of the bloodiest revolutions of modern history. The increasing demands of the *hacendados* versus their *arrendires*[2] set off the peasant movement in La Convención, Peru. The opposition of the rural elite to the renting of the Santa Clara estate by a peasant union in Ucureña, Bolivia, turned a small peasant organization into a radical, large-scale movement. Refusal to fulfill the moderate demands of cotton workers in the Laguna area in Mexico lead to a movement which resulted in a complete expropriation of the *haciendas* in 1936 (Huizer, 1967, p. 119-140; Senior, 1958). It appears, then, that some severe alteration in the conditions imposed by the traditional landed elite, rather than some spontaneous or internally generated "revolutionary" spirit in the peasants, creates the appropriate conditions for organized movements.

There are indications that it is the rigidly-negative reaction of the landholders to moderate demands which has contributed most to the awakening of the peasants, preparing them for collective action. Increasing harshness and terror often accompanies attempts to maintain the old order. Subsequently political and military forces arrive to rescue the landowners. Such incidents stimulate and bring to consciousness not only an awareness of the injustice which exists in the traditional oppressive conditions, but also a readiness to organize.

Some kinds of agricultural improvement can play a limited but important role in the awakening process. The above-mentioned examples of peasant movements were related to moderately successful agricultural development efforts: The *arrendires* in La Convención; the *sindicato* in Ucureña which had rented the land from the Santa Clara estate; the commercially-oriented agriculture of the peasants who worked the lands of *engenho* (sugar estate) Galileia. These were spontaneous development efforts undertaken by the peasants themselves. It is also likely that many of the current self-help and community development programs (including cooperative organization, agricultural extension, and supervised credit), which are discontinued or allowed to fail helped create the frustration out of which dynamic peasant organizations have emerged. The *status quo* is undermined by small improvement programs, but generally not radically enough to give the peasants the feeling that a new life is beginning for them. Too frequently, the traditional interests manage to get such a large share of the benefits that the programs lose their appeal for the peasants. In addition, there are often directly opposing forces limiting the scope and success of any program which might lead to drastic, local, social change. Almost predictably, it is exactly this type of opposition which often leads to the emergence of more radical movements seeking really drastic reforms. Of course, a great deal more evaluation of concrete cases is needed to bring out these relationships, and more knowledge of the dynamics of these processes may lead to more effective "political reform-mongering," as well as to community development programming.

The effects of pilot projects and other well-meant but half-hearted development measures are often misunderstood and greatly overestimated by the outsider. While visitors may be impressed by spectacular local projects, the peasants in surrounding areas are more likely to be skeptical. The publicity built around such show projects, and the constant influx of visitors, have an effect on the peasants which is more frustrating than satisfying. The discrepancy between promise and reality is perhaps too obvious.

Another source of frustration as well as a stimulant to action is rural community development programs which promote "popular participation;" the peasants get a taste of democratic ways of life different from their traditional, paternalistic society, one of the reasons, of course, why some large landowners and the governments influenced by them go very slowly on community development and literacy campaigns. However, development experts in Latin America are increasingly aware of the importance of social mobility and access to social and political power for the under-privileged majorities, and Latin American local government, as an expression of local power structures, is at last beginning to receive the critical attention it deserves.

Although there is great differentiation within the rural labor force, from landless proletariat through indigenous *comuneros*[3], effective organization is possible among all these types once frustration and awareness of opportunity exists. The group most difficult to organize is that composed of destitute peasants who live at or below the margin of subsistence, are highly dependent upon their *patrõn,* and live in isolated conditions or as migrant workers. Such rural people come into movements only when their lot becomes *more than unbearable,* and a violent explosion may result, without any organization.

Within the spectrum of "organizability" at the opposite extreme, are tenants or sharecroppers who have experienced a certain independence in managing their own plots. They are more apt to feel frustration and take the initiative in organizing. Eviction from land they have cultivated for many years without reimbursement for the improvements brought about, insecurity of tenure related to arbitrariness of the landowners, and high rents as such, are major causes for frustration. Many such tennants feel that the large share of the produce and cash which goes to the landowner is an unjust payment. The more alert ones are aware that the benefits produced by their toil are conspicuously consumed by the landowners in the cities, in luxurious housing and other status symbols, and this aggravates their anger.

III

Given a situation in which conditions for the organization of peasants and other rural workers are favorable, many factors can contribute to the actual springing up of an organization. The first steps toward organization are often taken by peasants who want to solve specific problems and deal with concrete grievances. The real impulse usually comes when those who are in a position to solve the problem or respond to the grievance refuse to do so, forcing the peasants to become more aware of their situation. This rigidity of the powerholders usually reflects their fear that giving in to any requests from below will seriously endanger the *status quo.* This consistently negative response, as in Ucureña (Bolivia) in the late 1930's, in Morelos around 1910, and at La Convención in the late 1950's, is one of the main reasons that the budding local movement looks for more drastic ways of supporting their demands.

Sometimes, a specific precipitating event, a concrete case of felt injustice, may produce a sudden growth in the unity and militancy of the peasants but in other cases, the process is more gradual. Under the surface, the desire for land is a basic driving force in most growing peasant movements. This comes into the open, however, only after the peasants have gained some experience in united action, and have come to believe that their aspirations are more realizable than they could have imagined when their traditional apathy still weighed heavily upon them.

Unquestionably, a *charismatic leader* who knows how to rally the peasants once the conditions for the creation of a movement are favorable is also important. One can probably say that there are many areas where favorable conditions for unionization exist, but where the lack of capable leadership prevents successful organization. A common misconception is that all peasant movements and organizations are created by outsiders, particularly, men from urban areas. Most of the important movements, however, have been started by indigenous leaders, that is, locally-born members of the farming classes, although it is true that they have usually had experience, generally urban, which has helped to prepare them for movement leadership. Emiliano Zapata had his army experience and a period of work in the city; José Rojas of Ucureña had experience in Argentina; Primo Tapia, in Hichoacán, was a *bracero* in the United States for some time.

Once a rudimentary rural organization exists, urban political leaders on the order of Hugo Blanco in La Convención, Francisco Julião in the Northeast of Brazil, and the Acción Democrática party leaders in Venezuela often assume the overall leadership, and help the organization to gain regional and national impact. On a number of occasions, however, authentic peasant leaders (such as Rojas and Zapata), with the important aid of school teachers, lawyers, and politicians, were able to remain in control. A cross-fertilization between peasant and urban-political leadership seems to be common. Here, as elsewhere, problems of developing "natural leaders" and of bringing capable organizers with labor union and political experience into rural areas would benefit greatly from comparative case studies, and insights into the kinds of urban experiences which peasant leaders find most valuable would be useful for future training programs.

It often happens that as a peasant organization achieves importance, government officials and political parties try to gain control of it for its voting power. Some groups may then use this control to strengthen the peasant organization against such opposing forces as the large landholders, as happened under Cárdenas in Mexico and apparently in the late 1940's in Venezuela. On other occasions, the political organization seeks to placate the peasants and meet their demands only to the extent needed to get their votes. In such cases, the peasant organization may become a more or less bureaucratic organism for the channelling of favors and benefits such as credit and jobs, while the official agrarian reform program grinds to a halt. This appears to be especially the case when the middle classes or a new elite develop an increasing stake in the "establishment," and fear that radical peasant demands will disrupt the whole social structure. Mexico after Cárdenas and Venezuela since the early 1960's may be such cases. The peasantry, feeling betrayed, may then become involved in new, radically-oriented, and independent movements which can be kept under control only by violent government repression. Comparisons among different examples of these processes may provide answers to the problem of balancing drastic reform, popular participation, and political stability.

The influence of politicans who gain control over peasant organizations can block the achievement of peasant goals, if such control deteriorates to the point of strengthening only the political power of some *caudillo*. Then, an agrarian program may become merely a device to gain support, only to be dropped when it is no longer needed. The tendency to follow one leader for better or worse – called *caudillismo* or *personalismo* – appears to be a remnant of a feudal social structure which continues to be influential in many Latin American countries. It is a serious obstacle to effective peasant organization in Latin America, but may be partially overcome through the strengthening of internal democracy within the organizations.

Among the various ways to increase the actual bargaining power of growing peasant organizations, direct action on concrete demands appears to be important. Peasant organizations and their leaders gain strength and experience by organizing a strike, a symbolic occupation of land, or a mass demonstration. Such undertakings are risky in the sense that they may fail and lead to disillusionment and repression, but the many cases in which valuable experience and unity were gained appear to justify the risks involved.

It is obviously useful to the cause of rural organization that government officials offer genuine support. The Cárdenas period in Mexico, the initial stages of the Acción Democrática (1945-1948) in Venezuela, and the MNR-stimulated movement all over Bolivia in 1952-53 are examples of this.

In cases where the authorities used public forces to defend the peasants, or armed the peasants themselves when the landowners violently opposed the implementation of the laws, the peasantry appeared to react in a constructive way, to the benefit of political stability in the country, as in the Cárdenas period in Mexico. President Cardenas, in order to be able to effectively distribute land to 770,000 peasants in six years in spite of the often violent opposition of the landowners, had to create the peasant militia. Sixty thousand rifles were given to the peasant groups between 1934 and 1940, supervised by about 200 regular army officers. At the same time, workers and peasants were organized into their respective national federations which formed part of the official party, at that time called *Partido de la Revolución Mexicana* (Party of the Mexican Revolution), later the PRI (Party of the Institutionalized Revolution). Several attempts by the conservative forces to overthrow the Cárdenas government failed because of the politically organized and armed support of the peasants and workers. The orderly change of government in 1940 also took place because of this support (Huizer, 1967, p. 82-88; Nathan, 1955, p. 100).

In various cases, peasant organizations have found support and guidance from urban labor and leftist political groups which helped to formulate and channel the peasants' demands into organized action. In the Valle de la Convención, Peru, the regional peasant federation received considerable advice and support from lawyers working with the labor unions of Cuzco. Hugo Blanco, who at a later stage became the secretary-general of the federation, had been a labor organizer. The peasant federation of the Cochabamba area received support, particularly in its efforts to spread all over Bolivia, from miners or peasants with mining experience.[4] The peasant organizations of the Laguna area in Mexico which provided the large scale expropriations of 1936, were built up with the assistance and guidance of the workers unions of the towns of Torreon and Gomez Palacio. The movement of peasants which led to many land expropriations and distributions in Northwestern Mexico in 1958 was led by labor organizers and teachers, mainly belonging to or sympathizing with the Popular (Socialist) Party, headed by Lombardo Toledano. In Venezuela, the labor organizers of the Acción Democrática party were influential in the peasant organizations which struggled for agrarian reform in 1958. The local grouping which grew into the *Ligas Camponesas* in Northeast Brazil, was founded by José dos Prazeres, a peasant's son with experience as a labor organizer. Francisco Julião, a lawyer in Recife, used his small estate and his position as a state deputy to help build the movement throughout Pernambuco and other parts of Brazil.[5] The relation between rural and urban labor movements needs much further study.

It should also be noted that various local organizations have purposely used forms of organization other than formal unionization in order not to alarm landowners. Peasant unions are sometimes disguised as literary clubs, civic action groups, or mutual benefit committees which show their true character only after they gain experience and some kind of recognized existence.

In peasant organizations, a distinction is made between *agitation* and *organization*. Agitation – the holding of mass meetings, rallies, and demonstrations – can be useful in drawing attention to existing abuses and the demands of the peasants for change and improvement. However, to obtain broad agrarian reform, more than this is needed. The building of an organizational structure which has at its disposal many forms of strategy and tactics is a long-term process. The important movements such as those led by Zapata, Hugo Blanco, Julião, Rojas, and Jacinto Lopez have all gone through this painful process of organization.

At the local level, it appears to be wise policy to base the strength of peasant organizations on nuclei of slightly better off peasants who have resources to fall back upon if they get into difficulties. Later on, they can gain massive support through concrete action by large groups of peasants who have no resources at all. This policy was successfully applied in the *Ligas Camponesas,* and it seems, also, that Zapata got a great deal of support from such local nuclei who took the risk of founding agrarian committees in Mexican communities. In Taretan, Michoacán, Mexico, a recent case study indicated that, initially, several efforts to form a peasant committee to petition for land from the local *hacienda* were unsuccessful. Opposition from the local clergy and the armed bands of the *hacienda*-owner scared the *peons*. Once the initiative was supported strongly by some of the local merchants and craftsmen and the sons of a better-off farmer in the community, and was linked to a regional peasants' and workers' federation, the movement succeeded and the *hacienda* lands were distributed according to the law (Landsberger and Hewitt, 1966; Alcantara, 1968).

In studying the factors which influence the organizational process, special attention must be given to the dynamics of the process, and it is important to do comparative analyses. Some organizations start in one place, and then spread like oil patches into the surrounding areas where essentially the same conditions prevail, such as in Ucureña in the Cochabamba Valley. It also happens that attempts to organize spontaneously occur in scattered communities or areas in a country. Such attempts can be incorporated into a nation-wide movement created by political leaders to gain support from broad masses for a reform program. The rest of the peasants in the country are then organized from above. The first of these types of processes is predominantly horizontal, while the other is to a large extent vertical. Most of the known cases appear to be a mixture of these two approaches (Quijano, 1967). The second (vertical) approach often follows the horizontal after it has achieved considerable success. This seems to have happened in a later stage of the Bolivian revolution, and also in Venezuela and many areas of Mexico.

In some countries, political groups compete with each other in gaining control of an existing more or less spontaneous movement. Occasionally, one political group takes the banner of such a movement to extend it nation-wide, while others create new, sometimes parallel, organizations, at the local and national level. Depending on the political structure predominant in a country, one political group, through official or other powerful support, can sometimes gain almost complete control over all the organizations. Elsewhere organizations with different political color exist beside one another in competition or – more rarely – in some form of coexistence or collaboration.

IV

Comparative study of many cases of successful peasant movements which achieved sufficient political influence or bargaining power to pressure effectively for agrarian reform and other demands may lead to recommendations for a dynamic development policy in the rural areas. Among the means applied by peasant organizations to obtain their goals are petitioning according to the law, peaceful invasions of land, and even armed defense against the counter-reform activities of the traditional elite. Through such acts, peasants may gain the political influence and participation which was long withheld from them. It seems from the few historical examples dealt with in this paper, that the fears of the authorities about adopting dynamic policies, as well as the intransigence of the traditional elites, leads to frustration and anger among the peasantry. The peasants then become willing to follow radical leaders, often bringing about, by violent means, the structural changes in society which policy makers hesitated to make when they had the chance to do so peacefully.[6] Only where national leaders such as Cârdenas in the 1930's in Mexico and Paz Estensoro in the early 1950's in Bolivia were prepared to take the risk of giving the peasantry immediate and full political participation and effective power, could structural changes, which are a *sine qua non* for modernization, be brought about effectively.

NOTES

1. Huizer, 1967, p. 113-116; Schmitt, 1965, pp. 14, 113-114, 180-181, 201. It is surprising that Erasmus in his book, *Man Takes Control,* gives practically no attention to this movement which took place while he did field work on the strategy of rural change in the Sonora area (Erasmus, 1961).

2. *Arrendire* is the kind of tenant who pays for his plot partly by rendering services and work without pay to the landowner, such as was the case in the Valle de La Convención in Peru.

3. *Comuneros* are the holders of communal land.

4. For further information, see Petras and Zeitlin, (1968).

5. This movement, and those which were created by several Catholic priests to compete with its increasing and radicalizing impact, brought much turmoil and "class-struggle" to the Northeast of Brazil, to which the *coup d' état* of March 31, 1964 was partly a reaction. Based partly on some faulty misinformation, both Leeds (1964) and Galjart (1964) misinterpret the character of this movement.

6. On the need for structural change, and the alternatives for policy makers in Latin America, see Prebisch (1963).

BIBLIOGRAPHY

Alcantara F. Sergio

1968 *El Proceso de Cambio Económico-Social en Tarentan, Mich.*, Tesis Profesional, Escuela Nacional de Antropologia e Historia, UNAM, Mexico (mimeograph).

Craig, Wesley W. Jr.

1969 "The Peasant Movement of La Convencion, Peru," in Henry A. Landsberger, ed., *Peasant Movements in Latin America,* Ithaca, New York: Cornell University Press.

Erasmus, Charles J.

1961 *Man Takes Control,* University of Minnesota Press.

Galjard, Benno

1964 "Class and 'Following' in Rural Brazil," *América Latina,* VII:3.

Huizer, Gerrit

1965 "Some Notes on Community Development and Rural Social Research." *Comentario* with Reply by Benno Galjart, *America Latina,* VIII:3.

1967 *On Peasant Unrest in Latin America,* A Collection of Notes for the I.L.O.-C.I.D.A. Study on the Role of Peasant Organizations in the Process of Agrarian Reform in Latin American Countries, Comite Interamericano de Desarrollo Agricola, Washington, D.C.

1968 "Peasant Organizations and Agrarian Reform in Latin America," Some Preliminary Generalizations, Paper presented at Second World Congress of Rural Sociology, Enschede, Netherlands.

– – – and Cynthia N. Hewitt

1969 "Bibliography on Latin American Peasant Organizations," in Henry A. Landsberger, ed., *Peasant Movements in Latin America,* Ithaca, New York: Cornell University Press.

Landsberger, Henry A.

1968 "The Role of Peasant Movements and Revolts in Development: An Analytical Framework," *Bulletin,* February, International Institute for Labor Studies, Geneva.

1969 *Peasant Movements in Latin America,* ed., Ithaca, New York: Cornell University Press.

– – – and Cynthia N. Hewitt

1966 *Preliminary Report on Cast Study of Mexican Peasant Organizations,* New York State School of Industrial and Labor Relations, Cornell University (mimeograph).

Leeds, Anthony

1964 "Brazil and the Myth of Francisco Julião," in Joseph Maier and Richard Weatherhead, *Politics of Change in Latin America,* New York: Praeger.

Nathan, Paul

1955 "Mexico en la Epoca de Cárdenas," *Problemas Agrícolas y Industriales de Mexico,* VII:3, Mexico.

Patch, Richard W.

1960 "Bolivia: U.S. Assistance in a Revolutionary Setting," in *Social Change in Latin America Today,* Council of Foreign Relations, A Vintage Book.

Petras, James and Maurice Zeitlin

1968 "Miners and Agrarian Radicalism," in James Petras and Maurice Zeitlin, *Latin America, Reform or Revolution?* A Fawcett Premier Book.

Powell, John D.

1966 *The Politics of Agrarian Reform in Venezuela: History, System, and Process,* Ph. D. Dissertation, University of Wisconsin, (unpublished).

1969 "Agrarian Reform or Agrarian Revolution in Venezuela?," in Arpad von Lazar and Robert Kaufman, eds., *Reform and Revolution: Readings in Latin American Politics,* Boston: Allyn & Bacon, forthcoming.

Prebisch, Paul

1963 *Towards a Dynamic Development Policy for Latin America,* United Nations, ECLA, E/CN/12/680/Rev.

Quijano Obregón, Aníbal

1967 "Contemporary Peasant Movements," in Seymour Martin Lipset and Aldo Solari, ed., *Elites in Latin America,* New York: Oxford University Press.

Schmitt, Karl M.

1965 *Communism in Mexico,* Austin, Texas: University of Texas Press.

Senior, Clarence

1958 *Land Reform and Democracy,* Gainesville, Florida: University of Florida Press.

ARISTOCRACY, OLIGARCHY, AND CULTURAL CHANGE IN COLOMBIA

Andrew Hunter Whiteford

The picture of a static Latin America divided into castes and cliques, impervious to the ideals of freedom and justice, unaware of the great changes that had taken place in the world until the emissaries of the Alliance for Progress proclaimed them, slowly awakening from its indifference or hypocrisy, has little to do with reality. (Uslar-Pietri, 1964, p. 78)

Cultural values exercise a subtle but pervasive effect upon our judgments and decisions, usually without our knowledge or perception. Attempts to describe and define the basic values shared by the people of the United States have differed somewhat in their interpretations but they agree that in our ideal culture, and to a considerable extent in our real culture, we hold in high esteem such concepts as *equality* and *democracy*. These "fighting words" affect our thinking about civil rights, union negotiations, school segregation, open housing, states' rights, and a hundred other issues. They also affect our attitudes and responses when we deal with other societies or other nations, and we are quick to condemn tyranny, dictatorship, or communism, which we have been taught to regard as incompatible with equality and democracy.

We also respond negatively to other terms which we regard as contrary to these cherished values, words such as *oligarchy* and *aristocracy*. We tend automatically to associate the term oligarchy with suppression, rigidity, and feudalism; and to regard the members of an aristocracy as effete, decadent, apathetic, rather stupid, and concerned only with preserving their own positions through the manipulation of the wealth, power, and prestige which they inherited from their ancestors and to which they have no actual right.

It is this sometimes unconscious but strongly negative response to terminology which has led many of us into an uncomfortable dilemma when we discover that our best friends in Latin America are usually aristocratic members of the oligarchy. The dilemma is intensified when we realize that almost all of the programs which we are urging upon our friends, through the Alliance and other instruments, are designed to cost them money through taxes, property through redistribution, and power through shared education and broadened enfranchisement. For many of us, the problem is resolved simply by concluding that aristocrats are passé, oligarchies are anti-democratic, and both will be swept away by the "wave of the future" or some similar historical phenomenon, and that our friends had better learn to adjust and adapt to the coming new world in which they will have our best wishes—but perhaps little else.

Our biased conception of aristocracies and oligarchies also leads us to the hasty conclusion that any government in which they participate must be antediluvian in outlook as well as oppressive in intent, eternally conservative and evoking its powers primarily to smother the progressive interests of the seething masses. It is difficult for us to realize that, in reality, the progressive force may be the government and one of its major problems is often the apathy of the citizens and their resistance to change. This "reversal" of roles is noted by the political scientist, Charles Anderson, who says:

> It is conventionally assumed that political power in Latin America has predominantly been used to reinforce the rigidities of existing social and economic institutions. However, it may be that the problem of government in Latin America is less that it has been used as an instrument of resistance to change, and more that it has been resisted in its effort to induce change. It may be that the Latin American state has been an inadequate vehicle of social and economic transformation in an environment where the aspiration to change of political leaders has not been shared by those whose primary life commitments are located in other social systems and institutions. (Anderson, 1966, p. 239)

To understand Latin America as it presently exists, we must be prepared to recognize that at least some governments, sometimes, attempt to conduct the affairs of the state for the maximum good of the greatest number, and that they do make efforts to attain improved conditions for the future of their countries. This is giving them no more than the benefit of a legitimate doubt, but it is more realistic than the sweeping, general condemnation which is often expressed.

Even if such an open-minded attitude toward the political organizations of Latin America is accepted, it must be recognized also that all governments of the area are not the same, nor are they equally representative or progressive. The problem I am concerned with here is whether those governments which tend to be oligarchic and/or in which members of a traditional aristocracy participate are *ipso facto* the most conservative and the most productive of programs which benefit only the privileged few. To what extent is there justification for suspicion toward oligarchies and aristocracies as forces which impede the solution of problems confronting Latin America today?

There do not exist, to my knowledge, adequate research data to answer this question, but I feel it might be helpful to examine its dimensions in one country. My choice of Colombia reflects my interest and experience in that country and the existence of certain relevant conditions: it is faced with many of the problems which are characteristic of Latin America, it is deeply involved in reform programs, its society possesses elements of a real aristocracy, and it has often been cited as an example of government by oligarchy. (Fluharty, 1957; Martz, 1962).

Instead of beginning with an examination of the aristocracy and its way of life, I propose to look at some of the major problems confronting Colombia today and to attempt to discover the role of the members of the Upper Class in the current endeavors to solve those problems. Are the aristocrats always the ones who resist change, are they always arch-conservatives who object to progress, are they interested only in the preservation of the *status quo* and their own privileges and position, and what role, if any, do they play in the government? An examination of their positions and attitudes *vis-a-vis* the problems of the day should answer some of these questions and offer some clarification regarding the nature of the contemporary aristocracy.

The Basic Problems

This section may be unnecessary. Readers who are acquainted with Latin America, its problems of industrialization, over-population, urbanization, employment, education, and land distribution and use, may pass over this review and go directly to the discussion of the aristocracy's role in the attempts to deal with them. For others, a brief review of some of the problems as they exist, especially in the Cauca Valley of Colombia, may reveal their complexities and the enormous difficulties involved in their solution.

1. *Industrialization and Economic Diversification.*

The Colombian economy suffers from dependence upon the world coffee market, and the country is presently attempting to encourage the development of other crops and resources. It is also encouraging the development of other industries, not only for the goods which they would produce, but also for the many jobs which would be created. Many factors, however, tend to inhibit their development and, although the present ten-year development plan represents a major effort, some observers already regard its prospects for success as no better than a somewhat similar attempt to encourage industrial growth in the first part of the 1950's (Glade, 1963, p.

In the upper Cauca Valley, Cali represents one of the fastest growing cities in Latin America. Here industry is developing because of the electric power resources made available through Colombia's major TVA-type project, the Autonomous Regional Corporation of the Cauca Valley (CVC). In the early period of the CVC, the Departments of Valle, Cauca, and Caldas agreed to cooperate in its foundation and participate in its program. However, Caldas and Cauca withdrew from the project, retaining an interest only in the agricultural extension service. (Posada and Posada, 1966, p. 165). Between 1945 and 1961, with the first increase in electrical power from the Anchicaya Hydroelectric Plant, the number of workers employed increased from 17,979 to 44,605, the productivity per worker rose 49 percent, and the number of factories in the Department of Valle rose from 800 to 1,584. (Posada and Posada, 1966, p. 114). This was just a sample of what could be expected with the increased availability of electrical power. During the same period, most other regions did not have this advantage, or even a similar prospect of such electrical power, and industrial development thus remained relatively stagnant. The neighboring department of Cauca lacked the power resources to encourage industrial development and possessed barely enough for its immediate needs. Without prospects of substantially increased electrical power, but with a constantly growing population, Popayán and similar provincial cities are faced with critical unemployment problems.

2. *Population, Urbanization, and Employment.*

For purposes of this brief review, these three concerns may be discussed together because they are related to each other and to the problems of industrial growth.

Colombia, with a population of 17.5 million in 1965 and an annual increase of 3.2 percent, is one of the most rapidly growing countries within the block which has the highest annual increase in the world. (Posada and Posada, 1966, p. 17). (T. Lynn Smith estimates that the population of Central and South America is growing two to three times as fast as the population of Mainland China.) (Smith, 1963, p. 142).

Such growth causes alarm largely because other developments do not keep pace with it, and the results are unemployment or under-employment, poverty, illiteracy, discontent, individual deprivation, and social tension. Even an annual economic growth rate which has averaged between 4.5 and 5 percent, which some observers regard as moderately high (Phelan, 1963, p. 5), is swallowed up by the increased population so completely that the result is a deteriorating standard of living for the masses and a widening gap between the poor and the wealthy (Posada and Posada, 1965, pp. 17-18).

Population pressure is evident in both the rural and urban sectors of Colombia, but the cities, with a growth from three million in 1950 to five million in 1960, and an estimated eight million in 1970 (Barraclough and Domike, 1966), have the greatest problems. The city of Cali exploded from 30,000 people in 1912 to 813,200 in 1964, an annual growth rate of 8.3 percent. Because of the job shortage and because many people do not possess either the skills or education for newly created jobs, a "disproportionate increase in urban service occupations of a highly inefficient type" results (Posada and Posada, 1965, p. 19).

3. *Education and Training.*

Urbanization alone will not raise the standard of living, and industrial growth may not occur unless literate and/or trained workers are available. This is one of Latin America's great deficiencies–and Colombia's. In spite of the country's long support of higher education, and its more recent dedication to compulsory education, the frenzied building of schools and the training of teachers is far outstripped, as is everything else, by the population growth. Education cannot expand fast enough to close the literacy gap in the near future. According to the census data of 1951 (the 1964 data were not available), only five percent of the population had finished university or secondary school and seventy-seven percent were functional illiterates with little or no schooling (Posada and Posada, 1965, p. 18).

Although the figures are not directly comparable, it is interesting to note that nine years later (1960) only fifteen percent of all the youngsters of school age were enrolled in secondary schools but the proportion had risen from 1957 when it was only eight percent (1951–five percent, 1957–eight percent, 1960–fifteen percent). At the same time (1960), one-third of those enrolled in secondary schools were attending some kind of vocational training institution (Lipset and Solari, 1967, p. 459). In spite of this slight improvement in the educational situation, the illiteracy of seventy-seven percent of the older generation must be remembered, as well as the fact that only a very few years ago less than one-sixth of the eligible young people were getting a secondary school education.

4. *Land Distribution and Exploitation.*

The complex pattern of problems surrounding the subject of Agrarian Reform is one of the most difficult and compelling which faces Latin America today. Parts of it touch upon every aspect of life; it arouses violent emotions and haunts every government. From the millions of words which have been written about the subject only a minimal number of comments need be presented here to focus attention upon Colombia and the upper Cauca Valley.

There can be no doubt that the ownership of land in Colombia is grossly unequal.

	Size of Unit	Percentage of Owners	Percentage of Exploited Land
SMALL	up to 20 hect.	84.0	15.0
MEDIUM	20 to 100 hect.	12.0	20.8
LARGE	100 to 500 hect.	3.5	33.2
VERY LARGE	over 500 hect.	.5	31.0

Approximately one-third of the land in use was in land units of over 500 hectares and belonged to a group of owners who constituted only half of one percent of all land holders in Colombia. In actual figures, 689,930 owners held 3,385,300 hectares in average holdings of 5 hectares each while 29,582 owners held 14,557,000 hectares in average holdings of 500 hectares (Aguilera Camacho, 1964). When these figures were presented in the national senate the comment was made that the distribution was undoubtedly even more one-sided that it appears here because many large land owners owned several large *haciendas* and were counted several times.

In the Cauca Valley, two percent of the landowners held 43.5 percent of the usable land, most of which was in units of more than 100 hectares. At the other extreme were seventy percent of the owners who were classified as *minifundistas* with holdings smaller than 5 hectares (Posada and Posada, 1965, p. 53). There is some evidence that the situation is becoming even more unbalanced. Between 1954 and 1959, the total number of farms in the Department of Valle decreased by 8,177, and the Posadas conclude that "there would seem to be a gradual trend toward greater concentration of land in fewer hands" (Posada and Posada, 1965, p. 53). Land distribution figures are not available for the Department of Cauca.

This extremely skewed distribution of land has its roots in the Hispanic colonial system of *encomiendas, repartimientos*, and *latifundios*. Its basic pattern of a bifurcated rural society, with a great mass of farm laborers dominated by a small, wealthy elite group of landowners, has persisted in most of Latin America until the present. This system has long been criticized and has often been the target for reforms of one kind or another; today it is regarded by many analysts as the major obstacle to economic, social, and political progress. The dysfunctional effects of the system are many and complex, and they have been discussed in detail in the literature (Fals-Borda, 1955; Freyre, 1946; Smith, 1965).

Problems resulting from the system include:

1. *Peonage.*

Farm laborers and *minifundistas* with farms too small to support their families have little alternative but to work for the *latifundista* on his terms. Through various kinds of contracts, debt peonage, obligations, etc., they may be bound to the *hacienda* for life—and their children after them. Indians, or *mestizos*, are literally disfranchised and without recourse.

2. *Impoverishment.*

Among peons, the standard of living is usually reduced to the lowest level of subsistance, with resulting disease and debilitation. More importantly, the people are deprived of purpose in life, or any prospect of improvement, and are denied the possibility of living like human beings. Education and opportunity for learning or improvement are almost completely absent.

3. *Instability, Insecurity, and Tension.*

Peons are not paid when there is no work, and many become migrant workers. "Permanent improvements such as buildings, or fruit trees, belong to the estate even when all the costs are borne by the tenant. . . .Residents of the large estates can be expelled at will in traditional areas where there is neither a strong central government, nor a labor union to defend them. . . .In some cases the administration's consent is required even to receive visitors from outside, or to make visits off the property." (Barraclough and Domike, 1966, p. 399).

4. *Ignorance and Stagnation.*

Educational opportunities are absent or scarce, and the majority of the peons are functionally illiterate; nor do they receive any training in crafts or work skills which will assist them in improving their value or their status. With no training, no education, and no experience, their attitudes become protective, their view remains narrow, and they often resist change and improvement because they have come to distrust anything new.

5. *Low Productivity and Uneconomic Operation.*

With a labor force which is apathetic, untrained, unenlightened, protective, and unambitious, as well as suffering from chronic infection and malnutrition, it is understandable that output is low. Most work is done by the same methods and with the same tools that were used more than a century ago.

Land use is a problem closely related to its distribution. Some aspects of agricultural inefficiency in Colombia have been touched upon and may be summarized—and over-simplified—by saying that the *minifundias* which belong to nearly eighty-five percent of the rural owners are too small to be productive, and the *latifundias* possessed by approximately four percent of the owners are so large that a more than adequate income can be derived from them by extensive (rather than intensive) exploitation, minimal investment, and application of the most rudimentary techniques. As a result, agricultural productivity falls far short of its potential and of the nation's needs.

> Agricultural production per head is lower today (in Latin America) than in the prewar period, and since 1960 the decline has been more marked. In most countries there has not been sufficient improvement in the agricultural sector to meet the growing demands for food, let alone to provide the surpluses required for economic development. (Pearse, 1966, p. 46)

The historical developments allowing extensive land ownership by a small number of families also led to absentee ownership and to an interest in cattle raising instead of crop agriculture. The political and social dominance of the *hacendados* allowed them to select for their cattle *haciendas* the flattest, most fertile, and most conveniently located land. As a result, pastures surround most Latin American cities requiring the food produced for the market to be transported from a distance.

> What has been generally true of Colombia as a whole is more specifically and emphatically true of the Cauca Valley: the rural population has been forced into the peripheral foothills, or even into the steep mountains so that the fertile level lands can be dedicated to cattle grazing. Wherever there are many cattle extensively grazed, there are bound to be few people. The rural hamlets, elbowed out of their natural area of potential expansion by large estates, frozen in their present form, have become places where surplus labor has its origin, but where it has no outlet. It is not to be suggested that human beings must live specifically on the land that in an extensive grazing economy fed a certain number of cattle; but, in a progressive country, potentially productive land should be made to increase the per unit yields of food value. Outmoded systems of land tenure must not stand in the way of bettering the standards of living. Onto the

> ancient cattle culture must be grafted a vigorous agricultural society of the twentieth-century pattern. (Crist, 1952. p. 28)

The expansion of population, both rural and urban, in recent years has aggravated the discrepancy between food needs and food production, and the wasted resources of areas such as the Cauca Valley have become national issues. Attempts by the Colombian government to divide the great cattle estates and make them more productive go back more than a century, but few results have been obtained (Adams, 1966, p. 45). Many have recognized a paradox in the best and most convenient land in the valley being used for pasture, and have often suggested moving the cattle to the hills and plowing the valley floor for intensive crop production.

> Despite this favorable endowment, two thirds of the rich land of the Valley were still in pasture as late as 1959. Cattle breeding, the main use to which these lands have been put, is on an *extensive* basis. With notable exceptions, most ranchers have simply let their cattle out to roam in open pastures. . . .Ranching is often done with a minimum of effort, differing little from that of centuries ago. Beef experts have estimated that cattle output could be at least tripled on existing lands. (Blasier, 1966, p. 389)

Productivity in the Department of Cauca is low in comparison with other parts of Colombia (Arroyo, 1953, p. 72). Arroyo noted that the amount of land in Cauca used for pasture was three times greater than that under cultivation, although income per unit from the agricultural land was much higher. In recognizing the need for greater productivity in both cattle and agriculture he said:

> But agriculture and even stock raising cannot develop and grow to cover the needs of internal consumption and exportation from Cauca while there exists, as a residue of an archaic right, the great green stains of the cattle *latifundias*, 2000 to 5000 hectares in extent, under the private domination of a single owner, or a family group, in locations adjacent to the cities and county (*Municipio*) seats and occupying economic locations which should be dedicated to agriculture. . . . (Arroyo, 1953, p. 72) (My translation: AHW)

Attempts to Cope with the Problems

Insufficient industry and lack of economic diversification, over-population, rapid urbanization and under-employment, deficient education and vocational training, dysfunctional distribution of land and its uneconomic utilization: this list, or any list which samples the problems facing Latin America, Colombia, and the Cauca Valley is overwhelming. The problems are so complex, so deeply rooted, so gargantuan in their scope, that they seem almost beyond solution. And yet, they must be solved in some degree if the countries are to progress, or indeed, continue to exist.

Failure of immediate solution is not the result of lack of concern, projects, or programs. At least three general approaches, theoretical or real, compete and combine with each other: 1. evolutionary progress–dependent primarily upon the effective use of private resources, 2. planning and administration of reform programs by the government, 3. armed revolution aimed at disposing of both existing governments and their problems, and beginning anew. The first two are not incompatible and are combined in almost every part of Latin America. The quandary in Colombia arises not from competition and antagonism between the private interests and the government so much as from the fact that the people in both tend to be the same. The significance of this personnel duplication will be explored later. The third proposed solution, armed revolution, is espoused by the enlightened and impatient youth, the idealistic and exasperated Left, and the hungry poor. They regard any kind of internal, peaceful reform as impossible, or too remote to be valuable; fundamentally they are driven by concern with the problems they face today, and they are convinced that any change would be preferable to the present conditions.

The revolutionists are not the only ones who doubt that adequate change can be achieved by allowing the traditional society to respond to problems in its own way and in its own time (Blaiser, 1966, p. 387). In any event, such a prospect is purely academic because government intervention has long since transformed the traditional society, and pure private enterprise hardly exists. To a remarkable extent the government is the society and the society is the government, and this very congruence makes the young men cynical and frustrates the administrators, native and imported, who assume the task of applying to the society reform programs formulated by the government. These administrators are constantly aware that members of powerful families possess the power to obstruct and circumvent government regulations; they are also aware that members of these same families were leaders in the government which designed the legislation, and may also sit on the controlling boards of agencies created to implement the legislation. These omnipresent people are an oligarchy, a term rarely heard in Anglo-America, but common and meaningful in Latin America. For the most part, the oligarchy in Colombia consists of old aristocratic families with mineral and cattle wealth, and with sons following their fathers into cabinet offices and governorships in both the Liberal and Conservative Parties. Other members are the new industrialists in the booming cities, and often the new industrialists are descendants, or relatives, of the old aristocratic *hacendados*. These are the people who have exercised political power in Colombia for generations, and these are the people who designed the reform programs and passed them into law.

For the purposes of this paper it is sufficient to note that the oligarchy in Colombia is a reality and to hope that someone will make a detailed study of its structure while it still exists. It must also be recognized that the oligarchy is far from being the monolithic structure outsiders consider it to be; it undergoes internal change and dissension, and it does not consist exclusively of members of the old landed aristocracy. It is these latter, however, who are my immediate concern, for they are the ones who are most frequently involved on opposite sides of the conflicts regarding reform, and it is their roles in the society which are most intriguing. If we can examine carefully the value systems and objectives which motivate them as a group, we may approach an understanding of them.

To deal with the many problems outlined in the preceding pages, Colombia has instituted many reforms. As mentioned earlier, various kinds of land reform programs were introduced during the 19th century, but the modern period of reform really began when Alfonso Lopez was president from 1934 to 1938 and again from 1942 to 1945. This period of liberal legislation has often been regarded as a Colombian reflection of the New Deal in the United States, but it is apparent that the national political tradition provided the basis for the majority of the programs which affected minimum wages, social security, income and real estate taxes, the national educational program, and land reform laws which legalized expropriation under certain conditions. Most subsequent social legislation has been built upon the accomplishments of this period, many of which appear to have existed on paper more than in reality because they were at most only partially implemented. However, they clearly reflected the views of some influential Colombians: that education was important, that industrial workers should receive fair treatment from employers, that land ownership was a social responsibility, and that everyone should contribute financially toward the operation of the national government. When the most recent land reform law was passed in 1961, it was regarded as "Latin America's most inclusive and far reaching instrument for restructuring a nation's agriculture. . . .Thus, Colombia took a step which progressive politicians and social scientists believe is essential to wipe out low levels of living in rural areas. . . ." (Feder, 1963).

The various Colombian governments have been aware of the problems of the country for many years, and they have taken legislative steps to ameliorate them. It is also apparent that almost every item of social legislation has met with massive resistance from the landed *hacendados* and often from the wealthy industrialists. *The Associación de Ganaderos* (National Cattlemen's Organization) opposed tax reforms, fought all land reforms, and consistently lobbied against developments such as the Cauca Valley Corporation. Almost everyone interested in the success of land reform has expressed disappointment at the success of the opposition in slowing down the program of the National Agrarian Reform Institute (INCORA) by diverting its activities from expropriation to colonization, by convincing it to concentrate upon irrigation and credit programs instead of broader land reform, and by persuading the government not to increase the financial resources of the Institute (Feder, 1964, p. 33; Adams, 1966).

The details of the virtues and deficiencies of the land reform program do not concern me here; it is enough to demonstrate that reform programs have been put into effect and that they have met with determined opposition from land owners and particularly from the cattlemen. I said that many of the aristocratic members of the oligarchy which enacted the reform legislation were also cattlemen, and it would be interesting to know whether the same people were on both sides of the controversy. I cannot prove that any given individual voted for the program in the legislature and at the same time actively opposed it in the *Associación de Ganaderos*, but, clearly, members of the same group, the aristocratic *ganaderos*, were on both sides. This undoubtedly reflects differences of opinion within and between families and probably some serious schisms, but there are more important aspects to the phenomenon which tell us something about the culture and the people.

Politics and cattle traditionally have been the major interests of upper class Colombian men. The church and the military have also attracted them, but only as instruments of power. In cattle *per se* they had little real interest, but the role of country gentleman, the estate owner, has traditionally held great prestige.

> The idea of wealth was formed by the contemplation of movable things and of men, of great flocks of sheep and goats on their treks from summer to winter pastures and back again, and of the *gran señor*, who, richly attired, with hands unsoiled by work of any kind, rode across the *Meseta* on his gaily caparisoned steed–and it is significant that the word gentlemen in Spanish means horseman.

> It was but natural that the Sixteenth Century Conquistadores should have imposed the manorial system on the New World, for that was the only method of landholding with which they were familiar, and they were happy to assume the attitudes and prerogatives of the manor lords of the Peninsula. The manorial system, with certain feudal traits, was implanted in the Cauca Valley by Belalcazar, the lieutenant of Pizarro. (Crist, 1952, p. 31)

Cattle and land wealth gave them education, allowed them to travel, supported their large houses and large families in the city, and permitted them the leisure to devote themselves to politics. In recent years, and particularly with the increase in urban population, the gentleman politician has been somewhat replaced by career men from the Middle Classes and by wealthy industrialists. Even these, when they reach positions of respectable power and affluence, usually buy *fincas* in the country and go through the gestures of being concerned with land and livestock; they may even go so far as to purchase colonial furnishings for their new "family estates."

But Colombian aristocrats were much more than cattlemen, and they were not really country gentlemen at all. In the main, they were people of breadth, culture, and sophistication who lived in the cities and coveted their *haciendas* for the purposes of status, leisure, and income. (Whiteford, 1964, p. 79; Strickon, 1965). Antonio J. Posada and his wife, Jeanne, both Colombians, describe very well the interest range of the aristocracy and part of the ideology and social process which has enabled this group to maintain its oligarchical position.

> The vast majority of Colombia's presidents, cabinet ministers, party leaders, and parliamentarians have, throughout its history, been writers, poets, doctors, philosophers, and more recently, economists. They are members of a highly sophisticated, urbane, aristocratic, and talented upper class, with excellent and broad humanistic educations. Rule by the intellectual is held in such high esteem that part of the myth allows the upward mobility of the talented of any class, who can manage to surmount the obstacles of entry into a restricted educational system and who adopt the manners, pure Castillian language, and outlook of the upper class.
>
> That some few, a sufficient minimum number, actually do accomplish this despite the obstacles placed in their way, tends to validate this myth. Another social mechanism which serves to reinforce this myth is the high reproductive rate among the upper classes. Not only

> does this ensure the availability of a sufficient number of talented, well-qualified persons born into the elite to justify its claim to right to rule, but results in the spilling over into the upper-middle professional classes, of members of large families, still socially 'accepted,' who may be marginal in financial wealth as compared with the upper class. This second group, possessing the same myth and world view, helps to support the ruling elite from below. (Posada and Posada, 1966, pp. 26-27)

The Posadas refer to the aristocratic upper class as the "ruling elite," and they too recognize it as a real and effective component of Colombian society–the oligarchy. This is not the place to become involved with terminology, but in Suzanne Keller's study of elites, she attempts to distinguish between aristocracy, ruling class, and strategic elites, and demonstrates that they are very similar and often overlap. One of her conclusions seems to apply to the Colombian situation.

> As long as the social core group was principally recruited from a small exclusive circle tied by economic position and kinship–that is, from an upper class–it was difficult, if not impossible, to distinguish between the strategic elites and the class that supplied most of their membership. (Keller, 1963, p. 59)

I believe, however, that it is less meaningful to regard the Colombian aristocracy as a "ruling elite" than as a social class as defined by Lipset and Bendix:

> . . . .strata of society composed of individuals who accept each other as status equals, and are hence qualified for intimate association. Men may change their occupational status by changing their job, but they can improve their social-class position only by being admitted to relationships of intimacy with those who already possess a higher rank. (Lipset and Bendix, 1959, p. 275)

As the Posadas have suggested, the Colombian aristocracy incorporates several elite groups which are separate entities in other societies. This overlap is particularly true of the traditional social structure of Cauca where the members of the Upper Class–the aristocracy–occupy most higher political offices, along with the important positions in the educational and ecclesiastical structure, and the select professions. They are not the only people in these positions, but they are the community members who have the widest range of national and international contacts, who are the best educated, the best dressed and best mannered, and who possess the best blood-lines. They are also the richest in wealth and in the inside knowledge of what is happening and going to happen. These same people are the intellectual and artistic elites too, not because they are always the most creative, but because they are the only ones whose tastes are "worth considering," and they do have training in music, literature, and the classical arts; some of them have been poets of renown. Every member of the class is expected to exhibit some grasp of these arts, but excellence in them is not sufficient to procure membership. A successful politician does not become a member if he is nothing more, nor does an artist, nor even a successful writer. The process is highly selective, and a young man with special talents who is not a member of the Upper Class is well advised to leave Popayán if he wants an opportunity to use those talents.

The aristocracy of the upper Cauca Valley appears to be far from either exhaustion or extinction. Although its members do not have the influence in Bogotá they may have had when the Mosqueras and the Arboledas headed both parties, and they filled the presidency and the archbishopric as well as ambassadorships, generalships, and governorships, there are still kinsmen in the cabinet and the senate, and the past president, Dr. Guillermo León Valencia, heads one of its old families. His father was one of Colombia's greatest poets, twice governor of the Department of Cauca, Rector of the University of Cauca, Colombian consul in Paris, and the presidential candidate of the Conservative Party. In past generations, every man in the aristocracy expected to go to the university and acquire a profession, to take his turn in political office and work within one of the two parties, to write essays or poetry, to enjoy life on the *hacienda* (at least on weekends), to spend some time abroad, and to participate in the social and cultural life of the community.

The young men of the present generation are less dedicated to party and political office than were their fathers, although some have moved into this area with the goal of a government career. This is a relatively new idea because, although many men of the older generation spent years in political offices, they always returned to their other roles. Those younger men without open political ambitions attend the university as did their fathers, but many of them also attend school and work for graduate degrees in the United States and Europe. Engineering, medicine, and science attract some, but others have taken a completely new direction and attend agricultural schools in order to undertake the personal, full-time supervision of the family estates. Some have even built new homes on the *haciendas* and live there with their families throughout the year, a complete reversal of the old manner of *hacienda* administration. Traditionally, the owner visited the *hacienda* during the summer and on occasional weekends, and the actual operation was left entirely to a *mayordomo*, or manager.

> One of the reasons for the relatively low income of many haciendas is the *mayordomo*, or manager. The typical *mayordomo* gets from 70 to 80 pesos a month for his work. In view of the responsibility involved, this is a very low salary. An American miner, who had bought a ranch, put the situation in the following words: 'Either the man in charge of an estate is so stupid that he is not even worth 80 pesos a month, or he is smart, and is worth a lot more. In the former case, the estate vegetates from year to year, as does the *mayordomo*; in the latter case, the *mayordomo* really improves things, and pockets the profits. His cows have twin calves year after year, whereas many of the owners' cows lose their calves. He makes money on all sorts of little rackets, and after ten or fifteen years he is able to have a nice house in town and to send his children to school. The owner receives his checks regularly, and comes out from Bogota every year for a week or so, to return to the capital feeling that all is right with his world. (Crist, 1953, pp. 35-36)

Adams describes the problems of absentee ownership in Colombia and points out that, in 1959-60, over one-third of the land in farms was operated by *mayordomos* and two-thirds of all the rural lands in an area near Bogotá were owned by people who lived in the capital. He concludes that this arrangement is conducive to low productivity and stagnation because of the lack of training and the absence of incentives for the *mayordomo*. It also leads to the selection of farm enterprises (such as pasturing cattle) which require little expertise or supervision (Adams, 1966, pp. 50-51).

The new approach, with resident owners trained in animal husbandry and agriculture, has meant that the threat of expropriation by the land reform program is now resisted with something besides a simple desire to retain patrimony. There is now a concern with the development of the land and, in many cases, there exists highly trained knowledge of how it can be done. The number of *haciendas* and owners involved in this modern type of program is undoubtedly still small, but the innovations of the younger men are very likely to be followed by the older generation which has already been casually experimenting with new and different pasture grasses, with crops suitable to higher altitudes, and with the introduction of new types of beef stock and, more recently, fine-blooded dairy cows. The university has had no interest in agriculture and the small "experimental farm" of the area produced little of value, but developments in the valley near Cali were always watched with interest. The *haciendas* of Valle had the advantage of the experimental station at Palmira and were looked to for leadership in new strains of plants and animals. An annual agriculture and livestock fair is now held in Popayán and it is chiefly the old *hacienda* families who compete for the prizes. The recent interest in the establishment of dairy herds has led to developments in cheese making, and a Milk Producers Cooperative has been established to pasteurize the 20,000 liters of milk which are now shipped daily to Cali.

Inefficient land use and antiquated techniques and practices are obviously detrimental to the national and regional economies, but it is too easy to account for their existence by charging the owners with lack of interest, ignorance, or deliberate resistance to progress. Andrew Pearse (1966, p. 55) has described very well the problems encountered by the landlord who wishes to introduce change to his traditional *hacienda*, whether for purposes of altruism, profit, or defense. He must train, encourage, and/or coerce his manager and unskilled workers in the values and techniques of the change, he must intensify his own surveillance, and he must be prepared to compensate his labor for the new operations involved. The *patrón* attempting to introduce change often finds that he has brought about structural and cultural changes which go far beyond the technical modifications intended to increase productivity: money wages are introduced, traditional resident labor becomes uneconomical, special skills have to be imported, education becomes necessary, and life becomes much more complicated. It can easily be understood why, without any advantages of technical aid or encouragement, the use of much of the land in Cauca remained simple and relatively archaic.

This is not the whole picture, of course. I do not intend to convey the impression that the aristocratic *hacendados* of Cauca were a group of enthusiastic progressives who were held in check only by the lack of technical assistance. Some were and some were not. There were ideological differences within the aristocracy; after all, they were the leaders of both the Liberal and Conservative parties. All landowners could be expected to be apprehensive and defensively critical of land reform and division, and it could be anticipated also that the old-line members of the Conservative Party would be particularly critical of a program which had been formulated by a Liberal administration. As Blasier (1966) and others point out, the principal of agrarian reform has now been accepted by all nations of Latin America, and even the most conservative *hacendado* hesitates to admit that he does not understand it, or that he disagrees with its broad objectives. Criticism tends to concentrate instead upon efficiency, legality, and bureaucratic personnel.

But some aristocratic landowners do believe in the program. Some recognize the national need for increased agricultural production and the political need for available land; although it is inimical to their immediate interest, they accept it as a lesser of two evils–the greater being Revolution and possibly communism. Others are ideological liberals who accept the logic and objectives of the reform programs but are deeply distressed at the affect they will have on their personal lives. These people are ambivalent and uncertain; some of them are capable of supporting the programs in public and voting against them in private, an indication of the discrepancy between their abstract liberal ideology and their pragmatic view of their own involvement. Almost all of them have considerable perspective upon the world as a result of education and travel, and they recognize the direction in which their society is moving. Traditionally, they are dedicated to the *patria* as well as to the *patria chica*, and they are aware that there are needs and demands which must be met for the good of Colombia. At least one indication that some aristocrats of Cauca were deeply concerned with the need for agrarian reform appeared more than fifteen years ago in the polemical review of conditions in the Department written in 1953 by Miguel Antonio Arroyo, a representative of one of the old families, *alcalde* of Popayán, and a professor of the university. To improve conditions in the department he advocated:

> . . . .the increase of bank credit, the development of commercial associations of small business, the parcelization of farm land adjacent to the centers of consumption, the progressive conversion of the old-fashioned cattle ranching by intensive [application of the principals of] modern animal husbandry and public projects of land improvement, and roads for the opening of unexploited regions. (Arroyo, 1953, p. 96)

He was an aristocrat and, as a matter of fact, so was Alfonso Lopez, and so are Alberto Lleras Camargo, Carlos Lleras Restrepo, and Guillermo León Valencia. Alfonso Lopez Michelson is an aristocrat; and he is also the son of former president, Alfonso Lopez, and the leader of the MRL (Movimiento Revolucionario Liberal), the left-wing faction of the Liberal Party which is regarded by many as communist. Laureano Gomez, arch-conservative friend of the Axis powers in World War II, was also an aristocrat.

There are aristocrats of every possible political persuasion, and throughout Colombian history these leaders have opposed each other politically for the principals of their parties but they have also married each other's sisters to cement the solidarity of their class. Their ties of kinship and culture link them together even while they dispute political matters. There are some clan feuds of long standing but even these families marry each other and they rally together whenever there are threats from the outside. One of the most important differences of belief among them currently is whether or not the threats of expropriation, revolution, and change are really serious and imminent. Those who are truly concerned with these threats supported agrarian reform legislation and other reforms because they believed them to be necessary; many of those who were less concerned tended to support the reforms also, because they were consistent with their 19th Century French-style liberalism and not because they believed that the programs would ever be implemented. (Hirschman's interpretation of the forces leading to the enactment of agrarian reform legislation leaves very little to be added) (Hirschman, 1963).

Those who might be regarded as complacent actually have some reason to feel that real progress is being made. In spite of the totally bleak picture which is usually presented in the literature, and in spite of the apparent difficulty experts have in agreeing upon an interpretation, or even upon the figures, for food production, land use, and most other important matters, evidence exists that conditions were being improved somewhat even before the recent reforms.

> . . . .considerable progress was in fact made in the late fifties. . . .namely, increased agricultural production in a variety of important lines (cotton, rice, barley, sugar cane, oil seeds). Imports of barley dwindled to a negligible figure and from a substantial importer of cotton Colombia became a net exporter. Increasingly, enterprising middle–or upper class–operators rented, or acquired, tracts of good flat land in the Sabana of Bogotá, The Cauca Valley, and the Tolima plains close to the Magdalena River and sowed them to commercial crops.
>
> The modernization of Colombia's agriculture along capitalistic lines thus made rapid advances in the late fifties. A number of basic economic forces were also at work, such as the growth of markets as a result of industrial expansion and urbanization. (Hirschman, 1963, p. 129-130)

Hirschman is not alone in his view that substantial growth has been attained. Dale Adams, in a cautiously optimistic evaluation of the land tenure reform, comments:

> Changes in Colombia's land tenure system have speeded up since the end of the Second World War. The conditions described in 1949-1950–extensive cattle farms in the flat areas and intensive crops on the hillsides–have changed substantially. In the flat fertile areas–such as the Cauca Valley, the upper Magdalena River Basin, the north coast, the Sabana around Bogotá, and some of the eastern plains–mechanized crop production is now common. Intensive dairy production and truck crops are well established around the principal cities. Land division through inheritance, cash rental arrangements, and land division through sales have been common in many parts of Colombia. Substantial increases in the production of rice, cotton, edible oil crops, sugar cane, and tobacco are partial results of these changes. (Adams, 1966, p. 47).

He concludes, however, with this cautionary statement: "In spite of the changes which have taken place in Colombia's land tenure system, its performance still fails to meet expanding social needs and aims." (Adams, 1966, p. 47).

I am in no position to evaluate the economics of the situation. It appears from the wealth of reports and reams of statistics that the problems confronting Colombia remain very pressing. It also appears that great attention is currently being given to them, some results are emerging and, further, the more or less gradual evolution toward modernity has been bringing about changes in the total culture pattern for some time. Many aspects of the old *hacienda* complex and its relationship to the land and the people have already been modified. Whether the earlier changes were sufficient to set the currents of progress in motion, or whether the recent programs have developed an adequate base for the accomplishment of reforms and the prevention of revolution, no one yet knows.

In attempting to understand the aristocratic oligarchs of Colombia, some consideration must be given to the influence of the Catholic Church upon their thinking. While some of them are liberals and some are conservatives, all of them have dealt with the church throughout their lives and are influenced by church policy even though some may reject it. The major impact of recent years has certainly been the awakening of the church and its new and dramatic position on social problems. Pope John XXIII said in *Mater et Magistra*:

> It is not enough to assert the natural character of the right of private property, but the effective distribution among all social classes is to be insisted upon. Rural workers should feel a sense of solidarity with

> one another, and should unite to form cooperatives. . . if they are to defend their products. . . .The rural workers can legitimately demand that their efforts be seconded and complemented by the public authorities. . . . (Quoted in Thiesenhusen, 1966).

This statement was received in most circles in Colombia like the proverbial bombshell. The long enduring and close relationship between the church and the Conservative Party was shaken and liberals of various stripes suddenly found themselves in a Holy Alliance with the church. Conscientious laymen were told that it was their religious duty to become their brother's keeper and to give active support to radical programs of social action. The effect on some conservative aristocrats was simply confusion, coupled with a new reluctance to be openly critical of programs which they had previously opposed as "communistic" or even "immoral." In Popayán, a liberal friend told me of some of the results and described one case in which a wealthy Conservative had been moved to subdivide a section of his land near the city and to sell the lots at a very low price with low interest loans for the construction of houses. This was not charity but an act of social concern instigated primarily by the new teachings of the church.

The church has also been very active in its own housing program and one of the women's organizations in Popayán raised money for buildings and the purchase of land. Participation in such programs is somewhat akin to the extensive charities in which such aristocratic women have always been engaged, but exposure to the complications of planning, construction, and financing of housing units made them much more aware of the problems which confront the government agencies and the people. The same thing is true of the school program for rural peasants in which many aristocrats have become involved partly because of church relations and partly because the peasants are the workers on their *haciendas*. They have been instrumental in financing and establishing a large number of primary schools in the rural areas, and the church-operated educational radio station, Sutatensa, is easily the most important means of instruction and contact with the outside world; small transistor radios are a vital educational instrument for the entire nation.

The church also sponsors and supports the Colombian Workers' Union, UTC, (Union de Trabajadores de Colombia). It has organized FANAL, the National Agrarian Federation, among the peasants, and the Jesuits have established a university for peasants (Universidad Campesina) in Buga. In addition to the effects of direct admonishment from the pulpit, in recent years, Catholic aristocrats are made aware through its programs that their church (or some parts of it) believes in social service. In this, the church accords with the objectives of the national government.

The children of rural families are also included in a kind of higher education program which is supported by the government through compulsary contributions from all employers, including *hacendados*. This program, known as SENA (Servicio Nacional de Aprendizaje), supports a wide network of vocational training schools. City boys learn shoemaking, iron working, carpentry, mechanics, etc., and country children attend boarding schools for courses in dairy and livestock farming, vegetable gardening, and poultry raising. SENA has expanded in Cauca in recent years and is a major effort toward the development of a trained and literate labor force which may eventually find employment in the new industries and in the intensifying agriculture. This brief survey of the programs of the Catholic church is far from complete, but it may serve as a reflection of the deepening social concern which affects many segments of Colombian life. The positive position of the church has not been accepted completely by all its adherents, but it has weakened the monopolistic hold of the radical political movements upon the peasants and the urban poor. There is probably truth in the lament that the church is "stirring up dissatisfaction" among the people, but the energies stirred by unrest may be directed toward overcoming the problems instead of simply tearing down the government. The poor may be convinced that there is hope; the aristocrats may not be induced to sacrifice their lands and privileges immediately, but they may be convinced that it is no longer acceptable for them to own everything.

It has been said that the small gains which the Colombian people have made in recent years have been yielded reluctantly and grudgingly by the oligarchy only under the pressure of political expediency. This is undoubtedly true, but there is nothing bizarre or unique about it; this is what happens everywhere. It must be noted, also, that the changes have come about while the oligarchy is still in control, not as the result of its overthrow. Its influence, then, is clearly directed toward the improvement of the public good, whether in desperation or through conviction.

> While traditional interests remain in control, several of these leaders look more to the future than to the past. And although they are not about to preside over their own liquidation, this group is giving increasing attention to the city's urgent social needs. They act partly from humanitarian reasons. No less important is the growing realization of what may happen if these needs are not met. As a result, the civic leaders of Cali have become somewhat more socially conscious and responsive to popular demands. (Blasier, 1966, p. 409)

The eventual test of the aristocracy will not be its survival, but the maintenance and continuity of Colombian society, involving a process of continuing responses and counter-responses between unlike forces attempting to establish a viable balance. In this case, the chief forces which must be balanced with the aristocracy are the rural peasants and the urban poor. Partially because of the long period of *La Violencia*, the peasants have changed their ancient outlook on life and many now have expectations and aspirations, as well as a sense of identity and potential power, feelings unknown a few years ago. With this development at one end of the social structure, the other parts cannot continue in their old forms or expect that the society will continue to function in the same manner as before. As no society is truly static, we can expect changes to occur in all parts of Colombian society, but the adjustments at each end must contribute to the formation of a working whole which will move toward the solution of their common problems, or the society will cease to function. All the problems will not be solved overnight, but as long as the various segments of the society are working toward a balance of interests there are possibilities of success.

It is always difficult to discuss the personality and character traits of any group of people because there is so much variation and so many exceptions to any generalization. In spite of this, it should be recognized that both past and recent history show that there are many Colombian aristocrats who are intelligent, dedicated, resourceful, and talented. They are also tough, adventuresome, and wily. There is no indication that a significant proportion of them is effete in any sense. The younger generation may be more radical in its thinking than the old, it may be less devoted to the cultivation of gentle manners and delicate courtesies, it may be more open-minded and more concerned with professional training than with the assumption of political office; all of these things may be, but this is the way of the world and it is no more degenerative in Colombia than in England or Italy. It may be the kind of change which is a "normal" response to current conditions and necessary for the transition from oligarchy to democracy. Colombia appears to possess the most important factors which Lipset finds are necessary for change, although he believes them lacking in Latin America.

> It would appear that modernizing societies require either strong values, or rules, sustaining achievement and universalism. *They need not reject their traditional value system if they can work out mechanisms to guarantee that a large section of the elite will be composed of men who are highly motivated and able to achieve.* However, much of Latin America. . . .[has] not succeeded in doing either. (Lipset, 1967, p. 44)

Conclusion. In beginning the research for this paper, I was disturbed by the apparent incompatibility between the caliber of the Colombians I have known over the past twenty years and what was reported as their continuing "failure" to make any progress toward solving national problems. I realized that it was impossible for me to document the intelligence, the idealism, the skills, and the dedication which I believe are possessed by many Colombians, so I turned to a closer look at the programs which they had designed and the results which had been achieved. From my general reading of the situation in Latin America as a whole and in Colombia particularly, I had been convinced that the economies of the entire region were not only static but actually were going backward. I was impressed and rather surprised to discover that the actual figures indicate that substantial developments have been taking place in Colombia and that real progress has been achieved. It is true, unfortunately, that the achievements have not been great enough to keep pace with the enormous growth of population nor have they been able to rectify the deficiencies and inequalities of past centuries; they have been inadequate for the situation but they are real and they do represent progress achieved under difficulties.

Those who insist that conditions in Colombia (land, income, industry, etc.) are declining constantly, and who further insist that this state of affairs is the result of repressive rule by an aristocratic oligarchy must face certain facts. With regard to this proposition of cause and effect, there are four alternatives: (1) An oligarchy rules and conditions are bad, i.e. the oligarchy is responsible for bad conditions; (2) There is no oligarchy and conditions are bad, i.e. some factor other than an oligarchy is responsible for the bad conditions; (3) There is no oligarchy and conditions are good, i.e. some factor other than an oligarchy is responsible for the good conditions; (4) An oligarchy rules and conditions are good, i.e. the oligarchy is responsible for the good conditions.

These statements cannot all be true because they are contradictory. If it is insisted that the old-line aristocracy of Colombia still exercises an amount of political power which is disproportionate to its numbers, it can (by my definition) be regarded as an oligarchy. I believe this is the case, at least in the Department of Cauca. I also accept the figures describing economic growth and the programs of social reform as indicative of substantial progress. I am forced to conclude that the government, and the aristocratic oligarchy which is part of it, must be given credit for its accomplishments. Instead of permitting our democratic biases to force us into an unnecessary rejection of our aristocratic friends we should, perhaps, recognize the educated, experienced, politically involved elite of Colombia and other countries of Latin

America as major national resources. It is not entirely the fault of the present generation that all the problems of the area have not been solved.

Such recognition does not necessarily imply that all oligarchies and/or all aristocracies are the best socio-political institutions for all time and in all places. This position would be equally as ridiculous as the acceptance of the cliché that they are always bad. To recognize that some politicians in Latin America are intelligent, effective, and honest is not to assume that they are the rule there any more than they are in other parts of the world. To understand that some Latin American aristocrats waver in their ideologies, express ideas which seem incompatible with each other, attempt to exert power for their own ends, and also espouse causes which appear inimical to their own interests is only to approach reality by discarding stereotypes in which everything is painted in basic colors.

Whatever the future may be, clearly many changes are occurring in Colombia and great changes have transpired in the past fifteen years. Whether the changes have been radical enough or effective enough to have a lasting impact upon the problems involved, and upon the consciousness of the people, is difficult to discern at this point. Culture change is always too slow for the young and radical and too precipitous for the old and conservative, and it is not necessarily desirable simply because it does away with traditional patterns and introduces modern styles. Nor is a way of life intrinsically evil, or unacceptable, or even dysfunctional, merely because it is not like our own. Many societies of the world accept our cultural diffusions and we should not be disturbed when they adopt our neon lights, use jet fighters, soft drinks, "modern managerial practices," and hair styles, but show less interest in our style of family or our particular brand of democracy. All aristocracies are not completely bad, nor are all oligarchies necessarily reactionary. We have our own in the United States, but those of other countries are more apparent to us and, therefore, less acceptable.

> The ways of a society are largely fixed by the myths and doctrines of a ruling few. Democracy differs from oligarchy not in the presence or absence of an elite who wield most influence, but in the closed or open, representative or unrepresentative, responsible or irresponsible character of the elite. Who these elites are, how they circulate, are among the most significant facts of the history of a society. (Lasswell, Lerner, and Rothwell, 1952:155)

In reality, the aristocracy constitute a kind of national resource which should be recognized and supported at the same time that the basis of political power is broadened and a wider segment of the nation begins to participate in the decisions of the government and in improved living conditions. The transitional phase of social change between aristocracy and democracy does not have to be the chaos of military revolution.

POSTSCRIPT

Since committing myself to this position, I have read James L. Payne's (1968) summary discussion of his research on political groups in Colombia, but I have not had the opportunity to read his complete report. I am aware that, according to any of his dimensions, there is no such thing as an oligarchy in Colombia. I respect his data and wish we had more, but I *feel* that his definitions are too tight and result in a conclusion that oligarchies are logical impossibilities. It would be difficult to demonstrate that any single group has ever possessed *exclusive* power in any country. As a rule of thumb, it might be said that an oligarchical situation would exist whenever any group (however defined) appeared to exert an amount of power, or had access to power, vastly out of proportion to its size as compared with other groups or with the rest of the population. In this sense, I believe that the Upper Class, the aristocracy of the Upper Cauca Valley, is clearly an oligarchy.

BIBLIOGRAPHY

Adams, Dale

1966 "Colombia's Land Tenure System: Antecedents and Problems," *Land Economics,* 42:43-52. Reprinted as Land Tenure Center Reprint No. 18, University of Wisconsin.

Aguilera Camacho, Alberto

1964 "Reforma y Contra-Reforma Agraria en Colombia," *Revista de la Universidad Libre,* Epoch IV, No. 18, December, Bogota.

Anderson, Charles W.

1966 "Political Factors in Latin American Economic Development," *Journal of International Affairs,* 20:235-53. Reprinted in Land Tenure Center Reprint No. 26.

Arroyo, Miguel Antonio

1953 *El Cauca es Así.* Popayán, Colombia: University of Cauca Press.

Barraclough, Solon and Arthur L. Domike

1966 "Agrarian Structure in Seven Latin American Countries: A report of ICAD," *Land Economics,* 42:392-424. Reprinted as Land Tenure Center Reprint No. 25, University of Wisconsin.

Blasier, Cole

1966 "Power and Social Change in Colombia: The Cauca Valley," *Journal of Latin American Studies,* 8:386-410.

Crist, Raymond E.

1952 *The Cauca Valley, Colombia: Land Tenure and Land Use.* Baltimore: Waverly Press.

Fals-Borda, Orlando

1955 *Peasant Society in the Colombian Andes.* Gainesville: University of Florida Press.

Feder, Ernest

1963 "The Rational Implementation of Land Reform in Colombia and its Significance for the Alliance for Progress," *America Latina, Centro Latinoamericano de Investigaciones en Ciencias Sociales,* 6:81-108, Brazil.

1964 "La Reforma Agraria en Colombia, Post Scriptum," *Revista de la Universidad Libre,* Epoch IV, 8:33-38.

Fluharty, Vernon L.

1957 *Dance of the Millions.* Pittsburgh: University of Pittsburgh Press.

Freyre, Gilberto

1946 *The Masters and the Slaves.* New York: Putnam.

Glade, William

1963 *Prospects for Political Stability in Colombia: A Critique.* Discussion paper No. 1, Land Tenure Center, University of Wisconsin, January.

Hirschman, Albert O.

1963 *Journeys Toward Progress.* New York: The Twentieth Century Fund.

Keller, Suzanne

1963 *Beyond the Ruling Class: Strategic Elites in Modern Society.* New York: Random House.

Lipset, Seymour M. and Reinhard Bendix

1959 *Social Mobility in Industrial Society.* Berkeley: University of California Press.

1967 "Values, Education, and Entrepreneurship," *in* S. Lipset and A. Solari, eds., *Elites in Latin America.* New York: Oxford University Press.

Martz, John D.

1962 *Colombia: A Contemporary Political Survey.* Chapel Hill, North Carolina: University of North Carolina Press.

Payne, James L.

1968 "The Oligarchy Muddle," *World Politics,* 20:3:439-53.

Pearse, Andrew

1966 "Agrarian Change Trends in Latin America," *Latin American Research Review,* 1:45-69.

Phelan, John

1963 *Prospects for Political Stability in Colombia.* Discussion Paper 1, Land Tenure Center, University of Wisconsin, January.

Posada F., Antonio J., and Jeanne de Posada

1966 *The CVC: Challenge to Underdevelopment and Traditionalism.* Bogota, Colombia; Ediciones Tercer Mundo.

Smith, T. Lynn

1963 "The Growth of Population in Central and South America," *In Study of Population and Immigration Problems,* Committee of the Judiciary, U.S. House of Representatives, Washington, D.C.

1965 (Editor) *Agrarian Reform in Latin America.* New York: Knopf.

Solari, Aldo

1967 "Secondary Education and the Development of Elites," *In* S. Lipset and A. Solari, eds., *Elites in Latin America.* New York: Oxford University Press.

Strickon, Arnold

1962 "Class and Kinship in Argentina," *Ethnology,* 1:500-15. Reprinted *in* D. Heath and R. Adams, eds., *Contemporary Cultures and Societies of Latin America.* New York: Random House, 1965.

Thiesenhusen, William C.

1966 "Chile's Experiments in Agrarian Reform," *Land Economics Monographs.* University of Wisconsin Press.

Uslar-Pietri, Arturo

1964 "No Panacea for Latin America," *In* J. Maier and R. Weatherhead, eds., *Politics of Change in Latin America.* New York: Frederick A. Praeger.

Whiteford, Andrew H.

1960 *Two Cities of Latin America: A Comparative Description of Social Classes.* Bulletin No. 9, Logan Museum of Anthropology, Beloit College. Reprinted by Doubleday, New York, 1964.

III

ISSUES IN RURAL AND URBAN LABOR

The many facets of economic development touch every group and reach into every corner of the nation, but perhaps the most profound challenges are those experienced by the country's labor force. Not only do new kinds of work appear and traditional trades disappear without warning, but the entire context of work–the relations between employer and employee and between the workers themselves, the relations between the family, the community and the job, the values attached to careers and occupations–is altered with disorienting speed. In Part III, we consider the impact of economic development on rural and urban labor.

The section opens with Solon Barraclough's elaboration of the thesis, both pessimistic and realistic, that the situation of rural Latin America labor is very likely to worsen with national economic growth. As he puts it, "it is hard to foresee any real decrease in the problems of poverty and under-employment in rural Latin America during the next two or three decades, and in some areas for much longer, even if the growth records of today's developed countries could be matched." This is given statistical support by Arthur Domike, also an agricultural economist and a long-time associate of Barraclough, who issues a similar warning.

> *It was contended at the outset that agriculture will prove the key to the Region's development. The chances for notably improving, or even maintaining, the rate of labor absorption by modern industry. . .are most dismal. But, in agriculture, the technical potential for new employment is more than adequate. . . .Nevertheless, without altering the landholding systems, employment increases will not occur.*

Comparisons between the agricultural and industrial sectors of the economy have long played a major role in the analysis of economic development. In this context, Barraclough launches a sustained attack on suggestions that the dual economy concept might be applicable to Latin America. Rather, he suggests, the distinction should be not between a modern and a backward sector, but between capitalist and non-capitalist sectors, and in any case, there is ample evidence that the large-scale farming operations which produce the bulk of the region's agricultural products are as "capitalist" as most urban factories, and perhaps more so.

This raises another point, one which also appears in several other essays in this section, that the usual conception of agriculture–labor force, organization of production, marketing–in Latin America (and in most of the Third World) is grossly oversimplified. This is, first, an empirical question which can be answered in short order with statistics on the size of rural landholdings, shares of commodity markets controlled by the larger producing units, the ratio of peasants and other smallholders to wage laborers, and so forth. Secondly, it requires careful definitions of the different agricultural systems found in Latin America, including peasants, part-time farmers and farm laborers, and plantations, with particular attention to the differences between agriculture in economically-advanced and Third World countries; James Blaut's essay meets some of this need, a task which is important because of the widespread tendency, considered a major source of error by many critics, to use the agricultural organization of advanced countries as the proper and necessary model for the developing nations. Finally, a sophisticated understanding of rural labor requires a thorough analysis of the dynamic processes through which peasant and other rural populations are incorporated into national systems undergoing rapid economic change. The outlines of such an analysis are presented here by the English sociologist, Andrew Pearse.

What Pearse stresses is that the peasant's choice is not WHETHER to accept the incorporation process, but rather among alternate ways of adjusting to it, all of which carry the strong likelihood that his level of living will worsen because of his weak bargaining position vis-a-vis the large estates, the rural middle-men and money lenders, and the urban entrepreneurs investing in corporate farming, what in the United States is called "agro-business." In a sense, then, Pearse takes a different route to arrive at a picture quite as gloomy as that painted by Barraclough and Domike.

The population explosion, the weak competitive position of Latin American agriculture in world markets, and the failure to carry out significant land reform are but a few of the reasons why rural labor and rural society in general are in serious trouble. In this light, it is noteworthy that the essays of Huizer, Barraclough, Domike, and others in this volume suggest in different ways that collectivization or, at least, the development of large-scale farm cooperatives, is a definite alternative and perhaps the only solution for the poorer countries of the continent. As Barraclough notes, concerning the collective-cooperative strategy of rural development,

> *I think we would have to see that this is a very real possibility if it's permitted, in the sense that it is the U.S. which is supporting the present power structure and would try to prevent it. The Cuban*

> *experience may turn out not to be an isolated phenomenon, but rather a forerunner of a socialist strategy for rural development in many. . .regions of Latin America.*

It is important to have a clear grasp of the problem for which Barraclough and others here outline possible solutions. The problem as they see it is unemployment, and especially rural unemployment. Why? Because, as Domike states the issue in the opening sentence of his essay, "economic and social development prospects in Latin America during the relevant future . . . depend largely upon changes brought about in the most traditional part of these societies, agriculture." Put another way, the problem is how to slow down rural-urban migration, keeping labor on the land and making it more productive. Domike suggests that industrialization is increasing its share of the labor force, but not at a rate rapid enough to reduce the importance of generating large numbers of new, rural jobs, largely, of course, in agriculture. The fact that many writers ignore or misunderstand this point is evidence that it is not the truism it seems to be.

Problems of employment and labor productivity are both rural AND urban, as David Chaplin notes in reporting on his research in Peru. He found, for example, that productivity is higher among urban workers for cultural and psychological reasons, on the one hand, and because of unionization and the greater enforcement of labor legislation in urban areas. He found, also, that productivity and morale, contrary to what one might expect, are often inversely correlated. "The most contented workers . . . worked in the least efficient mill, . . . while the most highly militantly organized 'radical' union developed in the mill with one of the highest productivity rates and the highest pay scales . . . ." Further, in contrast to other essays in this section, he suggests that "land reform as an attempt at social justice within the rural sector, and between it and the urban, does not seem very promising. At best, it can only 'buy time' for a regime committed to a program of rapid urban industrial development." In brief, Chaplin's description of the Peruvian experience provides a provocative introduction (witness the discussion which follows his paper) to the analysis of industrial labor in the development process.

RURAL DEVELOPMENT AND EMPLOYMENT PROSPECTS IN LATIN AMERICA

Solon L. Barraclough

One-fourth of the net annual increase in Latin America's total population must probably remain in agriculture, if we accept the slow growth rate of urban employment suggested by Arthur Domike.[1] For Latin America as a whole, this situation implies finding jobs on the land for over one-half million new workers each year (ECLA, 1966, pp. 41-51). Domike concluded that the possibilities for finding productive employment for these people now and in the foreseeable future depend mainly on the internal structure of agriculture.

These propositions should be examined more fully. To what extent are they valid for particular countries with differing levels of development? How rapidly will, or could, Latin American agriculture be modernized, and what labor requirements are likely during the process? What are the prospects for putting additional rural families to work through colonizing new lands? How rapidly can new non-agricultural job opportunities be created for the "surplus" rural population? How would alternative development strategies affect the incomes and employment opportunities of rural people?

I do not pretend to answer all of these questions here, and in any event, the answers depend largely upon political and social considerations such as those discussed by Huizer and Pearse elsewhere in this volume. I will try, however, to indicate some of the economic limits within which the answers must be found. These restrictions are determined by the general framework of agricultural development.

By agricultural development, we understand a process in which farming becomes a continually more productive and rationally organized component of a modern industrial system. Development implies a continual transformation in productive processes, cognition, organization and social structure. The process is far more complex than can be indicated by a few accounting aggregates and economic indices. It involves the transformation of a society's basic values and the whole structure of underlying social and economic relationships. There are, however, a few salient economic characteristics of the development process which are of particular interest to our analysis.

What happens during the change from traditional to modern society? First of all, farm production generally must increase more rapidly than total population and much more rapidly than the agricultural work force. Capital, new technologies, skills, and organization become increasingly important factors in farm production, while land and unskilled labor lose their traditional primacy. Farmers use progressively greater quantities of services, inputs, and consumption goods provided by other sectors of the economy. An ever-greater proportion of farm production is marketed to be consumed by non-farm people. Urban populations increase more rapidly than rural, and eventually agricultural population may even decrease absolutely. Farm production becomes more rationally planned and organized, in the economic sense, so as to obtain the greatest possible returns from available resources, technologies, and population. The living levels of farm people rise, at first slowly, but as development gains momentum, much more rapidly as redundant and underemployed rural labor migrates from the land to the cities.

What proportion of the benefits of increased productivity will accrue to the mass of farm workers and peasants? This depends only in part on the path and rate of economic development. The allocation of gains in income between investment and consumption determines how much is globally available for improving the material conditions of life. The question of who shall benefit, and when, from the greater net availability of consumption goods and services is a political matter about which economic theory has little to say that is especially relevant for rural Latin America. The absurdity of believing that the real questions of income distribution are answered by marginal productivity analysis does not require comment here. Fortunately, development is far too important a matter to be left to the economic technicians.

Agricultural growth is only a part of the whole development process. Arguments over the merits of "balanced" versus "unbalanced" economic development, and whether the agricultural sector can thrive while industry languishes, or *vice versa*, must be dismissed as academic hair-splitting. In the real world there will always be lags and leaps in the progress of particular sectors. Only in this way will traditional institutional rigidities be broken and new, higher productive levels be reached. On the other hand, one cannot imagine agriculture developing indefinitely while the rest of the economy stagnates, or the reverse. In the long-run, in any economic system, growth must be balanced in relation to demand and technology or it cannot continue. Even a superficial acquaintance with the concepts of input-output matrices should make this clear.

As other papers in this volume show, most of the Latin American rural population are in traditional *latifundia* and *minifundia* agricultural systems, with incomes and living levels very low by any criterion. Technology is often primitive and farm organization relatively unproductive.[2] This general impression can be highly misleading, however. Many areas of commercial farming are using modern technology. The great bulk of agricultural production comes from farms that are neither modern nor traditional, but somewhere in between. It is this great diversity of farming systems that makes generalization about agriculture in any Latin American country easy to criticize.

This paper has three objectives. The first is to review some of the currently fashionable theories of agriculture's role in economic development and examine their relevance for the various Latin American situations. The second is to attempt to analyze in a very general way the employment and income prospects of the rural population. Finally, I consider a few broad alternative rural development strategies consistent with the requirements of rapid overall economic development in various situations.

The Dual Economy Growth Models

Much conventional wisdom about agriculture's role in development is based on the assumption of a "dual economy," an assumption that requires detailed criticism here[3] because it dominates many of the currently fashionable economic growth theories, with broad implications for development policy. Unfortunately, in my opinion, many of these policies are inappropriate for Latin America because they are based on erroneous assumptions.

It is supposed in these models that, in the poor but developing country, there are really two sub-societies–almost "apartheid" in caricature. One of these, identified with agriculture, is stagnant and traditional. Neither labor nor capital is systematically hired for profit and, in fact, the struggle for subsistence, not profits, is this economy's driving motor. Labor is generally assumed to be redundant and available in practically unlimited supply for transfer to industry for a modest premium. Some analysts, however, assume full employment in agriculture but with a production function of diminishing returns, while in industry returns are increasing (Jorgenson, 1961).

In these models, the other sub-society, called industry, is assumed to be modern, profit-driven, and bent upon accumulating capital and more capital. It uses the most efficient techniques, reinvests most of its economic surplus, and achieves increasingly "rational" organization. This modern industrial sector, at first small, grows constantly relative to, and in part at the expense of, the subsistence agricultural sector, and eventually it absorbs the redundant and under-employed labor of the subsistence economy. This forces up the price of labor, assumed to be practically homogeneous in quality, in turn forcing agriculture also to adopt profit-making criteria; it must make more "rational" use of labor, capital, and technology in order to survive. Once this happens, the "take-off" into sustained economic growth is completed and agriculture is soon transformed.

The two sub-economies are assumed to trade with each other. If industry expands too rapidly, or agriculture too slowly, the terms of trade turn against industry, slowing its rate of expansion while making greater investment in agriculture necessary and profitable. Both sectors produce some surpluses (profits) above consumption which are invested for the most part in "industry," where returns are higher on the average.

Arthur Lewis, the most sophisticated of the dual economy theorists, carefully warns that he is really talking about "capitalist" and "non-capitalist" sectors, not "industry" and "agriculture." He believes they may roughly correspond in some developing countries, but admits that many agricultural producers may also be capitalists. Following Malthus and Ricardo, he allows a place in his scheme for a group of landlords who do not produce or invest but only consume. Lewis admonishes that "analysis is not prescription." Nevertheless, in his subsequent argument, he speculates that "in practice, failure of peasant agriculture to increase its productivity has probably been the chief reason holding down the expansion of the industrial sector in most of the underdeveloped countries of the world." (Lewis, 1958). To remedy this, he recommends research into peasant problems and the provision of adequate agricultural extension, credit, roads, and the like. While some of the other dual economy analysts are less careful than Lewis in their qualifications, they would probably agree with his general conclusions.

The relevance of these dual economy models for Latin America is at best highly questionable; the basic assumptions are a long way from reality, and consequently, and not surprisingly, the analysis fails to yield deductions and insights immediately useful for policy guidance.

In the first place, the notion that economic relationships between a peasant "subsistence sector" and modern industry can be usefully analyzed as a problem in the terms of trade, that is, primarily as one of price relationships, is rather esoteric for Latin America. An increase in food prices relative to those of industrial goods would undoubtedly benefit landlords, capitalist farmers, and some middlemen. It is doubtful, however, that such changes would be reflected either in peasant incomes or farm wages. The existing agrarian structure excludes the peasantry from participation in political processes and from any possibility of negotiating over wages or over the prices they actually receive for their marketed production. The increased proportion of national income going for food purchases would simply flow into the pockets of other social groups. The evidence we have indicates that this is, in effect, what happens, and this being the case, there is no reason to believe that improved price relationships for farm products would have any economic impact on the "subsistence sector."

Terms of trade analysis was developed to show changing economic relationships in the exchange of goods and services between two sovereign nations. It is also useful for measuring changes in exchange relationships between two monopolists or any other two groups both having "market power" within a national economy. But this kind of analysis does not contribute much to our understanding of the economic relationships between an unorganized politically-inert mass of *campesinos* and urban industry. This "subsistence sector's" economic relationships with industry are determined more by other social institutions than by institutions for marketing farm products. An analogous procedure would be to analyze the relationships between Negroes and Whites in the United States as a problem in terms of trade; it is theoretically possible, but scarcely relevant for either understanding the problem or finding policies to solve it.

Even granting the rather remote possibility that there may be significant exchange and bargaining between the "subsistence sector" and modern industry, (Lewis recognized that in many cases there may be none), identification of the subsistence economy with agriculture and the modern capitalist economy with industry makes little sense.[4] In Latin America, unlike what happened historically in much of Europe, the colonists and *conquistadores* established their cities and towns before they subdued the countryside (Morse, 1962). Almost immediately, however, they organized capitalist enterprises to exploit mines and the land (and the Indians and slaves who worked them) long before they began to organize urban manufacturing and other industries. Large-scale capitalist production in Latin America virtually began with the colonial plantations and *haciendas* (Bagu, 1949).

Urban industry, on the other hand, has seldom been distinguished in Latin America for its dynamic capitalist traits. Fostered originally by a protective mercantilist imperial system, only permitted in restricted fields where it would not compete with the home country, usually controlled by foreign investors and protected from competition by elaborate monopolies, tariffs, quotas, and franchises, its outstanding characteristics have been its high cost structure and its dependence upon paternalistic government. Profits, far from being relentlessly accumulated and reinvested, have frequently been repatriated, dissipated in consumption, padded pay-rolls, and bureaucracies, or securely invested in agricultural land and other real estate.

During the 1950's productivity per man in Latin American manufacturing industries was increasing only about two-thirds faster than in agriculture. The rate of growth in manufacturing employment was some twenty-five percent slower than in services and only about twice as great as in farming (ECLA, 1966, pp. 44-49). Marginal urban populations of unemployed and underemployed, and those employed at near subsistence levels in such activities as domestic services and petty buying and selling, not particularly vital for transforming the traditional society, have been increasing relatively more rapidly than has industrial employment or, for that matter, the rural poor. In countries such as Chile, the urban poor undoubtedly outnumber the peasantry and farm laborers.

The most dynamic industries have often been foreign subsidiaries. Their net economic impact on the local economy is greatly dampened because their production, purchases, sales, investments, and employment are frequently more attuned to the economic requirements of the industrialized home country than to the underdeveloped country in which they are doing business. In short, to identify urban industry as the principal dynamic and capital-accumulating sector in the developing Latin American nations stretches both facts and credulity.

To suggest that Latin American "agriculture" in some manner approximates the sluggish, non-capitalist "subsistence sector" of the dual economy models also requires both imagination and a disregard for reality. Capitalist farm organization is the rule in contemporary Latin America. Subsistence-type peasant farming, even if broadly defined, is limited mostly to marginal areas and is dominant in terms of production only in a few regions such as parts of the Andean highlands.

There are, to be sure, many traditional large estates or *haciendas*. These are technically backward, and their owners depend heavily upon quasi-feudal labor services, rents, and tributes for their incomes. But these estates can hardly be described as subsistence operations. They often market a sizeable surplus, and profits are almost always an important management objective. The traditional *hacendados* are more akin to Malthus's and Ricardo's landlords whose primary function is to consume than to the prototype capitalists with their passion to produce, accumulate, and invest.

Most of the region's agricultural production reaching national and international markets, however, originates on farm units which can be called capitalist by any common-sense meaning of the term, not from subsistence peasant holdings or traditional *haciendas*. The operators of these enterprises make a profit calculus, within the limits of their knowledge and the local institutional setting, and they guide their farm operation accordingly. They generally use commercial credit of some kind. The large capitalist producers, such as the wine growers of Chile or the cattle producers of Brazil and

Uruguay, have easy access to private banks and public credit agencies. Small producers have to depend more on middlemen and the larger landowners for their capital. Many large plantations, such as the foreign-owned sugar and banana companies, have their own sources of capital. New technology and purchased inputs are used to some extent wherever available and profitable for the owners.

If they are large, these capitalist farms usually hire all or part of their labor for cash wages. Even so, many continue to use their monopoly positions in the labor market, (where such a market can be said to exist), to pay very low wages or to continue many of the traditional "forced" labor arrangements still common on the traditional *haciendas*. The CIDA studies found many situations of this kind in Brazil and Chile. Small commercial farms may depend largely on family labor but these operators nonetheless behave like rational businessmen. CIDA studies in Antioquia, Colombia; in Panachachel, Guatemala; in Coastal Peru, Ecuador, and many other places found many highly efficient small capitalist producers.

These capitalist farmers (large and small) may frequently be more addicted to good living and conspicuous consumption than either the development ethic or the Protestant Ethic would consider proper and desirable. But they can hardly be considered as either traditional landlords passively collecting and consuming rents or as peasants whose economic activities are primarily governed by the requirements of survival and custom.

It is difficult to make precise quantitative estimates, but from two-thirds to three-fourths of the agricultural production in Latin America undoubtedly originates on commercial farms. Even in countries such as Peru, Guatemala, and Ecuador, where subsistence-oriented peasant farming and the traditional *haciendas* include well over two-thirds of the rural population, the bulk of agricultural production reaching urban and world markets comes from commercially-oriented "capitalist" farm enterprises of one sort or another. It must be concluded that the "subsistence sector" not only does not dominate Latin American agriculture in terms of production, but also in most countries it is of negligible economic importance except as a source of unlimited cheap labor.

The main criteria for defining a "sector" in social or economic analysis is that its members have some common characteristics with respect to the problem at hand that cause them to act or react in a predictably similar way. Presumably we are looking for stable relationships that aid in understanding the development process and might possibly be influenced by purposeful design. But this is not the case for the "agricultural sector" in Latin America. Instead, changes in prices, markets, credit terms, technology, taxes, land tenure, and political structure affect the consumption, production, and investment patterns of different agrarian groups very differently. Often the effects on different groups of an increase in food prices will be in opposing directions; for example, the incomes of commercial farmers would tend to rise, while wage laborers in agriculture would suffer a reduction in their real incomes because of higher food costs.

In the CIDA studies of land tenure and development, as a working hypothesis, we tried to identify at least six different agricultural groups: 1) the traditional landlords of multi-family size farm units; 2) market-oriented large capitalist farmers; 3) small (family and sub-family) commercial farmers; 4) subsistence-oriented small farmers; 5) landless laborers tied to the estates by traditional tenure arrangements obligating labor services for usufruct rights to land, and 6) landless laborers working for cash wages. The intractability of the available data and the complexity of the actual situations encountered everywhere made this attempt only partially successful. It showed, nonetheless, the need for much more rigorous and functional concepts concerning the agrarian sector and for more adequate empirical data. Without these, it is idle to hope that the economics of agricultural development may be brought from the realm of academic speculation into that of programs and policies.

For the economist to lump together in analysis all the groups depending on land for their livelihood as the "agricultural sector," treating the resulting accounting aggregates and indices as real variables in development equations, may conceal more than it reveals. It is not too different from the military planner who prepares his campaign only on the basis of the total number of men in the armed forces without ever examining their composition, organization, training, equipment, or morale. It makes for ready calculations, but poor strategy and tactics.

We must conclude that the dual economy models purporting to analyze the terms of trade between agriculture and industry during development are in many respects irrelevant for understanding Latin American agrarian problems. The theoretical insights derived from the models concerning some of the possible consequences of a surplus of labor in rural areas, however, are much more pertinent. To ignore these, or to deny the existence of rural unemployment and under-employment by defining it away, as Theodore Schultz (1964) seems to do, leads to a very unrealistic appraisal of the rural development problem.

The fact that in most developing countries surplus labor is available in relatively large amounts has been largely forgotten, ignored, denied, or its importance belittled by many neo-classical economists. Even so, earlier analysts such as Malthus, Ricardo, and Marx recognized very well some of the implications of this phenomenon of early capitalist growth. Partly as a result of Lewis's celebrated article on "Economic Development with Unlimited Supplies of Labor" and Ranis and Fei's[5] later mathematical elaborations, it is again recognized that widespread unemployment and under-employment is the rule rather than an exception during the earlier stages of industrialization as it is occurring in Latin America and many other parts of the world. This fact has important implications for development planning.

The ubiquitous labor surplus found in Latin America, rural and urban, is now usually attributed to "disguised unemployment in traditional agriculture," the "population explosion," and *marginalidad*. Actually, it is much more realistic to view the phenomenon as a by-product of the incorporation of traditional rural societies into the orbit of national and international markets and the "modern" institutions emanating from the developed nations. The impact of modern medicine, for example, reduces mortality while birth rates remain high. As new communications, education, and consumer goods penetrate rural areas, they increase aspirations and social consciousness. A flood of cheap but functionally superior manufactured products displace artisans and craftsmen. Unskilled farm labor is increasingly replaced by machines on modernizing farms. At the same time, low-cost foodstuffs and agricultural raw material become more and more available from modernized farms and from imports, forcing peasant production out of many traditional markets. Large-scale migration to urban areas becomes commonplace as, on the one hand, the traditional rural organization and its relative security disintegrates, while on the other, the pull of the cities with their minimal conveniences and opportunities seem to offer the only alternative to the displaced peasants and rural workers.

Malthus and Ricardo attributed the apparently ever-growing labor surplus of their day, and the persistence of dire poverty, both urban and rural, to the "Iron Law of Wages" and the working man's incurable habit of unlimited procreation. They saw little hope for a brighter future, although Adam Smith was relatively optimistic. Marx was more perceptive in his analysis of the causes of this "reserve army of the unemployed." He saw the tendency of advancing industry and technology to leave large numbers of workers and peasants without stable jobs as the traditional society disintegrates. That he failed to foresee all the adaptive capacities of the social system he was criticizing to cope with the problem later on within the industrialized countries should not make us overlook the large doses of truth in his analysis. He based his prediction of ever-increasing unemployment on a particular historical situation and remarked that "... every special historic mode of production has its own special laws of population, historically valid within its limits alone." (Marx, p. 693). One could reasonably argue, along with Galbraith (1967), that the mode of production within the "developed" and industrialized countries has changed in fundamental ways and, for that reason, Marx's prediction for them went awry. It might, nonetheless, still be very pertinent for present-day Latin America where the social structure has many similarities to that of Nineteenth Century Eastern and Southern Europe.

The present tendency to ascribe widespread under-employment in developing countries to the inherent nature of traditional agriculture, if it is rural, or to "marginality," if it is urban, instead of to the unplanned impact on the traditional society of modern industry, institutions, and technology from the developed countries is, of course, superficial.[6] But this should not lead us to deny the problem's existence or its consequences.

Employment Prospects for Surplus Rural Labor

Under-employment in Latin American agriculture is so evident to anyone with first-hand knowledge of the agrarian situation that it is difficult to take seriously the academic debates about whether or not it really exists. The CIDA studies showed that, by any common-sense definition of under-employment, from one-fifth to over one-third of the workers in Latin American agriculture are practically surplus. That is to say, the same output could be obtained from two-thirds of the available work force, with *present* levels of technology and capital, provided some adjustments were made in farm organization. Schultz, by assuming immutable farm organization, concludes rural under-employment scarcely exists, but it is hard to believe that peasants who have productive work in their fields only a few months of the year, or plantation workers who are paid only to cope with peak labor requirements, are anything but under-employed.[7]

The prospects for increasing agricultural employment and incomes immediately in most of Latin America are sharply limited by the persistence of traditional land tenure structures.[8] Potential entrepreneurs have few opportunities to develop their talents because of the rigid rural class structure and the monopoly of land, water, and other resources by a few large owners. One does not have to resort to "achievement motivation" or other psychological and cultural explanations to account for the absence of a more dynamic agricultural expansion in the face of growing demands for food and ever-increasing agricultural imports.[9]

Following a relatively drastic land reform, agricultural production in Mexico has increased since 1940 more rapidly than in any other Latin

American country, although a major part of these gains occurred on privately-owned farms as a result of new investments. In Mexico, Bolivia, and Cuba, peasants' and farm workers' real incomes have unquestionably risen significantly, in part as a consequence of removing the rents and tributes formerly collected by large land owners and also because some public services have been redirected.[10] In Cuba, Bolivia, and Mexico, rural employment opportunities undoubtedly increased following reform. In Chile, both employment and cultivated area have practically doubled on expropriated large farms, while peasant incomes on these same estates went up by nearly 200 percent the first year after they were "reformed."[11]

Even if restrictive and monopolistic land tenure structures were to be profoundly reformed, however, the agrarian problem in Latin America would persist for many years. Sufficient land is simply not available in many areas such as the Andean highlands. Here every farm family could not possibly have sufficient area to employ all of its labor productively. Continuing rural population growth will intensify the problem in other regions even where land resources are not now the limiting factor. To provide every farm family with adequate capital and modern technology to increase its production by more than minute amounts is a short-run economic and administrative impossibility in most Latin American countries. Moreover, present social and political structures preclude agricultural policies that make the most productive use of even the limited available resources and services (Barraclough, 1967).

Colonization of new lands offers no panacea either. Expansion of the intensive and extensive margins of cultivation is limited by the same economic and institutional parameters. The dream of settling surplus rural population in the Amazon jungles or the Colombian *llanos* is in the words of the geographer, Preston James, "the 'El Dorado' of the Twentieth Century."

In the United States, we take great pride in the fact that every farm family, on the average, supplies food and fiber for some fourteen or fifteen non-farm families. This is not only a function of technology, skill, and capital, however. (The average value of reproducible farm capital such as machinery, livestock, and buildings in the United States is about US$30,000 per family, while in Latin America it probably does not average even five percent of this.) The high United States productivity per farmer can only be explained by the fact that its agriculture is an integral part of a highly complex industrial system. It must be remembered that a corollary of the high productivity per farmer in the United States is that some fourteen or fifteen non-farm families are required to supply each farm family with the goods and services needed for its production and consumption. Economic growth "is a social product that owes as much to the jurist as to the inventor" (Tawney, 1932, p. 130).

In any event, agricultural modernization cannot be expected, in itself, to increase farm employment. Modern agricultural technology is predominantly labor-saving. Oshima's argument (1963) that technological advances in agriculture generally require the employment of more labor is not realistic for Latin American conditions.

More indicative of the probable outcome of agricultural modernization in Latin America is the recent history of the Mississippi delta. During the twenty-year period from 1940 to 1960, traditional sharecropper tenure and mule technology in the region were largely replaced by mechanized methods. At the same time, the use of better varieties and fertilizers greatly increased yields. Labor requirements per hundred pounds of cotton in this period fell by some eighty-five percent, and per bushel of corn by sixty-five percent. Despite increased total agricultural production in the area, total farm labor requirements dropped during the period so rapidly that in 1960 they were only about ten percent of the level existing twenty years before. The proportion of skilled labor had risen drastically. During the change-over from the traditional to modern technology, seasonal labor demands had first increased sharply and then declined. The rural population was reduced to about one-third of its 1940 level as many people migrated to the cities (Day, 1967).

The prospects of urban job opportunities expanding rapidly enough to provide alternative work for Latin America's growing "excess" rural population appear even slimmer than those for finding them sufficient agricultural employment. At least, this is the situation unless the whole strategy of Latin American development is drastically revised.

In the first place, urban industrial growth does not seem to be creating many new jobs in manufacturing. Recent Chilean experience showed that each three percent increase in manufacturing output required only a one percent growth in employment. A new factory in Medellin or Sao Paulo will generally adopt the labor-saving technology of industries in present-day Detroit and Pittsburgh, not those of Nineteenth Century Birmingham and Manchester.

Secondly, the economic historians do not hold out much hope that economic growth rates greatly in excess of those now prevailing in Latin America could be maintained for long periods. Reviewing the growth rates of some of today's principal industrial countries (United States, Great Britain, Russia, France, Germany, and Sweden), Kuznets (1965, p. 307) found no three-decade period since the middle of the last century in which gross product grew by more than three percent per capita. Sustained rapid growth of gross national product, say, four to five percent per capita for two or three generations, has yet to be proved possible. But growth rates of this order would be necessary for Latin America as a whole to develop the economic capacity to modernize its agriculture substantially within the next half century and to provide the rural and urban "marginal" population with incomes comparable to those of today's farmers and industrial workers in the United States or Western Europe. This is true even assuming that the present pattern of income *distribution* could also be modified to resemble those of present day England or France.

Theoretically, a relatively quick solution to the problem of rural under-employment and low incomes could be found, perhaps in twenty to forty years, depending upon the degree of industrialization already achieved. The only requirement would be really effective "all-out" effort. The gains in income from more productive technology and organization would have to be ruthlessly reinvested and all political, social, and cultural obstacles to rapid development would have to be overcome, or assumed away. Thus, R. M. Goodwin (1961) shows that theoretically, even the poorest underdeveloped country could reach a level of sustained and growing per capita consumption of some ten times its starting level after only about forty years of intensive effort, if it tried hard enough and intelligently enough. And it could do this without foreign aid. But to do so, the marginal savings rate would have to rise to about seventy-five percent during part of the "take-off" period and an average of as much as seventy to eighty percent of gross national product would have to be ploughed back into capital goods during the last decade of the "big push". Politically, it is hard to envision any "mobilization effort" that could extract such sacrifices from its participants. In any case, the social and institutional obstacles to such a break-neck transformation could not conceivably be overcome.

Despite these practical difficulties, Professor Lauchlin Currie (1966) must have had some such model in mind when he proposed solving Colombia's agrarian problems almost overnight by rapid industrialization and outmigration. For Currie's solution to be effective within a ten to fifteen-year period, migration out of agriculture would have to be over three times greater than its present rapid rate in Colombia–which would be a "big push" indeed. Moreover, the political changes required for such an effort could hardly be made without one of the most thorough-going revolutions in social structure that ever took place anywhere.

No matter whether the goals of income growth are assumed to be very high or to be the more modest ones of the Alliance for Progress, the problem of finding productive employment for the growing agricultural work force during the coming decades does not appear amenable to a ready solution either in Latin American agriculture or in the cities. At least, this is the situation unless sufficient structural changes could be effected to mobilize this available "surplus" manpower for development purposes such as the public works, new housing, factories, schools, and other requirements of accelerated modernization.

If Latin American integration were to become a political and economic reality, the rural employment problem would appear a little less formidable than at present. The inclusion of Brazil and Argentina, with their great expanses of potentially productive agricultural land and substantial industrial bases, would provide the economic planners with greater latitude than is possible for countries such as Bolivia, Peru, or Haiti taken by themselves. The greater size of the market would enhance conditions for growth in both agriculture and industry. Venezuelan oil, Chilean copper, and Brazilian coffee could aid in solving the balance of payments problems of less-fortunately endowed countries.

The fundamental problem, however, would not be greatly altered. Half the Latin American population is agricultural. While the agrarian problem is most difficult, in the economic sense, in the least urbanized countries, such as Guatemala and Ecuador, it is, in fact, universal. Regional integration and intra-regional migration would offer no panacea.

There still remains, however, one other possibility for dealing with the rural employment problems: massive migration to the industrialized countries. Out-migration played a crucial role in the Nineteenth Century economic development of Europe (Thomas, 1954). One-third of the population of Ireland, for example, emigrated to America following the potato famine. Today, in Latin America, Puerto Rico has sent more emigrants to New York than the number of people remaining in agricultural pursuits on the island.

Migration to the heavily industrialized United States, as has recently occurred from Puerto Rico, would offer possibilities for mitigating the rural employment problem in the more heavily populated rural areas of Latin America. At the same time, the United States would receive a massive infusion of vigorous new immigrants, (one would have to think of a million or more immigrants annually), similar to those waves of immigration in the last century that made it one of the world's most dynamic nations; and it would acquire some new problems.

Today's political realities, however, seem to exclude this possibility. United States immigration policy is becoming more restrictive. Latin America has been brought under the quota system, while Mexican migrant labor has been practically excluded. Professionals and capital from Latin America can enter easily, but not unskilled *campesinos*. In any case, from the viewpoint of many Latin Americans such a massive out-migration would be unacceptable.

It is hard to foresee any real decrease in the problems of poverty and under-employment in rural Latin America during the next two or three decades, and in some areas for much longer, even if the growth records of today's developed countries could be matched. To achieve a more rapid diminution of agrarian employment and income problems would require political decisions and changes in economic and social structure that appear extremely unlikely, at least for the near future.

The consequences of an increasing excess labor supply and persistent poverty in most of Latin America are difficult to foresee in detail, but less so in broad outline. The economic transformation that required some two centuries in Western Europe has already been pretty much accomplished by Japan and the Soviet Union in less than half that time. Now China and several other countries are attempting to speed the process still further. As social tensions increase in Latin America, and the gap widens between it and the industrialized countries, and, internally, between the rich and the poor, it seems unlikely that either its elites or the mass of its citizens will accept a continuation of the *status quo*. They would not be content to follow the same torturous development path associated with unplanned "capitalist free-enterprise" and "economic liberalism" that Europe was on when Malthus, Ricardo, and Marx were drawing their dismal conclusions. Some kind of planning or "mobilization system" to speed development in Latin America seems almost inevitable. Whether it will be authoritarian and repressive or based largely on popular support and democratic participation remains to be seen.

What is difficult to understand is why so many economists and other social scientists working on Latin American problems maintain that what is now happening to the peasantry is not only inevitable but also, by implication, in some sense even desirable. Dr. Pangloss could not appear more optimistic than some of our colleagues (Tout est pour le mieux dans le meilleur des mondes possibles). Perhaps the explanation lies in Galbraith's (1967) observation: "One of the small but rewarding vocations of a free society is the provision of needed conclusions, properly supported by statistics and moral indignation, for those in a position to pay."

Rural Development Strategies

As we have seen, the twin problems of widespread rural poverty and under-employment are likely to grow more serious in most of Latin America as development proceeds. The belief that they will simply go away as soon as some mythical "take-off" point is reached fairly early in the course of the industrial growth of a poor country does not stand up either to critical analysis or to empirical testing in the real world. Having painted this gloomy picture, we have an obligation to reflect on what might be done about it. Are there rural development strategies that would mitigate these problems?

In common usage, "strategy" means a general plan for waging a campaign to attain particular objectives. It implies a sequence of coordinated decisions and actions. It combines the use of intelligence, guile, and force to win the battle.

The concept of strategy, however, seems to have two rather distinct meanings in the literature on development. On the one hand, it is seen as a conscious overall plan for reaching predetermined goals of economic growth and social change; it is a matter of finding the appropriate consistent set of policy "means" to arrive at the desired ends. On the other hand, development "strategy" is often seen by social historians as merely the path of social and economic change actually followed, but resulting from essentially uncoordinated policies and pressures (Moore, 1966; Hobsbawn, 1962). It is an *ex post facto* rationalization of what happened. Less astute observers than those mentioned here sometimes infer that things were planned that way. As Galbraith notes, in social matters it is customary to attribute to intelligence what, in reality, was brought about by circumstances.

Whether development strategy is regarded as a plan of how to get from where one is to where one wants to go, or as a rationalization of how he got to where he is from where he was, the elements to be considered are about the same. The operating unit for which social and economic decisions are made must be defined. The destination must be identified. And the route has to be mapped. In the present essay, I shall consider strategy as a conscious plan for development and not merely as a prediction of the probable course of Latin American social and economic change.

Rural development strategies have to take account not only of where the rural society is and where the planners want it to go, but also of who decides what and who does what during the operation. In other words, a strategy should indicate the roles of different social groups and their responsibilities and rewards during the development process. Otherwise, it is hardly realistic to speak of a "strategy;" instead, one is indulging in wishful thinking, game playing, or mere description.

The accepted convention among developers is to consider the nation-state as their principal planning unit. This has many drawbacks, but the alternatives do not seem any better. C. Wright Mills (1959, pp. 134-35) justified this choice of the unit of analysis as follows: "In choosing the national social structure as our generic working unit, [one adopts] a suitable level of generality, one that enables us to avoid abandoning our problems and yet to include the structural forces obviously involved in many details and troubles of human conduct today."

Nonetheless, there are two objections to using the nation-state as the basic unit for development planning. The first, but less convincing, of these is that the state may not really correspond to a national society at all. It may merely perform limited services for a collection of essentially autonomous local societies under the umbrella of its general tutelage. According to this argument, the local society or region should be the first object of development strategy because the crucial decisions that can now be made directly affecting farm modernization must be taken at the local level. This approach, however, ignores the fact that the state in Latin America does represent a very real power structure within which the local society must function. The nation-state exercises a monopoly of legitimized force in its territory. It sets the limits of local initiatives of all sorts. Local development plans that are not part of a larger national strategy would be unrealistic.

The second objection, however, is more serious. The sovereignty of the nation-state itself is seriously compromised in the important decisions affecting national social and economic structure. Latin American nation-states are an integral part of an international political and economic structure whose center of gravity is now in the United States. Louis Halle (1965) argues that the nation-state as it evolved during the last two centuries is already an anachronism. The international concentration of economic and political power has proceeded so far that when it comes to the decisions that really count for national development, the "independent" but underdeveloped nation often finds its areas of decision circumscribed. Its "sovereign power" is in many respects a formalism. If its development strategies contemplate fundamental changes in the political structure or in property relationships, for example, they are, in effect, revolutionary. To the extent that Latin American countries are incorporated into a broader economic and political power structure, effecting some kinds of changes at the purely national level may be most difficult.[12] This is not just a problem of international politics, for the huge, international, economic conglomerates are often so tied up with local economic interests that they have a tremendous power to resist change.

In spite of this conceptual inadequacy, we will continue to talk about national development strategies for lack of a better alternative. Nationalism is still one of the most dynamic political forces in Latin America. The "state," in theory if not in fact, can choose whatever development policies it wishes.

An effective Latin American common market and political union could change this in the future, as could the formal political and economic integration of the region with the United States. A much more important change could be the acquisition of real powers over its members by the United Nations, making it a truly world-wide political system that could direct development and utilize the vast economic capacity of the industrialized countries for this purpose.[13] None of these events seems likely for the immediate future.

The goals of rural development strategy are not subject to precise definition while profound conflicts of interest concerning their nature exist in every Latin American country. There seems to be general agreement, however, that a principal objective should be continually increasing agricultural production and productivity per capita, accompanied by improved living levels and incomes of the mass of the rural population. A second goal is generally presumed by Latin American intellectuals to be one of the greater "social justice"–of a narrowing of the gap between the peasants' and rural workers' incomes and opportunities, on the one hand, and those of the rural well-to-do and the employed urban population, on the other. For our purposes we can suppose that the broad goal of rural development in Latin America is to achieve rural productivities, income levels, and rates of growth comparable to those in today's industrialized countries.

Rural development strategies in the developing countries must be adapted to such initial conditions as their income levels, economic structure, and degree of urban growth.[14] These parameters vary greatly in Latin America from country to country. The possibilities for rural modernization are obviously different in a poor and largely agrarian country with a weak civil service, a largely illiterate peasantry, and few trained professionals as compared with a rich industrialized country such as the United States or France with isolated areas of rural poverty and backward agriculture. Most of Latin America falls between these two extremes. Haiti and Bolivia are poor agrarian states, while Argentina has some of the characteristics of a rich urban nation with serious rural development problems. Perhaps an even better example of rural development problems in a poor area of a rich country is Puerto Rico which is closely integrated with the United States. Taking as our principal indices average per capita income levels and the percentage of population depending on agriculture, Venezuela, Uruguay, Chile, Mexico, and Cuba are all relatively more developed and urbanized than are Colombia, Brazil, Peru, Ecuador, Paraguay, and most of Central America (Inter-American Development Bank, 1966).

In this brief discussion of strategies we concentrate only upon the economics of rural development. While various alternatives are presented, combination strategies are always possible. How to bring about the changes in political structure required to make any of the proposed lines of policy effective calls for a far more talented strategist than this one.

For the poor agrarian countries, rural development strategy must take into account that it may be at least two generations before any real progress can be made toward modernizing agriculture and improving rural incomes on a wide scale. The most pressing economic problems are to increase food production and to mobilize capital for investment. As most of the population is rural and a substantial part of gross national product originates in agriculture, rapid industrialization must depend in part on using cheap rural labor and on capturing some of the agricultural surplus for investment purposes. In a sense, agriculture must be exploited.

As there is no industrial production to speak of in these countries, it is not possible to offer farmers "packages" of industrially produced modern inputs, unless it is to a very limited group of producers. For the same reason, few additional incentives for agricultural production can be offered in the form of consumer goods. As the government is probably poorly staffed and ineffectively organized for new activities, there is little chance of reaching most farmers with credit and technical assistance for years to come. Nor is the government in a position to organize rapidly the administration of cooperatives or collective farms; the required trained people do not exist nor does the necessary infrastructure. Meanwhile, rural population rapidly increases, partly because relatively few urban jobs are available. Social tensions in the countryside are bound to increase unless something is done to provide the peasantry with at least minimal security and a sense of participation.

Traditionally, in the poor agrarian countries of Latin America, rural development strategy, to the extent that one existed, relied on large landowners and foreign investors to increase food production, mobilize labor, and accumulate capital. We have seen that this has not given entirely satisfactory results. Nevertheless, it must be recognized that some economic growth has taken place in this way, as is made obvious by the fact that there are almost no completely agrarian countries left and only one-half of the region's population and considerably less of its gross economic production is now agricultural.

Some of the general lines of an alternative strategy that could be followed now become clearer. Farm production increases at this stage must be obtained primarily through making fuller use of labor and land because "packages" of new inputs cannot be had. Only very simple technological changes such as improved seeds and better transport and marketing systems can be expected to have a wide short-run impact in these really backward countries. The limiting factor preventing immediate production increases for most of the peasants is not a shortage of capital, technology, education, or labor, but land. The control of land is crucial. Tenure conditions must be reformed to encourage greater mobility of resources, more intensive land use, and a more diversified cropping pattern, all of which result in greater employment and production.

Mobilizing surplus rural labor to produce more food, to aid in public works, or to construct new industries requires the use of compulsion or incentives. Whether compulsion is exercised by traditional landlords or by some other group, the result is inevitably one of increased stress and unrest. On the other hand, as we have noted, the additional consumer goods to offer as incentives for putting forth more labor are simply unavailable and cannot be for some time.

The strategy, in this case, must be to secure peasant support and cooperation by offering them something that is available and which they want. This generally means aiding them to obtain their own land which, in rural Latin America, represents economic security, social prestige, and political power. As a minimum, a land reform which would take power from the traditional rural elite and grant land to the peasants could be expected to secure their passive acquiescence to a period of continued deprivation, while development proceeds in other areas. This apparently was one of the great accomplishments of the Mexican *ejido*—buying time. If the reform is carried out with full peasant participation and accompanied by skillful programs to gain peasant support of broader development goals, it may be possible to obtain their active participation in various "community development" projects. Reports from China indicate interesting experiments along these lines.

The *latifundia* systems in Latin America have proved to be inefficient, not only in production, but also in investment capital accumulation, the one line a landlord system is widely supposed to be good at. An alternative means of getting capital from agriculture is an effective agricultural tax system. But this has had scant success in Latin America as in most poor countries, although it was very successful in Japan. Generally, the political structure in Latin America does not permit such taxes and the administrative machinery is inadequate to collect them even if the political will to do so did exist. The third possibility of obtaining capital for development from agriculture is to keep food prices relatively cheap in order to hold the real costs of industrialization as low as possible. Even in poor countries, storage and import policies can be used effectively to keep down food prices and thus reduce the real cost of maintaining urban labor. State-controlled purchases and prices for farm products delivered to the cities were used in Russia and many other countries to keep food costs relatively low.

Of course, such a strategy would only have a chance of success as part of an all-out program of industrial growth and overall development. Also, its success would be enhanced if the peasants could clearly see other groups of the population also making big sacrifices. To ask the peasants to continue with practically nothing while many other groups grow fat with the early gains of economic growth is to invite disaster.

For less poor countries that are already partially industrialized and urbanized, or as development gains momentum in the very poor countries that we have just been considering, the possibilities for alternative strategies become more varied. The objectives of increasing food production and accumulating investment capital remain the same. The situation has changed, however; now more industrial goods are available both for farm inputs and for consumption. Government and public administration are more effective and flexible. Trained technicians and professionals can be found in much greater numbers. Access to land is no longer the principal factor limiting agriculture growth; the greater availability of capital and new inputs make possible the adoption of new technologies. While the land may be less important in itself as a factor of production, its control still may be crucial if archaic land tenure institutions restrict the access of most farmers to credit, services, and markets. Agricultural research is now vitally necessary to provide information concerning new technologies adapted to local conditions.

At this stage, an objective of rural development strategy must be to develop numerous dynamic centers of agricultural growth that use "packages" of modern farm inputs. The role of the agricultural entrepreneur assumes great importance. Conceivably the traditional landlord elite, if it still exists, could take leadership in agricultural modernization. As we have seen, in Latin America this is most unlikely for institutional and sociological reasons. Moreover, political pressures against such a solution are mounting as new urban groups gain ascendancy and the *campesinos* become more incorporated into political parties and other national institutions.

A second alternative during this stage of development is to encourage the growth of a new class of commercial farmers drawn from the existing medium-sized land owners and the larger and more enterprising peasants. They can be helped to acquire the best lands, capital, technical assistance, and access to markets. This strategy presupposes the prior elimination or at least partial elimination of the traditional rural elite as a class; this seems to be what happened in Mexico following its land reform. The danger with this strategy is that the process will get out of control as the new elite gains political strength and the largest group of the rural population remains practically without employment opportunities on *minifundia*, on traditional *haciendas*, or simply as unattached landless laborers.

The workers on these new commercial farms will necessarily remain a minority for some time. They may also be subject to harsh working conditions. The new elite may acquire sufficient power to frustrate effective tax reforms. It may also adopt many of the traditional prerogatives of its *hacendado* predecessors, turning to luxurious consumption and prestige investments instead of adopting an ethic of capitalist accumulation.

A third alternative in this situation is to use the state bureaucracy as the principal modernizing elite, working through cooperatives and state or collective farms. The necessary entrepreneurship is drawn from the civil service and the more dynamic elements of the peasantry much as in the previous case. The incentive system, however, is different; the rights associated with land ownership are sharply curtailed and, in fact, private ownership might be prohibited altogether. Economic incentives in the form of additional income and consumer goods will still be required to stimulate effort and innovation.

During this stage of rural development the use of price policy to keep food costs down in order to encourage industrial expansion becomes much more difficult and hazardous. It will be necessary to provide farm producers with adequate price incentives or some effective substitute, in order to encourage the more dynamic farm managers to adopt new technologies and to invest in farming. Agriculture itself must begin to industrialize. Probably an increasing reliance on taxes, especially land taxes and income taxes, is called for to mobilize capital for necessary public investment and to restrict consumption.

The economies of scale in farming that were of little consequence in traditional agriculture now become important.[15] Development strategy must devise institutional arrangements to provide the advantages of scale to small commercial producers. These would include such measures as government aid to cooperative marketing services, technical assistance, and research. The strategy could alternatively rely increasingly on large farm units; these might be large, commercial, private enterprises or various forms of cooperatives, group farming, or state farms. The administrative difficulties of adopting this latter course are, to say the least, formidable.

As farming becomes more modernized, organization and work discipline become more exacting. The level of rural education must be raised rapidly. A growing supply of technicians and professionals is required. For example, in Chile and Cuba where there were relatively more trained specialists for rural work than in most other Latin American countries, the shortage of trained manpower nonetheless became a severe bottleneck as soon as vigorous rural development programs were initiated.

As under-employed agricultural labor remains a serious problem in these countries, it will be necessary to take measures to utilize it in public works, community development projects, and small rural industries. It is no longer vital, however, to rely almost entirely on unpaid peasant labor contributions, as there are many more possibilities of providing the whole rural population with some consumer goods. The economy is developing to a point where central planning and "Keynesian" programs of public works and fiscal policies could be used more effectively to mobilize resources than was the case in the poorer agrarian countries. In fact, there is even the danger of "over-extension" of the economy in some lines with the result that local farm labor shortages might appear, especially in harvest seasons, as has happened recently in Cuba. It is hardly likely, however, that most surplus rural labor would find employment in the absence of effective development planning. Neither commercial agriculture nor industry could possibly provide sufficient jobs if structural reforms and development planning are not carried out effectively.

In the richer industrialized countries, the possible strategies for rural development become much more varied. Alternative urban job opportunities can now be created rather easily for the rural population. There will generally be a net exodus from agriculture and rural areas. Capital is relatively abundant and can be transferred to agricultural areas from urban industry without slowing economic growth. The limiting factors for increasing the incomes and productivity of poor farm people are no longer inherent in the country's economic capacities. Limits are solely the consequence of inadequate institutions and policies.

In this situation, there are countless alternatives for attacking the problems of rural backwardness and poverty. As there are no Latin American countries sufficiently developed to be in this relatively happy situation (from a strictly economic viewpoint), I shall not discuss it. In any case, the recent literature on the poverty problem in the United States and other advanced countries is vast. Suffice it to note that while the economic difficulties of eliminating rural poverty in the industrialized countries are not formidable, the political obstacles may be as obdurate as in the poorest developing nations.

This sketchy outline of alternate rural development strategies has concentrated on the strictly economic limitations to more rapid growth. We have ignored political problems which of course, are fundamental. The definition of the roles, responsibilities, and rewards of the various social groups during development is much more a political than an economic matter.

If anyone is naive enough to think that Latin American countries now have rational development strategies directed towards widely agreed upon national goals, he should immediately abandon this myth. There are, in reality, a multitude of policies affecting agriculture and rural life, often highly contradictory. They seldom add up to a strategy of any type that could speed rural development.

Economic policy is an output of the political system. It is there one must look for the major possibilities and obstacles facing rational development planning.

This paper has dealt with only a few of the problems of accelerating the economic development of rural Latin America and providing employment for rural people. If we are correct, however, in believing that the current social tensions in the region are more accurately viewed as a result of the economic "progress" that is taking place than as a consequence of stagnation, it becomes imperative to re-examine the accepted formulations of what constitutes the "development problem." Possibly, continued and even greatly speeded-up rates of growth in material wealth and output are unavoidable, barring world-wide self-destruction, for "underdeveloped" regions well-endowed with natural resources and population, such as Latin America. While public policies can marginally influence the speed and timing of modernization in the Latin American countries, the fact that they will become increasingly developed economically can hardly be reversed. Their incorporation into the modern industrial world seems certain although the terms of their entry remain in doubt.

In this context, one suspects that economists should find it at least as important and interesting to analyze how alternative development strategies affect the interests of the various social groups involved as to concentrate only on the growth of gross national product. In oversimplified terms, the problems of participation and distribution should receive at least as great a priority as those of output, always recognizing that "distribution" is really an index of a much more complex social reality. That they do not may, more than anything else, reflect the fact that those groups with the most power to influence policy are not particularly anxious to have widely publicized the facts about who benefits and who pays during the development process.

INFORMAL AUTHOR'S SUMMARY: BARRACLOUGH

I have tried to do three things in my paper: First, I look at some of the current economic development models. Then, I consider the problem (similar to the one Domike has written about here) of describing the real trends in Latin American rural and urban employment. And, finally, I discuss some of the alternative strategies, in a very broad sense, for rural development that might have some relevance for the Latin American situation.

My viewpoint is that of an outside, alien observer, like most of us here, but I also take the point of view of Pearse and Blaut, that is, the peasant standpoint. Thus, I'm concerned, first, with the impact of alternate policies on the peasants, and secondly, with the policies of the development planners who are interested basically in one thing, getting Latin American development moving as rapidly as possible.

In the paper Horowitz prepared for this volume, you'll note that he distinguishes between two concepts, *development* and *modernization*, and I can see what he is driving at. It is very much in the minds of the Latin American developers to ask whether they are going to have some sort of modernization based upon an integration with the U.S. economy, a spillover from U.S. productivity, especially of consumer goods, and a position of economic dependence, or genuine national development, where the national state in Latin America has its own independent economic base, and can really bargain from a position of economic strength. I think Horowitz is correct in making this sort of distinction. Most of the developers with whom I work are contemptuous of any change that is merely an integration with the U.S. economy, a spillover of consumer goods from the industrialized center's productive capacity; the Puerto Rican experience is just about the "lowest" thing that can be brought up in most university planning discussions about Latin American development. In my paper, then, I have tried, with a little empathy, to present some of the views of Latin America's more nationalistic developers.

Now, the first point I want to make is that most of our models of economic development are two-sector models where (you have to read this stuff to believe it) one spells out very elaborate mathematical deductions from the assumption of a traditional, agricultural sector and a modern, capitalist, industrial sector, and goes on from there with irreproachable mathematics to arrive at one's conclusions. Unfortunately, agriculture isn't that simple! It's not the traditional non-capitalist sector of the Economics textbooks by any stretch of the imagination. When my wife read a copy of my paper (she is something of an economist and sociologist), her comment was, "Well, this is the silliest thing in the world you can take to a group of anthropologists and sociologists because there will be no one there who has ever taken such a model seriously, or would even think of constructing a model on such a set of assumptions." But, economic models are based upon these assumptions and the economic policies of AID, the World Bank, and the various planning agencies in Latin America are based in part on deductions made from them.

The one who has been writing on this with the most sophistication, I think, and doesn't fall into these errors, has been Arthur Lewis, from Jamaica. Even so, he does build his model on the assumption of a capitalist, industrial sector and a traditional, agricultural sector. The problem really becomes extreme in the Ranis and Fei model (Ranis has been an advisor for AID), which contains the built-in assumption that agriculture uses practically no capital, but has only land and labor as productive factors; only after modernization is far along, and agriculture becomes commercialized, does capital become an important factor at all. I would say that these models are just not applicable to Latin America. I don't want to talk about India or China; I don't know enough about them. But they are not at all applicable to Latin America.

In the first place, in the studies of land tenure which the Inter-American Committee for Agricultural Development (CIDA) made, we were able to quantify to some extent the different groups dependent upon agriculture directly for their living, and we were also able to do something about estimating the amount of production coming from the different groups. Of course, the situation is variable. In Argentina there is almost no group of consequence that could conceivably be classified as a peasantry, or even as a subsistence wage-labor sector. On the other hand, in the Andean Highlands, we estimate that more than eighty percent of the rural population is made up of very small producers who are pretty much subsistence-oriented, in the sense that Pearse uses the term, and probably selling between 20 and 40 percent of their production, one way or another, on the market. But, while this is three-quarters or more of the population, most of the production reaching urban or export markets in these countries doesn't come from this group at all, but from much more commercially-organized farms. Some are small and some are large, but they use purchased inputs, which I think is the decisive factor for classifying agriculture as modernizing or not. I think the other indices don't really reveal the degree of farm modernization very much, and I particularly don't think it is very useful to deal only with the size of the farm operation. This has been a very misleading dichotomy, large versus small farms. In reality nearly all of North American commercial farming is based on large operations even though most of the farm units are family operated. It is quite possible to have the advantages of scale even in poor countries, with very small units, through an infrastructure of cooperative marketing and cooperative services. I've seen this done very effectively in Israel and Egypt, for example. I don't think the dichotomy of size of holding is always useful.

The use of purchased inputs is a fundamental variable. From half to three-quarters of the rural population in Latin America is made up of smallholders or landless laborers of one kind or another on the large farms. Now here you can break down these categories into commercially-oriented and subsistence-oriented groups, with the former acting very much like the small farmers of Japan and the United States, but they are very much a minority, although you'll find quite a few of them near the cities. Similarly, the farm laborers can be divided between those on large modern farms and those on traditional *haciendas*. There are the laborers on very commercial plantations and farms such as most of Cuba and Puerto Rico, and those on traditional estates who are paid mostly by the use of land and other farm resources, and live under many quasi-feudal relationships.

Now, quantitatively, most of the rural people, especially in the Andean countries, a good part of Brazil, and a good part of Central America, live on large, traditional *haciendas* or in communities of traditional subsistence-oriented smallholders, but most of the marketed production comes from the relatively few heavily-commercial large plantations and estates and small farms.

I was in a farm area of Venezuela with a large irrigation project just recently, and learned that it produces 33 percent of all the rice consumed in Venezuela; this production comes from just over 100 large farms, very heavily capitalized, and several smaller ones that are producing much less. But, it's very easy to make a big production impact with a highly modernized nucleus of production, if you can get the inputs and put them into production.

To return to my original point, I don't find the dual models of agriculture and industry very useful. In many cases, the same people who are investing in industry are also the landlords who have large commercial farms, which should suggest that it doesn't make much operational sense to identify agriculture with subsistence alone in analyzing political and social structures or in constructing economic models.

But, there is an aspect of these dual models that is very useful; this is the one that Lewis, especially, has developed in respect to the unlimited supply of labor. There is, for all practical purposes, an unlimited supply of unskilled labor in the countryside and, also, in the cities of Latin America. The official figures don't show unemployment as well as they do in the United States: it's probably a lot worse than they indicate. In Chile, the official figure is six percent unemployed, in Venezuela it is sixteen percent, and it varies from country to country. But this is based mostly on how you state the question. The real rate of unemployment, in the sense of people available for work at a salary that is close to what is the accepted subsistence level in the cities or in the rural areas, subsistence in a social sense, not physical subsistence, is for all practical purposes indefinitely large. This is the result of the processes that Pearse describes, that the traditional agriculture sector is being disrupted very rapidly, the people are leaving, are getting into the labor market in one way or another, (usually not getting into the city immediately, but into smaller towns or the more commercial farms, and then from there to the cities). They're there, and they'll be with us, as Domike infers, for a long time. It's going to vary from one region to another, but in the Andean region, these unemployed might be with us for fifty or sixty years, even if things go well. In some of the more developed countries, the "unlimited supply" of labor might conceivably dry up much more quickly.

In my paper, I cite the analysis that Marx made of the situation in Ireland and Great Britain in the last century; his analysis of the factors causing the army of unemployed that was available for work at low wages, barring other institutional interventions, remains quite good. I wouldn't go along with all of Marx's predictions, but his analysis is much better than most of those I've seen in the current Economics literature which speaks of disguised underemployment as an inherent characteristic of traditional agriculture. This is really nonsense as you learn if you live enough in traditional areas and study what people actually do. Most of the underemployment is a result of the social changes taking place.

Now, my paper offers an illustration of how the process operates: I worked a long time in the Mississippi Delta, and saw the active farm population decrease by ninety percent in the last twenty years with no decline in production. The number of families living on farms has decreased by sixty-six percent in the last twenty years, and there are very good studies by the USDA documenting this. This is what happens when you get modern inputs in any large quantity, and I would contend that it won't make any difference whether the farms are large or small. It's going to depend on the market, the availability of inputs, and a great many other factors.

This can also be influenced somewhat by the type of inputs that become available. The present tendency, since we seem to have a lot of productive capacity for big tractors in the United States these days, is to ship tractors as fast as we can. I've recently sat through the loan negotiations of the Chilean government, both in the Inter-American Bank and the AID, and both agencies centers of power at the national level? And I raise a second possibility, which is that the real centers of power that have to be manipulated are in the United States, and not at the national level. We've seen a great many recent examples that lend some support to this hypothesis. The outcome of the Bolivian revolution was frustrated in the eyes of many Bolivian nationalists in part because of the ability of the United States to maintain a post-revolutionary power structure that probably would not have developed if it hadn't been for U.S. support. The Guatemalan revolution and agrarian reform were directly overthrown by a *golpe* openly supported by the CIA. We have all sorts of examples of economic decisions being made by the International Monetary Fund and other international financing agencies, the big copper companies, and the big oil companies, which are often more influential in determining the path that Latin American countries take in their development than the political decisions that, with the present economic and social structure, can be taken at the local level. A great many of my Latin American colleagues feel that if they're going to have any real development, they will have to find some way to influence economic and political decisions in the United States.

I return now to national development strategies. Here, I tried to typify three initial situations: 1) The very undeveloped situation of which India might be a better example, but Haiti, Guatemala and Bolivia are good examples in Latin America. Here the alternatives aren't too broad, for there aren't many purchased inputs (including the advice of experts) to give or sell to the farmers unless they are donated or borrowed from abroad. They just aren't available! (There is no industry whatsoever in Bolivia capable of manufacturing fertilizers, farm machinery, and similar modern inputs, or at least there wasn't until recently.) Neither are there enough consumer goods available to pay people for additional effort unless they are obtained in large quantities from abroad. As a result, the government planner, assuming he has political backing for his plans, is limited to working through the existing power structure and trying to mobilize agricultural resources through the landlords and the few new commercial producers. Or, he has to do what the Chinese did, which was to throw the whole system over and purchase the peasants' support by giving them land. Land is the only available resource that rural people want, and that can be used to help organize them for greater production. But, in most of the Latin American countries, this extreme backwardness is not the case. There is already some industrial base and some capital, and most of them are involved in some exporting and importing; they can import capital too, and there are aid programs. There is often considerable latitude for planning rural development.

Among the countries that are less poor, the alternative strategies that might be followed are more numerous. One is to work through the traditional elite of large landowners, and let them take the lead in modernization. Another is deliberately to throw them out, as the Mexicans did, that is, throw out the landlord system, and put all the emphasis in rural development on getting inputs to the better entrepreneurs, letting the rest shift for themselves. In Mexico, they have most of the peasantry "on ice" in the *ejidos* where they aren't any worse off than they were before, and probably are better off in many ways, although they're not adding as much to the production of the country as is a smaller number of commercial farmers. This strategy is one which, if I had to make a prediction, I would see as most probable in the present Latin American context. It is a viable strategy for development, but not appealing from the peasant's standpoint because it leaves at least half of the peasantry, and I would guess a great deal more than half, completely on the margin of the development process. They hang onto their plots, they don't have the use of modern inputs, they're not really incorporated into the economic structure of the country. There isn't any way to bring them into the modern economy *soon* even if one goes to central economic planning, which one might combine with this second alternative.

For this reason, many of my colleagues in Latin America are thinking of the third alternative of modernizing the peasantry through a cooperative farm system in which entrepreneurial talent is brought to the rural areas by the bureaucracy. In Chile, for example, the Christian Democratic Party is very much committed to this third strategy.

There is a lot of pressure from the technicians in Latin America to adopt the cooperative-collective strategy. They're completely frustrated, and they're not only perfectly willing to accept such a system, but a few are even willing to go out and throw bombs for it or at least have someone else throw them, if they think there is any chance of getting it. They feel that this would be a way to get development going while avoiding the waste effort and luxury consumption they now see going on around them. I think that we have to see that this is a very real possibility *if it's permitted*, in the sense that it is the U.S. which is supporting the present power structure and would try to prevent it. The Cuban experience may turn out not to be an isolated phenomenon, but rather a forerunner of a socialist strategy for rural development in many other regions of Latin America.

When one considers the richer countries, the economic problem becomes very much less. There is enough productive capacity, enough consumer goods to pay for high productivity, and enough modern inputs available to maintain economic growth. It's not worth discussing this situation here in any detail.

are forcing more tractors and the like on Chile, when you come right down to it, than Chile can absorb in the short run without causing more unemployment. This is going to continue and, if the United States ever stops making tanks and military equipment, South America will be flooded with tractors. Therefore, I'm sure that displaced labor from the rural areas is going to become even more available in the future.

For Latin America as the whole, about fifty percent of the population is in the rural areas; this is true, not for Central America especially, not for Guatemala, which is three-fourths rural, but for Latin America as a whole. The annual net migration out of agriculture is just about half of the natural increase. In the heavily-urbanized countries of Chile, Argentina and Uruguay, the net increase in the agricultural population is only about a half-of-one-percent annually, but as you get up into agrarian countries such as Guatemala, it gets close to three percent annually.

My paper discusses a series of alternative development strategies, and I want to emphasize that all of them are considered real alternatives by at least some Latin Americans. They aren't all being discussed in the United States as real alternatives, but in Latin America they're being discussed very seriously in a great many circles. In choosing strategies, we must remember that the difference in development levels among Latin American countries, in the strictly economic sense, is very great. At one end of the scale, we have Bolivia and Haiti, and at the other end, Argentina, Venezuela and Puerto Rico. The problem of finding a workable strategy is completely different at these two extremes. It's also different in a situation such as Chile which has only twenty-seven percent of its labor force in agriculture and has quite an industrial base now, as compared with Peru, which still has between fifty and sixty percent of its labor force, in one way or another connected with agriculture, and where the industrial base is flimsy.

There is a point that must be made before I comment further on strategies. I suspect that most nationalists in Latin America want to build a national productive base that will make their economy a real economic power, and not dependent upon the United States or some other metropolitan, industrial center. Without question, this is a primary goal of most of the Latin America intellectuals, to the extent that they have specific goals.

But we have to consider another question, one which Horowitz discusses in more detail in his paper, and that is the unit of planning. I believe that we must reject the idea that the basic planning unit can be a village, a river valley, or even a region. There are a great many reasons for this. First, one just can't make the decisions needed to manipulate the variables that could drastically change the path of economic development, at the local level. Aren't real

The main point I want to make is that from the economic standpoint, all of these strategies are viable. However, if the emphasis is on really rapid growth, and one can imagine the existence of the necessary administrative capacity and political conditions, one will obviously choose a system that will maximize productive investment and keep consumption at a minimum, that will use as fully as possible available resources of labor and capital. This means central planning, and it probably means some sort of collectivization. I wouldn't rule out such a possibility for much of Latin America.

NOTES

1. See the paper by Domike in this volume.

2. My analysis draws heavily upon the CIDA Studies of Land Tenure and Agricultural Development. The Inter-American Committee for Agricultural Development (ICAD or, in Spanish, CIDA) was formed under the Alliance for Progress to coordinate the agricultural programs of five international agencies: FAO, ECLA, IDB, OAS, and IAIAS. CIDA (1966); See also, S. L. Barraclough and Arthur Domike, (1966c) and S. L. Barraclough, (1966b).

3. The economics literature analyzing models built around the dual economy concept is extensive. A few of the better known writings are Boeke (1953), Lewis (1958), Ellis (1961), Jorgenson (1961), Ranis and Fei (1961, 1964), Oshima (1963), Nicholls (1964), and Mellor (1967).

4. For some recent criticisms of "Dualism," see Andre Gunder Frank (1967) and Rudolfo Stavenhagen (1966).

5. Ranis and Fei explain that their model, which assumes an excess of labor in the initial period, leads to a more precise formulation of Rostow's "Stages of Growth" theory. The validity of Rostow's theory and Ranis and Fei's model for Latin America must be questioned. They offer no evidence that the under-employment which they posit for the initial stage of development was not really a result of earlier industrial penetration of the traditional society, or that it is an initial condition in agrarian society, rather than the result of an early stage of growth. Nor does their model show that the labor surplus would disappear when agriculture becomes commercial, thus producing a "turning point," unless one accepts their assumption that the "subsistence sector" and the "agricultural sector" are really synonymous. We have seen this to be erroneous for Latin America. If agriculture were really part of the industrial sector and not the subsistence sector, it follows from Ranis and Fei's own model that the labor surplus would persist until the "subsistence" sector finally atrophies completely–if it ever does–and not merely until a fictitious "turning point" or "take-off" is reached when agriculture becomes commercialized. If the "agricultural" and "subsistence" sectors are not the same, there would be no reason to invest in the "subsistence" sector because of the improving terms of trade for farmers implied in the model. One might logically infer from their model that only organization of the industrial

workers through which they attained real bargaining power could cause the incomes of unskilled labor to rise in industry as long as there existed a substantial labor surplus. But the incomes of the "subsistence sector" would not rise even then unless it also was able to organize and exert political influence to obtain transfers from other groups. Substantive structural changes would be required to eliminate unemployment and allow the "subsistence" sector real economic participation during the development process (Ranis and Fei, 1961, 1964).

6. Lewis, as usual, avoids such errors. He explicitly recognizes that even if disguised unemployment does not exist already, the development process will create it (Lewis, 1958, p. 25).

7. For further comments on Schultz's argument, see Balough (1967, pp. 74-78).

8. I have tried to analyze, in two recent papers, some of the relationships among agricultural development, agricultural employment, rural-urban migration, and land reform. The conclusions presented here summarize a few of the points discussed in more detail in those works (Barraclough, 1966a and b).

9. CEPAL-FAO estimates show that agricultural production must rise by about 4.3 percent annually, (the present rate is 3.2 percent), during the next fifteen years if economic development in Latin America is to proceed satisfactorily, food imports are to be reduced, nutrition raised to minimum standards, and some income redistribution achieved. If the agricultural population, net of migration, were to continue to increase by about 1.5 percent per year, productivity per farm worker would have to increase by about 2.8 percent annually (as against the actual 1.7 percent). At the same time, production per hectare would also have to rise by nearly three percent per year (present rate 1.3 percent). It would require drastic reforms and much else to achieve such goals (CEPAL, 1966).

10. In Cuba and Puerto Rico, agricultural labor shortages have risen during harvest season on the sugar plantations. Many other factors besides land reform, however, have contributed to this situation.

11. FAO-ICIRA, (1967).

12. If this appears exaggerated let us reflect on the contemporary history of Guatemala, Brazil, Santo Domingo, Cuba, and Bolivia, for example.

13. This optimistic view assumes a really democratic United Nations dedicated to the ideals of the United Nations Charter. One can easily imagine, however, that the United Nations might become an even more powerful instrument for maintaining the *status quo* than was the established church or the Holy Roman Empire in previous epochs. The history of international organizations, past and present, is not encouraging in this respect.

14. Much of the following discussion is based on the author's participation in a FAO-organized Panel on Rural Development in Areas of Small Farming held in Rome in May, 1967. The author is particularly indebted to Professor Dennis Bergman for suggesting this scheme for presenting alternative rural development strategies.

15. John W. Mellor, (1966, pp. 364-75); Kenneth L. Bachman and Raymond P. Christensen, "The Economics of Farm Size" and "Comments" by S. L. Barraclough (pp. 263-266) and Earl O. Heady (pp. 258-262) in Southworth and Johnston, (1967).

BIBLIOGRAPHY

Bagu, Sergio

1949 *Economia de la Sociedad Colonial,* Buenos Aires: Editorial El Ateneo.

Balough, Thomas

1967 *The Economics of Poverty,* New York: MacMillan.

Barraclough, S. L.

1966a *Economic Implications of Rural-Urban Migration Trends From the Highland Communities,* Cornell University.

1966b "Agricultural Policy and Land Reform," Conference on Key Problems of Economic Policy in Latin America, Chicago (mimeo).

– – – and Arthur Domike

1966c "Agrarian Structure in Seven Latin American Countries," *Journal of Land Economics,* Vol. XLIII, No. 4.

Boeke, J. H.

1953 *Economics and Economic Policy of Dual Societies,* New York: Institute of Pacific Relations.

CEPAL

1966 *Estudio Economico de América Latina.*

CIDA

1966 *Relaciones entre la Tenencia de la Tierra y el Desarrollo Socio-Economico del Sector Agricola en: Argentina, Brazil, Chile, Colombia, Ecuador, Guatemala y Peru,* Washington.

Tenencia de la Tierra y Desarrollo Socio-Economico del Sector Agricola: Informe Regional (Appendices) unpublished.

Currie, Lauchlin

1966 *Accelerating Development,* New York: McGraw-Hill.

Day, R. H.

1967 "Technological Change and the Sharecropper," *The American Economic Review,* Vol. LVII, No. 3.

ECLA

1966 *Estudio Economico para America Latina,* United Nations.

Eicher, Carl and Laurence Witt

1964 *Agriculture in Economic Development,* New York: McGraw-Hill.

Ellis, Howard S.

1961 "Las Economias Duales y el Progreso," *Revista de Economia Latinoamericana,* Año I, No. 3, Caracas, Banco Central de Venezuela.

FAO-ICIRA

1967 *Evaluación Preliminar de los Asentamientos de la Reforma Agraria de Chile,* Ediciones ICIRA, Santiago, Chile.

Frank, Andre Gunder

1967 "Sociology of Development and Underdevelopment of Sociology," *Catalyst,* (University of Buffalo), No. 3.

Galbraith, J. K.

1967 *The New Industrial State,* Boston: Houghton Mifflin Co.

Goodwin, R. M.

1961 "The Optional Growth Path for an Underdeveloped Economy," *Economic Journal,* Vol. XLII, No. 284.

Halle, Louis

1965 *The Society of Man,* New York: Harper and Row.

Hobsbawn, Eric

1962 *The Age of Revolution: 1789-1848,* New York: New American Library.

Inter-American Development Bank

1966 *Socio-Economic Progress in Latin America,* Sixth Annual Report.

Jorgenson, Dale W.

1961 "The Development of a Dual Economy," *The Economic Journal* Vol. LXXI, No. 282.

Kuznets, Simon

1965 *Economic Growth and Structure,* New York: Norton.

Lewis, W. Arthur

1958 "Unlimited Labor: Further Notes," *The Manchester School of Economics and Social Studies,* Vol. XXVI, No. 1.

1960 "Desarrollo Economico con Oferta Ilimitada de Mano de Obra," *El Trimestre Economico,* Vol. XXVII (4), No. 108.

Marx, Karl

Capital, New York: Random House, Modern Library.

Mellor, John W.

1966 *The Economics of Agricultural Development,* Ithaca, N.Y.: Cornell University Press.

1967 "Toward a Theory of Agricultural Development," *in* Herman M. Southworth and Bruce F. Johnston, *Agricultural Development and Economic Growth,* Ithaca, N.Y.: Cornell University Press.

Mills, C. W.

1959 *The Sociological Imagination,* New York: Oxford University Press.

Moore, Barrington, Jr.

1966 *Social Origins of Dictatorship and Democracy,* Boston: Beacon Press.

Morse, Richard

1962 "Some Characteristics of Latin American Urban History," *American Historical Review,* Vol. XLVII, No. 2.

Nicholls, William H.

1964 "The Place of Agriculture in Economic Development," *in* Eicher and Witt (1964).

Oshima, Harry T.

1963 "The Ranis-Fei Model of Economic Development: Comment," *American Economic Review, Vol. 53.*

Ranis, Gustav and John C. H. Fei

1961 "A Theory of Economic Development," *The American Economic Review,* Vol. 51.

1964 *Development of the Labour Surplus Economy: Theory and Policy.* New Haven: The Economic Growth Center, Yale University.

Schultz, T. H.

1964 *Transforming Traditional Agriculture,* New Haven: Yale University Press.

Southworth, Herman M. And Bruce F. Johnston (Eds.)

1967 *Agricultural Development and Economic Growth,* Ithaca, N.Y.: Cornell University Press.

Stavenhagen, Rodolfo

1966 "Seven Erroneous Theses about Latin America," *New University Thought,* Vol. 4, No. 4.

Tawney, R. H.

1932 *Land and Labor in China,* London: Allen and Unwin, Ltd.

Thomas, Brinley

1954 *Migration and Economic Growth,* New York: Cambridge University Press.

INDUSTRIAL AND AGRICULTURAL EMPLOYMENT PROSPECTS IN LATIN AMERICA*

Arthur L. Domike

Economic and social development prospects in Latin America during the relevant future (say, the next two generations) depend largely upon changes brought about in the most traditional part of those societies, agriculture. The capacity of agriculture to contribute to development depends, in turn, on reforming the land ownership patterns and the complementary power structure. This hypothesis carries obvious implications for public policy, some of which have been examined in previous publications and in companion papers in this volume.[1]

In exploring this issue, our attention will be concentrated on the problem of creating employment in manufacturing industry (as the leader of modern sector growth) and agriculture (the major traditional sector). Emphasis on creating employment (rather than on expanding production) gets us immediately to the nub of the development problem: How can the marginal populations be incorporated into the modern, "capitalist" sector?

Our goal here is not to treat all the relevant issues exhaustively; but, by calling attention to employment needs and potentials, to influence the priorities given to research and to development strategy analysis. There is an obvious difficulty in treating these problems at the regional level. We may adequately map the forest, but the trees will not be seen. Each country of Latin America differs in economic, technical, and institutional limits on its agricultural and industrial growth. Few would seriously assert that Bolivia, Guatemala, or Peru are ready for accelerated development. Some respected economists, on the other hand, feel that Mexico's agrarian revolution has created the conditions for relatively unfettered future growth; Venezuela, the Region's big winner in development roulette, would also seem capable of sustained self-generating expansion. Our failure to give close analysis here to intra-regional and country differences must nonetheless be forgiven in view of our intention only to outline the general problem, rather than appraising any particular country's policy approach.

The presentation is in three parts. We first examine some of the recent history of and prospects for improving employment levels in the modern sector, non-agricultural industries in the Latin American region.[2] The problems associated with increasing productive labor absorption in agriculture are then explored. Some conclusions about research and policy priorities are drawn in the final pages.

We may begin our inquiry with three questions. How is the labor force in Latin America now distributed among sectors? What have been the tendencies in recent years? And, what are the possibilities for overall improvement in the rate of labor absorption in the modern (particularly industrial) sectors?

A framework for our observations is provided by the Lewis-type, dual economy model. (We need not, however, embrace all the conclusions of Lewis's (1954) analysis as relevant to Latin America.)[3] This model requires us to identify and quantify sources of employment in the traditional or "subsistence" sector and in the modern or "capitalist" sectors, i.e., "that part of the economy which uses reproducible capital and pays capitalists for the use thereof."

As a first approximation to the subsistence sector, we lump together agricultural employment, artisan or cottage industries, and the "non-basic" services. Manufacturing (meaning factories), mining, construction, commerce, government, and "basic" services are grouped in the modern or capitalist sector. The classification is based upon both per-worker average product and convention. The main difficulty with fitting concepts to the available data is separating capitalist from subsistence agriculture. (This issue is further explored in Section II below.)

The Region's 1962 active labor force[4] numbered about seventy million–or approximately the same as that of the U.S.A.–out of a working age population of 144 millions and total population of about 210 millions.[5] Some forty-eight million workers are engaged in subsistence occupations in which productivity averages less than $700 per year per worker (see Table I). About a third of subsistence employment is essentially urban, that is, in "non-basic" services and artisan workshops. The other thirty-two million subsistence workers depend upon agriculture for livelihoods.

These workers (plus those without any remunerated employment) contribute little to overall production and less to demand. Their technology is primitive; the marginal labor productivity in these occupations approaches zero; seventy to ninety percent of the family income is spent for subsistence-level food and shelter.

"Modern" industries where productivity and most incomes are higher – mining, factories, infrastructure services, commerce, construction, and government – employ twenty-two million persons in the region. The key

TABLE 1 – WORK FORCE AND PRODUCTION IN SUBSISTENCE AND MODERN SECTORS OF LATIN AMERICA, 1950, 1962, AND PROJECTED 1985

	Production per Worker[1]			Active Work Force: Number (Millions)			Active Work Force: Annual Increase	
	1950	1962	Annual Rate Change (%)	1950	1962	1985[2]	Number (000's)	Rate (%)
TOTAL	$ 858	$1092	+ 2.0	51.3	69.7	138.0	1534	3.0
Subsistence Sector								
Agriculture	396	511	+ 2.2	27.4	32.4	50.8	415	1.5
Artisans	317	353	+ 0.9	3.9	4.6	7.6	68	1.8
Non-basic services[3]	712	647	– 0.8	6.2	11.0	28.4	391	6.3
Total, Sector				37.5	48.0	86.8	874	2.3
Modern Sector								
Mining	3118	5443	+ 4.8	.6	.7	1.2	11	2.0
Manufacturing	2009	3001	+ 3.4	3.5	5.1	10.8	128	3.7
Construction	765	735	– 0.3	1.9	3.2	7.9	106	5.5
Basic Services	1691	1833	+ 0.7	2.1	3.7	9.4	129	6.0
Commerce	1922	2123	+ 0.8	4.0	6.5	15.7	207	5.2
Government	2042	1810	– 1.0	1.7	2.6	6.2	79	4.7
Total, Sector				13.8	21.8	51.2	660	4.8

SOURCE: CEPAL Estudio Economico de America Latina, 1964, New York, 1966, pp. 45, 48.

[1] In 1960 U.S. dollars.

[2] Projection based upon rates of labor force growth by sectors from 1950 to 1962.

[3] Includes "Servicios varios" and "actividades no especificades."

capitalist sector, of course, is factory manufacturing. Economic growth will spring from and feed on expansion of factory production in modern (or at least, supra-marginal) factories. Today, those directly engaged in factory work make up about nine percent of Latin America's total work force, or one-quarter of its urban workers.

Turning to our second and third questions, the tendencies in rates of job formation and labor absorption in the capitalist sector offer a basis for at least mild optimism. But, as we shall discover, these trends cannot be expected to persist. Between 1950 and 1962, the working age population increased at about the same rate as the total population, three percent annually. New jobs in the modern sector during that period absorbed about forty-three percent of the eighteen million work force increase–an annual rate of job formation in the capitalist sector of 4.8 percent.

The subsistence industries, on the other hand, retained some fifty-seven percent of the total work force increase, for an annual job growth rate of 2.3 percent. However, jobs in "non-basic services" – the urban catchall for the effectively workless and under-employed living near subsistence levels – increased at the most rapid annual rate of all sectors, 6.3 percent.

The rate at which non-agricultural employment is absorbing increments of the labor force has increased importantly in the period since 1950, as compared to the 1925-50 period. Forty percent of the workforce increase from 1925 to 1950 was absorbed in agriculture, while from 1950 to 1962, only twenty-six percent of the new workforce stayed in agriculture. New urban jobs – both subsistence and capitalist – provided seventy-four percent of recent workforce increases (CEPAL, 1964, pp. 43, 47).

Unfortunately, when these increases in industrial employment are cast in absolute terms and compared to other standards, euphoria vanishes. The thirty-five year period 1925-60 saw an increase of 35.7 million in employment, of which 5.3 million were additions to factory jobs. This latter increase was about one-seventh of the total job increase and about one-quarter of the addition to urban employment. CEPAL points out that if industrial employment had even maintained its proportion of urban jobs, the industrial job total would have been 12.8 million instead of 10.0 million in 1960. When Latin America's industrial employment is contrasted with that of France, Britain, Italy, and Sweden at similar stages of their development (about 1900), the difference is even greater. By CEPAL's estimate, Latin America's level of manufacturing employment should have then been about fifteen million (CEPAL, pp. 35-36).

Returning to more recent history, we can see several sharp changes in labor force structure and composition associated with "premature" urbanization of the population. By one set of estimates, the total population of the Region appears to be increasing annually at about three percent, rural population at 1.5 percent, urban population at six percent, and "marginal" urban population at fifteen percent (OAS, 1967, pp. 7-10). Less than half the Region's people are now rural residents, that is, living on farms or in towns and villages of less than 1,500 to 2,500 persons (depending on national census definitions). But the rate of increase in total rural population is still substantially more than the increase in total employed farm labor force. One apparent cause of this phenomenon is that the young, rural workers make up the bulk of the urban migrant group.

The most obvious explanation for the relatively rapid capitalist job formation since 1950 is the deliberate industrialization policies of most Latin American governments. The new factories were able to produce for pre-existing domestic markets which were reserved to them by restrictive import regulations. Even the most optimistic forecasters, however, do not predict that increases in factory employment in the near future will be greater than the 1950-62 regional rate of 3.7 percent. In Brazil, Furtado notes (1965, pp. 252 ff), the annual rate of increase in the industrial work force since the mid-1940's has been less than three percent. In Chile, industrial employment grew by two percent a year from 1950 to 1960, but this was only one-third the rate of increase in industrial output. Bolivia's factory production is worth twice as much now as in 1950-54, but employment has actually declined.

The projections of labor force disposition to 1985 offered in Table 1 may assist in summarizing the results of this brief look at the region's employment history.[6] If present population and workforce growth rates persist at three percent (a near certainty), and the unprecedented, high 1950-62 rates of industry labor absorption continue (a much less certain and admittedly optimistic projection), factory employment would more than double and the total modern sector employment would rise by about thirty million by 1985. The labor force available for farm employment would increase by eighteen million, but this increase means a decline from forty-six percent to thirty-seven percent of the total labor force. Finally, about twenty million more persons would join the urban underemployed in services and artisan work.

What likelihood should we assign to this sort of projection, particularly to the probability that the modern sector will provide progressively more job opportunities in the near future? On the bright side, we can recognize the possibility of multiplier effects. Factories create secondary demands in construction, service, government, and the domestic raw materials industries, each of which, in turn, employs labor. The direct employment multiplier of new industrial employment is tremendously variable from place to place and industry to industry.[7] Over the medium term, it may be about 1.0. Over the 1950-62 period, about one-quarter of the modern sector's new jobs were in manufacturing. A 1.0 ratio would mean about half this increase in modern sector employment was directly attributable to factory manufactures and half autonomously determined.

To balance against such an industrial job multiplier, however, we must weigh the destruction or reduction in the employment opportunities of artisan and cottage manufacturers when more capital – intensive factory techniques are introduced. Without "luddistically" decrying automation whenever hand spindles are replaced, we must recognize that labor-intensive employment is lost when more capital-intensive techniques are introduced, particularly in stagnant economies. One serious estimate of this "displacement ratio" of factory to artisan employment is at 7-8 to one (Pan American Union, 1967, p. 106).

It should be added that much artisan employment is located in rural areas or at least outside principal urban centers, while factories cluster at the metropolis. This distribution means that the competitive shifts to factories diminish the opportunities, however modest the numbers may be, for productive rural or semi-rural employment. This result, of course, adds push to the movement from rural areas.

The major factors limiting growth of industrial employment opportunities, however, originate in the limited output markets. In selling nationally, most manufacturers even in the more developed countries face small and undynamic markets. They are selling in economies in which, typically, fifty to eighty percent of the families receive yearly money incomes of $500 or less. Sales of services and commodities not essential to bare subsistence depend upon the discretionary spending power of that small proportion of the population in the middle and upper classes.

Hopes, such as those of Laughlin Currie (1966), that "big pushes" of development in Latin America can be led by industrialization combined with the rapid mechanization of agriculture cannot be seriously entertained at least by the present generation of worriers.[8]

Manufacturers producing for export face the full force of competitive world markets. Regional market protectionism is now receiving much public attention, and may eventually assist some of these manufacturers, but optimism is obviously dangerous. Many domestically-oriented manufacturers still enjoy "infant industry" protection by which they are insulated from the world's competitive winds. This insulation, unfortunately, only reinforces a tradition in the region of mercantilistic and protection-riddled policies promoted by the region's less enlightened entrepreneurs. Even if there were serious potentials for internal market growth, the typical entrepreneurial approach would probably be to skim the cream off the market with high prices and low volume.

Without serious effort, a broader list of factors negative to rapid industrialization on a more or less "free enterprise" basis could be compiled. We have not mentioned, for example, balance of payments and foreign assistance problems, nor how decisions of foreign, i.e., U.S. and European-dominated industrial complexes, can interfere with the plans of home-grown industrial developers. On this count, the world industrial balance gives few advantages to Latin America. Total manufacturing output of the seven CIDA-study countries, shown in Table 2, is scarcely six percent of that of the United States.

There are several possible answers to our earlier question concerning prospects for expansion of productive employment to handle the growth in the Region's available labor force. The most optimistic answer would find industrial and other modern sector jobs increasing at the same rate they have in the last couple of decades. In such a situation, the working population left with urban subsistence employment would more than double (reaching thirty-six million by 1985), but so would the numbers of workers in modern industries, (reaching fifty-one million by 1985). The likelihood of this happening is not great, however, since the high rate of modern sector employment growth used for these projections resulted from not-to-be-repeated programs of fostering import-substituting domestic industries. In few countries of the Region does one find income distributions and investment levels which offer possibilities for inducing growth and higher employment.

A short-range answer to our question might be based upon the possibility that massive civil disorders and repressions will replace the current relatively quiet period. But since this eventuality cannot be conveniently programmed, it is better that economists not try to estimate the consequences.

II

Before offering estimates of the Region's capacity to absorb labor productively in agriculture, we ought to present the problem in a wider context, that is, recognize the influence which agriculture has on the rest of the economy, and vice-versa. Then, some attempt will be made to answer the central question, based upon findings of research still under way.

TABLE 2 – CONTRIBUTIONS OF AGRICULTURE AND MANUFACTURES TO GROSS DOMESTIC PRODUCTION, CIDA STUDY COUNTRIES AND USA, 1960 (MILLION DOLLARS)

Country	Agricultural Production	Manufactures	Total Gross Domestic Production at Factor Costs
Argentina	$ 1,783.6	$ 3,439.1	$ 10,592.9
Brazil	2,613.2	2,390.4[a]	9,267.7
Columbia	1,276.5	628.5	3,693.1
Chile	452.0	693.2	3,764.5
Ecuador	303.6	132.7	843.2
Guatemala	319.0	133.0	1,039.0
Peru	451.6	390.6	2,076.5
Total, Seven Countries	$ 7,199.5	$ 7,807.5	$ 31,276.9
United States	$16,656.0	$121,000.0	$409,100.0

SOURCE: Pan American Union "América en Cifras," Vol. 4, Washington 1966. Conversions to dollars at the following equivalents: Argentina, 82.7 pesos; Brazil, 205.14 cruzeiros; Colombia, 6.7 pesos; Chile, 1.053 escudos; Ecuador, 15.15 sucres; Guatemala, 1.0 quetzales; Peru, 26.8 soles.

a Includes mining, construction, and basic services.

There is an unreal quality to most current theorizing about agriculture's role in the development process.[9] Most unreal, perhaps, is the theory built on the presumption that economic development in traditional societies can be understood in isolation from the political and social power distribution.[10] Another peculiarity of the debate is a seemingly endless concern over whether agricultural output would decline in a developing country if labor were *withdrawn* from farming. From a practical point of view, a decrease in the labor force in farming is the least probable of all possible near-term assumptions for Latin America. We can, therefore, leave aside any theoretical concern with this argument.

More help in understanding the interplay between agricultural and industrial development and employment is provided by Dorner (1967). The institutional arrangements under which the agricultural resources are exploited, he holds, are not only relevant but also often crucial in determining levels and types of employment in the sector. This proposition obliges us to give attention to both the amounts of land, labor, and capital within agriculture, and its distribution among tenure systems. He lists five ways in which the development of the economy is conditioned or determined by the rural landholding and tenure institutions. These are (1) the effect of tenure structure upon the nature and use of political power, (2) its effects upon rural income distribution and consequent effective demands, (3) its effects upon investment in agriculture and consequently upon the composition and growth of farm production, (4) its effect upon movement of capital into non-agricultural sectors, and (5) its effect upon the rate of rural-urban migration.

The fundamental distinction to observe among tenure systems is that between "smallholders" and "estates" (Pearse, 1966, pp. 45-79). Scale of the enterprise, with the concomitant differences in work organization, forms the basis for this distinction. The legal tenure status of the farm operator is also often relevant. Further groupings might be based upon the degree of commercial orientation toward production and marketing activities. The important varieties of estates include the traditional *hacienda*, the plantation, and the *estancia*. The traditional *hacienda*, dependent upon Amerindian or *mestizo* labor, with traditional labor organization and low levels of capital and technology, has been the dominant form of estate in the highland regions generally and in pre-revolutionary Mexico and Bolivia.

The plantation "came into existence to produce for the market and make profits for its owners, and its internal arrangements are derived from the natural pursuit of this end." This is Lewis's "capitalist" portion of the agricultural sector, and it is still dominant in the tropical zones of the Region.

Labor is typically imported; Negroes from Africa and Hindus from India replaced the reluctant, rebellious, or scarce native American Indians. This form of plantation has been important in Brazil's north, in Colombian and Peruvian coastal areas, in the Caribbean (including the Guayanas), and, of course, the American South.

Another sub-form of the estate is the *estancia* of the Continent's southern cone – Argentina, Paraguay, Uruguay, and southern Brazil. They are seldom as capitalistic or efficient as the modern plantation. Livestock is produced extensively on these units; laborers are used in small numbers, demanding little supervision.

Most of the Region's most productive and readily accessible land resources are in some form of estate, and access to the complementary inputs is even more completely concentrated in the owners of the estates. In the rural areas, the control of employment potentials is in the hands of this group.

Smallholdings take on a variety of forms, but two types are basic, the traditional *minifundia* and the "independent" smallholder. The former have a symbiotic relationship with the estates which may vary from indentured servitude (in the Ecuadorean and Peruvian Altiplano, for example) to something approaching a market relationship of renters and owners (some areas in Chile).

The independent, European-type, family-scale farm can be found in significant numbers in the pampas of Argentina, in southern and western Brazil, and in parts of Colombia and southern Chile. However, the preponderent number of smallholder farms are the *minifundia*, whose land is a precarious cession from an estate, too meagre to afford more than subsistence.

A way to estimate the employment capacity of agriculture in the Region would be to determine the feasibility (considering agronomic and market conditions) and probability (considering the political and tenure situation) of increasing both per-worker agricultural productivity and the number of workers employed. Generalizations of such measures for the entire Latin American region must be very naive, heavily qualified, or both. We venture estimates here only because the topic demands it, and, fortunately, the CIDA studies permit more serious estimates than had previously been possible.[11]

The CIDA study countries – Argentina, Brazil, Chile, Colombia, Guatemala, Ecuador, and Peru – include about two-thirds of both the total and the rural population of the Region (see Table 3).[12] In the seven countries, some twenty million people (not including working farm wives) earn their living in agriculture. They are distributed about half-and-half between estates and smallholdings. Of the ten million estate workers, some

TABLE 3 – DISTRIBUTION OF TOTAL AND WORKING POPULATION, CIDA STUDY COUNTRIES, 1960 (THOUSAND PERSONS)

Country	Total Population	Rural Population	Working Age Population	Economically Active Population	Agricultural Active Population	Manufacturer Employment[1]
Argentina	20,009	5,664	14,199	7,599	1,466	1,422
Brazil	70,119	37,648	48,761	22,651	11,688	1,950
Colombia[2]	17,482	9,143	11,438	5,138	3,020	281
Chile	7,374	2,346	4,946	2,389	728	217
Ecuador	4,476	2,864	2,788	1,443	800	30
Guatamala[3]	4,284	2,846	3,172	1,427	750	20
Peru	9.907	5,208	7,925	3,125	1,540	109
Total, Seven Countries	133,651	65,719	93,229	43,772	19,992	4,029
Proportion, Total (Percent)	100.0	49.2	69.0	32.8	15.0	3.0

SOURCE: Rural population and active agricultural population, from CIDA reports. Other data, Pan American Union America en Cifras, Washington, 1966, with interpolations as noted in footnotes.

1 Reference years as follows: Argentina 1954; Brazil 1962; Colombia 1963; Chile 1957; Ecuador 1955; Guatemala 1953; Peru 1956.

2 Assumes a 3.6 percent annual increase of working age and exonomically active population from 1951 to 1960, and a rural/total population ratio of .528. See, CEPAL, "Algunos Aspectos del Crecimiento de la Población de Colombia". (E/CN12/618), Santiago, 1962.

3 Assumes a 3.1 percent annual growth rate of working age and ecomonically active population from 1950.

TABLE 4 – MEASURES OF LABOR SURPLUSES AND DEFICITS IN SUBFAMILY UNITS AND ESTATES, CIDA STUDY COUNTRIES (THOUSAND WORKERS)

Country	"Excess" Labor on Subfamily Units	Labor "Deficit" on Multifamily Units (Estates)	Measure of Net Labor Force Deficit or Surplus
Argentina	302	520	128
Brazil	1,149	43,798	42,649
Chile	76	2,002	1,926
Colombia	1,367	2,318	951
Ecuador	402	58	– 344
Guatemala	338	332	– 8
Peru	473	1,230	757
Total, Seven Countries	4,199	50,258	46,059

SOURCE: Compiled by Ernest Feder from CIDA country reports. Derived by applying land/labor relation of family-scale farm units in each country to other holdings of other scales.

5.1 million are tied to work on large holdings by formal or *de facto* contracts which grant them use rights in exchange for specified tasks or days of labor. Another 4.6 million workers are landless or temporary cash hire workers.

It was uniformly observed in all the CIDA study countries that the labor intensity with which land was worked declined as the scale of farm unit increased. For the seven countries taken together, 77 percent of the total agricultural land is held and operated as estates, but the estates employ only 47 percent of the agricultural labor force. The land of the very large units (those with 12 or more full-time workers) is proportionately the least intensively worked; with 53 percent of the land area, they employ only 18 percent of the labor and have only 16 percent of the cultivated land (including improved pasture and fallow).

Feder estimates that if the land-labor ratios prevailing on family scale units (units employing two full-time workers) in each of the CIDA study countries were to hold on estates, it would be possible to absorb *five times* more workers than are currently employed in the agriculture of the seven countries. Instead of 9.7 million workers, some 50 million could be absorbed (see Table 4). It is apparent that Brazil, with its huge land area, offers the greatest potential for using additional labor on existing farms – quite apart from the possibility of opening virgin country to settlement.

Applying the family-scale land-labor ratios to existing sub-family scale units provides a complementary measure of workers in *excess* of those who might earn *adequate* family incomes from such land. These data suggest that with similar production levels, higher per-capita worker incomes might be produced on the land of the *minifundia* with slightly more than one million workers instead of the 5.3 million now engaged.

Joining together (by heroic assumption) the estimates of excess and deficit workers, we find room to believe that the labor force in agriculture could be substantially greater within the present largely traditional agricultural zones, and could be much more productive and better remunerated. Support for this belief can be found by comparing Latin American land use intensity to that in other regions (U.S. Dept. of Agriculture, p. 64). The number of agricultural workers per 100 arable hectares in Japan in 1960 was 250, in the UAR and Taiwan the ratio was 167. In Brazil and Costa Rica, the ratios are 71.4 workers per 100 ha.; in Chile the ratio is 11.8 per 100 ha.

The most easily cited difficulties in bringing about improved land-man relations are the political-geographic. Excess workers in Ecuador are unlikely to be accommodated in the Argentine, nor Guatemalans in Brazil. But the social-institutional limitations to improvement are also immense. We have suggested elsewhere that the difficulties in bringing about change in either estate and *minifundia* management techniques require more than gentle persuasion. The present management and technology did not develop by accident, but grew out of and were fitted to the aspirations and motivations of the people involved. From the CIDA studies it was concluded:

> It is inconvenient for the large estate owner, given the social, economic, and political status he occupies in society, to modify his farming operations. It would require a considerable amount of his attention to do so. It would require more capital investments. And it probably would involve some changes in the tenure status of his work force. His non-farm political, professional, or business interests, the fact that he often leaves the farm operations in the hands of a hired manager while he devotes his time to other affairs, and the fact that his savings have been invested in non-liquid, inflation-proof assets limit his possibility of managing his farm business progressively.
>
> *Minifundia*, including those in *comunidades*, are fragmented independent holdings and, in a latifundia complex, have a fixed land base and virtually no access to productive factors other than labor. The common motivation of production is survival. These people must, at the same time, find room for that part of the increasing population which does not migrate. In the *altiplano* of Guatemala, for example, where population is increasing by three percent per year, one study shows average arable land per small farm to be 1.1 hectare, most of which is on steep hillsides. This is land enough to occupy only about ten percent of the available family labor force, even at the low levels of technology used. Under such circumstances, labor is necessarily applied with increasing intensity to the fixed land base. In brief, the combination of rapid population growth, a rigid tenure structure, a paucity of technical aid or capital, and a lack of employment alternatives, explain the *minifundia's* high yields from land and low yields from labor. The predictable consequence is low gross labor incomes and disguised unemployment. (Barraclough & Domike, p. 403)

We will not attempt to offer here more refined estimates of agricultural employment prospects on a country-by-country basis. We can, however, give some attention to the region's two ecologically and socio-economically "extreme" situations: the tropical lowlands and the *Altiplano*. In the tropics, man is scarce and land appears almost as a free good. In the highlands, on the other hand, are concentrated the greatest poverty, worst land tenure conditions, and poorest agricultural resources. A rapid overview of these two important sub-regions may sharpen our awareness of strategic and research priorities.

In the tropical lowlands of Latin America, we do not expect to find the poverty of people and resources, the "overpopulation," or the institutionalized rigidities in property and power systems that so thoroughly inhibit change in the Altiplano. There are serious lacks in transport and other infrastructure, of course, but these cannot be considered insuperable handicaps if there are real prospects that these regions can productively absorb the increasing populations.

Odd as it seems, given the immense territories involved (12.2 million Km^2) and the amount of resources presumably awaiting exploitation, there is very little reliable information on the productive potential of the tropical regions. Fortunately for our immediate purposes, a study now under way, directed by Michael Nelson[13], can at least help us put dimensions on the situation.

The rural population (1960-64) of the tropical and sub-tropical lowlands of South and Central America and Mexico is about thirty-eight million, of whom some twenty-seven million are in Brazil with its huge Amazon Basin. Accepting the most pessimistic of Nelson's assumptions regarding the quality of the soils, existing cover, technology, production, and size of farm units, it would still be possible for more than double the present population in the tropical regions to work productively in agricultural and forestry enterprises. If more optimistic but still reasonable assumptions were to prove realistic, more than 300 million people would be able to live in the area. In other words, the natural resource base of the tropical regions could provide productive employment for from ten to sixty million additional families.

But we must recognize that, however bright the long-term prospects for expanding employment opportunities in the tropics, they need not mature in the time and the manner that will solve the development problem. Massive exploitation of these latent resources requires capital, planning, politically powerful support, and luck. Furthermore, to incorporate these lands into high labor-absorbing, market-oriented types of settlements will require some modification of the ideological and technological preconceptions now prevalent (cf. Dagon and Panero, 1968).

Some experience with publicly-assisted smallholder settlement already exists, of course, and the experience could serve as a guide to a labor absorbing development policy. But the preference for large-scale private land developers is still very strong, and the assurance of "adequate" private returns is by no means consistently compatible with high rates of labor absorption. The better and more accessible lands are most likely to be exploited with capital-intensive techniques, leaving the marginal lands for spontaneous or assisted settlers. Or, where significant surpluses are being generated by the smallholders, money which could go into the rapid capitalization of agriculture is often captured by politically and/or economically strategic persons. Changing this system will be neither technically nor politically easy.[14]

What, then, of the other end of the spectrum, the *Altiplano*, the highland region. Parts of Bolivia, Peru, Ecuador, Colombia, and Guatemala are typically included in this category. Surely, if the employment problem could be relieved for the people living in these areas, either *in situ* or through migration, the Region's problems as a whole would seem much less.

The *Altiplano's* population of about eighteen million is overwhelmingly dependent upon agriculture and other subsistence sector employment. The area shelters about one-fourth of the rural population of the entire continent, while population growth rates, at three percent, and urban migration, at one-and-a-half percent, are about the same as for the Region.

In addition to the usual long list of obstacles to rapid industrialization, the *Altiplano* suffers extra penalties from high transport costs, lack of skilled workforce, generally difficult climate, thin or non-existent infrastructure, and poor local markets. True, there is cheap labor, and agricultural and mineral raw materials are available in substantial amounts. The industrialization opportunities lie in the possibilities for processing these materials beyond the minimum necessary to reach external markets. Recreation and other service employment is not a real possibility.[15] To all but the most "panglossian," then, there appear only the faintest opportunities to increase non-agricultural employment and production.[16]

By the process of elimination, agriculture becomes the only serious possible source of expanded employment and incomes *in situ*. In the *Altiplano* areas of the four CIDA-study countries (Peru, Ecuador, Colombia, and Guatemala), some 95,000 estate operators, 3.5 percent of the farm-dependent families, have 73 percent of the total land area under their direct management and another substantial part in cession, or rented to workers (see Table 5). The other 96.5 percent of the families – some 2.6 million smallholders and landless workers dependent on farming – provide the labor force, living off the wages and/or the usufruct of the land cessions of estate operators. If estates were as intensively operated as smallholdings, it would be possible to double production per family, even assuming no changes in techniques of production.

Significant production increases depend upon improving yields per land-unit. Present technology on both highland estates and smallholdings is,

TABLE 5 – CONCENTRATION OF LAND HOLDINGS IN HIGHLAND REGIONS OF PERU, ECUADOR, COLOMBIA, AND GUATEMALA, 1960

Highland Region	Number of Families		Land in Farms		Cultivated Land	
	Number (Thousands)	Percentage of all families in agriculture	Thousands of hectares	Percentage of land in farms	Thousands of hectares	Percentage of cultivated land
Peru:						
Estate Operators[1]	28	2	12,210	80	548	37
Small Holders[2]	930	92	3,050	20	850	63
Landless Families[3]	70	6	–	–	–	–
Ecuador:						
Estate Operators[1]	7	2	2,162	70	298	35
Small Holders[2]	253	85	858	30	550	65
Landless Families[3]	40	13	–	–	–	–
Colombia:						
Estate Operators[1]	54	15	11,719	68	769	27
Small Holders[2]	961	78	5,537	32	2,124	73
Landless Families[3]	80	7	–	–	–	–
Guatemala:						
Estate Operators[1]	6	2	1,580	64	293	64
Small Holders[2]	302	94	891	36	517	36
Landless Families[3]	12	4	–	–	–	–

SOURCE: Solon Barraclough, "The Development of Highland Communities in Latin America," Cornell University, March, 1966 (mimeo). From CIDA data.

[1] Owners or operators of estates large enough to provide year-round employment for more than four families of permanent laborers at prevailing local levels of income.

[2] The small holdings consist of the operators of sub-family sized parcels (minifundia), the "comuneros" – residents of the Indian communities, and the holders of "family-sized" parcels. Of these three groups, the family-sized holders have about half the land in small holdings, but make up less than ten percent of their numbers. Many of the small holders have insecure tenure arrangements, being renters, share-croppers, or squatters.

[3] The number of families of landless laborers is very roughly estimated and includes permanent laborers on the large estates, most of whom cultivate small parcels of land the use of which they receive in lieu of wages.

with the most rare exceptions, primitive; human rather than either animal or mechanical power predominates, and fertilizers, insecticides, and improved seeds and breeds are virtually unknown. The minimum requirement for improving technology would be more services of all sorts to the peasants. Because all services now provided by these governments (excepting credit) are so poorly supported, even their reallocation would be of little assistance in increasing production. Barraclough points out that if Ecuador's 118 extension workers worked with all 440,000 producers, they would each be attempting to aid 4,000 families, or at least fifty times more than the number generally considered desirable.

There are severe market and market structure limitations on agricultural improvement. Local suppliers and buyers are often the *hacienda* operators themselves, so that the chances of a peasant benefiting from increased production are remote. Market prospects are poor for the few commodities that are technically feasible in the *Altiplano* (such as potatoes and sheep), and comparative advantages over the other regions simply do not exist, except perhaps for llamas and goats.

The other alternative is, then, outmigration from the traditional agricultural areas. This movement could improve incomes both to those who stay and those who leave. Of course, *Altiplano* peasants have taken seasonal work away from their home sites since colonial times and earlier. More permanent migration to new agricultural areas, particularly to the tropical frontiers, has been promoted with particular fervor in Bolivia, Colombia, and Peru. Although these efforts should not be considered failures, the average number of migrant families successfully settled annually is of the order of hundreds and not thousands.

Special local situations and extraordinary efforts by national governments apart, the conclusions drawn by Barraclough (1966a, b) for the *Altiplano* seem to hold. Economic development will in the best circumstances be a long, arduous, and costly process. Extreme poverty and sacrifice will probably continue to be the lot of the rural highlander for a long time to come.

Despite these reservations, it may be fairly concluded that the potential for great expansion of agricultural employment does exist in Latin America. However, the political and institutional limitations on growth are enormous and equally apparent, and prospects for their alleviation discouraging. From the indicators and studies now available, it seems feasible to expand agricultural employment in tropical regions sufficiently to absorb the entire demographic increase and more. But in those areas of greatest demographic pressure, particularly the *Altiplano*, inherent economic potential is so poor, and the land tenure situation so inequitable and rigid, that both short- and long-run employment prospects are meager. We will not extend our comments on the cost and effectiveness of programs to foster migration from the *Altiplano* to the tropics; an evaluation of such activities is being carried out in the Nelson study mentioned earlier.

Two policy alternatives gain special priority in consequence of the foregoing analyses, agrarian reform and tropical land settlement. Democratization of the rural landholding and political systems would seem to be essential prerequisites to improving employment levels in most of the traditional agricultural regions. Land redistribution alone, we know, will not increase output very much. But, by helping to break down the oligarchic rural power structure, reform could bring changes in official attitudes and priorities, and lead to creation of broad-based rural development programs. This change implies great improvements in the quality and quantity of official programs in the rural areas, and a shift from the traditional clientele. If we must judge from history, the likelihood of this sort of reform occurring in the absence of revolution is very small.

The second serious policy alternative, tropical settlement, still lacks serious evaluations of past experience. On the basis of current knowledge, however, it would seem essential to encourage the widest possible popular participation in the programs, and avoid both the massive capital investment approach and the approach that permits completely undirected smallholder settlement. In land settlement, as in other important activities of man, no simple "formula" approach works. Man's ingenuity and intelligence have a place even in the jungle.

III

The conclusions to be drawn from this overview of the region's employment and development problems must necessarily be cautious. There are great gaps in both our theories of development and our usable knowledge about Latin American agriculture. We cannot overcome these deficiencies in one blow, perhaps not in one generation. Some conclusions, however, may be drawn.

It may appear unconventional, not to say politically unwise, to insist that Latin America's development problems be understood in terms of employment needs.[17] We nonetheless persist, since by using the conventional measures of progress it can be made to appear that there is economic progress in Latin America; in the world where real people live, however, matters are clearly worsening. Gross domestic product and agricultural production have shown gains in Guatemala, Nicaragua, and tropical Bolivia, but it requires selective blindness to believe that this means that greater numbers of these populations are better off. The Venezuelan gross domestic product grew by 7.3 percent per year from 1960 to 1966, but the combined under- and unemployment rate is still about thirty-two percent (cf. Seers, 1964).

It was contended at the outset that agriculture will prove the key to the Region's development. The chances for notably improving, or even maintaining, the rate of labor absorption by modern industry, we have concluded, are most dismal. But in agriculture, the technical potential for new employment is more than adequate, measured against both the numbers now in subsistence industries and demographic increases. *Nevertheless, without altering the landholding systems, employment increases will not occur.* Quite the contrary, opportunities for work may even decline, and the distribution of incomes in the sector will become even more unequal and less conducive to development. Where land reform occurs, the effects on employment and incomes will be very limited unless more and better services are provided to the farmers. In tropical settlement, the same order of limitations may prevail, unless particular attention is given to the employment criterion.

Members of the present and future "surplus" rural labor force fortunate enough to have a choice can continue in the countryside as precarious hirelings on some micro-parcel, or join the urban under-employed. Lack of rural work opportunities will combine with the inherent attractiveness of urban centers to bring the number of rural-urban migrants over the next twenty years to 50 million persons.[18] If the number of migrants is now enough to panic planners and politicians, the future will give them even more trouble. But if there is sympathy to be spent, it might more appropriately go to the millions whose lives will be shortened and misshapen by lack of opportunity and hope.

The urgency that social scientists attach to problems is not easily separated from the measures they use to describe the problem. Economists and planners in Latin America have summarized the development problem in terms of the rate of increase in Gross National Product. In this way, they ignore the essentially-human problem of development. Our concentration here on the problem of jobs needed to match population increases offers a more central, even if still incomplete, measure of development.

In this matter, Gunnar Myrdal (1968, p. 982) has shown by example and aphorism that social scientists should not accept the conventional definitions and wisdom; indeed they cannot do so and retain their claim to the profession. In his newest work, *Asian Drama* (which we can pray will become a model for a similar analysis of Latin America),[19] he points out:

All knowledge, like all ignorance, tends to be opportune and to advance the cause of special interests – as long as investigators fail to observe the necessity of working with specific and explicit value premises. There is a convenience of ignorance that enters into our observations and inferences and tends to fit them into a conception of reality conforming to our interests. Recognition of this fact does not, of course, imply that all our observations and inferences are faulty, but it does mean that we should scrutinize them carefully.

NOTES

*The views presented here do not necessarily represent those of the Food and Agriculture Organization of the United Nations.

1. See the studies prepared by the Inter-American Committee for Agricultural Development, under the title *Land Tenure Conditions and Socio-Economic Development of the Agricultural Sector* for Argentina, Brazil, Chile, Colombia, Guatemala, Ecuador, and Peru. Also, see Sonon Barraclough and Arthur Domike (1966, pp. 391-424). This general hypothesis was perhaps best expressed by Gunnar Myrdal (1965).

2. The definition of the Latin American Region used here is that generally employed by the United Nations; it includes Cuba and other Caribbean states except for the former and present British, French, Dutch, and U.S. colonies and possessions.

3. Cf. W. Arthur Lewis (1954; 1959). In Barraclough's paper in the present volume, the inadequacies of this model in the Latin American context are noted.

4. The data on the active labor force reflect employment opportunities, including those in lowest productivity, subsistence income occupations. They do not include (except in Bolivia and Haiti) working farm wives. More significantly, they fail to show adequately persons out of the market, i.e., unemployed and not seeking work, for which virtually no reliable measures exist. At the aggregate level, a tendency toward increased unemployment is seen in the declining ratio of the active labor force to the working age population (See, CEPAL, 1965, p.47).

5. If the territories and new countries under British, French, Dutch, and U.S. control or influence were added to the Latin American region, another 7.4 million total population and 2.8 million active labor force would be included.

6. The regional population and manpower projection offered by the International Labor Organization indicates that the expected annual increase in active population from 1960 to 1970 is about 2.9 percent or more than two million persons; from 1970 to 1980, the projected rate is 3.2 percent or just short of three million new members of the labor force annually. The comparable numbers for North America are 1,350,000 for the first decade and 1,700,000 for the second. In the ILO projections, all former and present territories and colonies are included, so that the data are not precisely comparable to the present estimates. The ILO also projects higher rates of labor force participation (ILO, 1966).

7. Very little empirical research of any sort has been carried out on employment multipliers, even in the United States. It would be important to discover not only the amount of new employment generated by additions to industrial output, but also the type and location of such jobs. Two recent studies of the U.S. situation give some indication of the difficulty of making such estimates and, from a substantive point of view, the very weak relationship between increased production and employment opportunities for the less skilled laborers. See Wadsworth and Conrad (1965), and Anderson (1964).

8. Another presentation of the same idea, which may represent a trial balloon for U.S. AID policy, is L. H. Berlin (1967).

9. For a competent review of the most commonly encountered views on this theme, see John W. Mellor (1966).

10. Barrington Moore (1966) offers an antidote to such theories. He draws upon the experience of England, France, the USA, China, Japan, India, Germany, and the USSR to support the hypothesis that the distribution of land and the relation of the landholders to the political power structure are crucial determinants of both the rate at which a nation modernizes and the political system through which modernization occurs.

11. The summary data used here from the CIDA country studies were compiled by Ernest Feder, who has also prepared various yet-to-be-published

analyses on this question. Any misinterpretation is the responsibility of the present author.

12. Because the detailed country data in the various CIDA studies were not all derived from 1960 censuses, the work force and population estimates here are not strictly comparable to the data on Table 1.

13. The estimates offered here have been kindly provided by Nelson, but responsibility for their possible misuse is, of course, the present author's. The study is being supported by the Resources for the Future Foundation and the United Nations.

14. It is fatuous to expect "official" programs of tropical development to reach more desirable social and economic results than are reached with private entrepreneurs if no improvement is achieved in the type of administration. A contemporary case is the Brazilian agency charged with the protection of Indians in the interior areas. To take control of these lands, officials in charge of the program allegedly engaged in "massacres of whole tribes by dynamite, machine guns, and sugar laced with (*New York Times*, March 21, 1968). A novelist's treatment of a similar situation is given by Peter Matthiesson (1965).

15. In Mexico and the Caribbean, on the other hand, the tourist trade has entered as an important economic activity. Whether this brings expanded income and employment to the population, or becomes an enclave activity benefiting foreign investors rather than the local population (as in pre-Revolution Havana) depends largely upon government policy.

16. For a similar view, see Solon Barraclough (1966b). As noted earlier, industrial employment in Bolivia is less now than in 1950-54 in spite of a doubling in level of output and a reported excess manufacturing capacity of thirty to forty percent.

17. A strong argument in support of giving high priority to investments which increase rural employment opportunities is offered by Fred Dziadek (1967).

18. To the individual, of course, the escape to the city may be a liberation. I. L. Horowitz almost rhapsodizes:

> The movement from ruralism to urbanism may appear as simply a matter of change to social scientists, but for the mass of people it is a matter of emancipation. Women are emancipated from domestic obligations; children are emancipated from the work force; laborers are emancipated from the vagaries and tyrannies of the land; and human relations as such are emancipated from strict economic necessity. (1966, p.338)

19. There is the opportunity for a global analysis of similar scope to come out of a recently initiated study of manpower planning and employment policy in Latin America sponsored by the International Labour Organization. The UN-FAO is about to publish the first findings of the World Indicative Plan, which treats problems of employment, with emphasis primarily upon agricultural production and trade prognostication.

BIBLIOGRAPHY

Anderson, W. H. Locke

1964 "Trickling Down: Relationship between Economic Growth and the Extent of Poverty among American Families," *Quarterly Journal of Economics,* Vol. 78, pp. 511-24.

Barraclough, Solon

n.d. Conference paper, "Rural Development and Employment Prospects in Latin America."

1966a "The Development of Highland Communities in Latin America," Cornell University (mimeo).

1966b "Economic Implications of Rural-Urban Migration Trends from the Highland Communities," Cornell Latin American Year Conference (mimeo).

– – – and Arthur Domike

1966 "Agrarian Structure in Seven Latin American Countries," *Land Economics,* Vol. 42, No. 4, pp. 391-424.

Berlin, L. H.

1967 "A New Agricultural Strategy in Latin America," *International Development Review,* pp. 12-14.

CEPAL

1965 *Estudio Economico de America Latina, 1964,* New York: Economic Commission for Latin America.

1966 *The Process of Industrial Development in Latin America,* New York: United Nations.

Currie, Laughlin

1966 *Accelerating Development,* New York: McGraw-Hill.

Dagon, R. and R. Panero

1968 "An Approach to Large Scale Agricultural Systems in South America," Croton-on-Hudson, N.Y.: Hudson Institute.

Dorner, Peter

1967 *The Influence of Land Tenure Institutions on the Economic Development of Agriculture in Less Developed Countries,* paper prepared for the meeting of North Central Land Economics Committee.

Dziadek, Fred

1967 "Unemployment in the Less Developed Countries," AID Discussion Paper No. 16, Washington D.C.: U.S. Agency for International Development.

Furtado, Celso

1965 *Political Obstacles to Growth in Brazil,* London: Chatham House.

Horowitz, Irving Louis

1966 *Three Worlds of Development,* New York: Oxford University Press.

Inter-American Committee for Agricultural Development

n.d. *Land Tenure Conditions and Socio-Economic Development of the Agricultural Sector.*

International Labor Organization

1966 "Manpower Planning and Economic Policy in Economic Development," Eighth Conference of American State Members of the International Labor Organization, pp. 28-40.

Lewis, W. Arthur

1954 "Economic Development with Unlimited Supplies of Labor," *Manchester School,* Vol. 22, pp. 139-91.

1959 "Unlimited Labor: Further Notes," *Manchester School,* Vol. 26, pp. 1-32.

Matthiesson, Peter

1965 *At Play in the Fields of the Lord,* New York: Random House.

Mellor, John W.

1966 "Toward a Theory of Agricultural Development," *in* H. Southworth and B. Johnson, eds, *Agricultural Development and Economic Growth,* Ithaca, N.Y.: Cornell University Press.

Moore, Barrington

1966 *Social Origins of Dictatorship and Democracy: Lord and Peasant in the Making of the Modern World,* Boston: Beacon Press.

Myrdal, Gunnar

1965 "The United Nations, Agriculture, and the World Economic Revolution," *Journal of Farm Economics,* pp. 889-99.

– – –, Assisted by David Wightman, Paul F. Streeten, George W. Wilson, *et. al.*

1968 *Asian Drama: An Inquiry into the Poverty of Nations,* New York: Pantheon Press.

Organization of American States

1967 *Social Aspects of Urban Development,* Washington D.C. Document CIES/1138, Meeting of IA-ECOSOC.

Pan American Union

1966 *America en Cifras,* Vol. 4, Washington.

1967 *Industrialization in Latin America: Priority Problems.* Doc. CIES/1138 Add. 2, May, Washington (mimeo).

Pearse, Andrew

1966 "Agrarian Change Trends in Latin America," *Latin American Research Review.*

Seers, Dudley

1964 "The Mechanism of an Open Petroleum Economy," *Social and Economic Studies.*

U. S. Department of Agriculture

n.d. "Changes in Agriculture in 26 Developing Countries, 1948-1963," Foreign Agricultural Economics Report, No. 7.

Wadsworth, H. A. and J. M. Conrad

1965 "Leakages Reducing Employment and Income Multipliers in Labor-Surplus Rural Areas," *Journal of Farm Economics,* Vol. 47, pp. 1197-1212.

INDUSTRIALIZATION AND LABOR IN PERU*

David Chaplin

The relation between a man's occupation and his total self changes during the industrialization process. When a nation's economy is non-industrial, the social status of most men determines their work, with the two being highly integrated. In urban-industrial societies (whose essential or "final" structure is never certain since built-in change is one of their characteristics), occupations seem to determine social status, although pre-industrial "survivals" still function. During the transitional era, especially in urban areas, the relationship between status and occupation is indefinite, as we shall see in the present paper which focuses on one Latin American country, Peru.

The reasons for the lack of clear integration between work and "life" during the transitional stage are many. For one, the rural migrant is leaving not just an economic sector of his society, but also a culture. His milieu changes so much that it is debatable whether he has moved upward or downward in social class terms. On arrival in the city, he enters a world in which the upper class ideal is still not to have any job at all, but rather to consume ostentatiously. The growing middle class, in turn, attempts to reach this consumption ideal by holding several full-time jobs at once (only to be frustrated by inflation). In Peru, middle and upper class persons still tend to be judged more by style of consumption than by occupation. Most middle class men carry a variety of calling cards, presenting whichever one is most appropriate at the moment, a practice which may be seen as a form of alienation from work. The better paid factory worker in Peru, in fact, appears to be over-committed to his job, and his alienation focuses more on his government or on "politics."

In order to examine more fully the development of industrial work in an urban context in Peru, we shall take up the following topics: plant location, labor legislation, labor recruitment practices, the "brain drain," labor conflict, and land reform.

Plant Location

Location is a central issue. The greater success which urban textile factories (the major branch of manufacturing in Peru[1]) have enjoyed in recruiting and holding a satisfactory labor force as compared to the "decentralized" plants is apparently due to several factors:

1. Their workers are city-born or voluntarily self-selected migrants from rural areas;

2. These workers are part of a largely-commercialized world in which most necessities and luxuries cost money which paid labor can provide; they are thus exposed to a wide range of consumer goods which have effectively eliminated any mythology of a fixed level of wants, the age-old justification for paying only subsistence wages to "native" workers;

3. They are exposed to a constant inflationary spiral. Rising prices on goods and services *alone* will drive the worker to seek the relatively highly paid factory work, even in the absence of any great personal ambition, simply to preserve a customary standard of living;

4. Most of them also find themselves in urban areas without the protection of a traditional *patrõn*, but with a variety of voluntary associations such as unions, political parties, and social clubs to assist in the modernizing process of psychological emancipation from paternalism.

In addition, in Peru the rural-urban wage differential is far greater than, say, in the United States. This difference is due partly to payment partially in kind in rural areas, and also to the very unequal enforcement of the generous labor and social security laws. The differential enforcement of these laws has made the urban manufacturing labor force the most privileged of all blue collar occupations (Economic Commission for Latin America, 1959, p. 11). In addition to this "pull," more than sufficient "push" out of rural areas now exists because of population growth, the scarcity of arable land, and the absence of a significant amount of land reform which might have succeeded in making agricultural work more attractive. It is noteworthy that in Peru there is practically no genuine deep nostalgia about rural life among the Indian population. Most highland Indian migrants today seem to be thoroughly disenchanted with their ancestral areas which, unlike many areas in Asia and Africa, have been under overwhelming European cultural and political domination for over four hundred years.

Rural employers, on the other hand, have long suffered from a high degree of labor turnover and absenteeism, and most of the pre-World War II literature on labor recruitment characterized such problems as *universal* in underdeveloped areas (Moore, 1959, pp. 306-7). However, this literature refers largely to mines and plantations, almost always in rural locations, and obviously, rural employers could not enjoy the advantages listed above.

My own data indicate that even from 1900-1945 the Lima mills did not suffer significantly from such problems. In fact, an objective view of labor-management relations during this period, and even to the present, would have to credit or debit management with much of the responsibility for what labor instability existed. Peru's textile mills internally, and the textile industry as a whole, are poorly organized (Haour, 1959), although relatively better than those of many other Latin American countries (United Nations, 1951, p. 105). Most firms are over-integrated – from spinning to finishing and even retail sales – and poorly structured in terms of the ratio of spindles to looms and the productivity of both compared to the capacity of their finishing machines. As a result, production is often interrupted owing to poor management. In addition, the textile industry all over the world has been undergoing a chronic overproduction and reorganization crisis throughout the history of Peru's branch of this industry.

It would be especially inappropriate, of course, to locate market-oriented, consumer goods plants – such as textiles – far from well-populated areas. We may, then, justly attribute the low productivity and poor working conditions in the rural plants not only to their environment, but also directly to their management's reasons for choosing such locations, usually a preference for cheap and docile workers above all else. Rural locations arrest the development of the usual sequence of stages of participation and adult socialization which prepare a worker voluntarily to seek and remain in factory work. This sequence involves a positively reinforced cycle in which a few of the self-selected migrants, usually the better educated and more ambitious, gradually work their way to the "top," in terms of realistic opportunities, by passing through truck ownership, street vending, and other such commercial activities on their way to the best paid manual jobs in factories. (Only a minority of migrants enjoy such success, but this is the group of concern in this paper.) In any case, rural factory labor is usually used inefficiently.

In recruiting labor, very few of the textile factories made use of such "classic" labor recruiting tactics as *enganche* (shanghai-ing), *yanaconaje* (sharecropping), *la repũblica*, and *faenas* or *mitas* (types of corvẽe labor), and when they did, the results were poor. They did not need to use such techniques largely because they were located in urban areas with a ready-made labor supply.[2] Those that did use these tactics sacrificed much to achieve labor discipline and low wages. In one rural case, girls were recruited directly from Japan under the control of a Japanese ex-army officer. Another technique was the renting of an *hacienda* from the *Beneficencia Publica*[3] in order to inherit the traditional work obligations of the resident Indians. In the only current example of this latter method, the factory was taken *to the hacienda*, the workers were not taught Spanish, and were paid one-fifth of the prevailing urban provincial wage. As a result, I found there the highest morale, (thanks to the successful reconstruction of traditional paternalism), and the lowest productivity of any textile mill in Peru.

In general, during the first period of the development of manufacturing in Peru – 1900-1940 – when the mines and coastal *haciendas* wrestled with a shortage of labor and resorted to most of the above "classic" recruiting techniques, the urban textile mills had no need of such methods.

Labor Legislation

A directly related factor in labor recruitment is Peru's outstandingly progressive labor and social welfare legislation. I shall not attempt a detailed analysis of Peruvian labor laws, but shall instead offer an interpretation of their general significance, based on my field research and background study. It may be said that Peru's labor legislation was passed in its generous and progressive form:

1. Because of a desire on the part of influential Peruvians to assert Peru's membership in "Western" civilization (cf. Lizarraga, 1957);

2. Because of the pressure of the Aprista Party and its labor union support;

3. Because governments opposed to the Aprista Party tried to wean away the same group of workers;

4. Because most Peruvians do not accept either the desirability or reality of a "free" market-determined level of wages and working conditions;

5. Because in the earlier stage – especially under Benavides – manufacturers were still so weak a group that the government could afford to buy labor peace at their expense.

This legislation represents, for the most part, a sincere attempt to avoid all the abuses of workers which accompanied Western industrial development and to award workers in advance all the material benefits available in the most economically developed societies. (It must be noted, however, that most of this legislation was decreed during military dictatorships rather than passed by democratically elected congresses.)

The results have been:

1. The wholesale promulgation into law of the most advanced ideas proposed by the International Labor Organization as desirable (but not necessarily immediately realizable) goals;

2. Because the government is financially and administratively incapable of the thorough and uniform enforcement of its labor code, laws are enforced only in urban areas and/or where unions are strong. (I do not feel this latter aspect to be regrettable since it has served in the past to favor the most dynamic sector of the economy);

3. The law, in theory, replaces the traditional paternalism enjoyed or suffered by a large segment of the pre-industrial labor force with a state paternalism, without forcing the favored segment of the labor force through an era of "self-respecting individualism."

Few modern observers would argue that the working classes in developing countries *should* undergo all the exploitation and abuses experienced in Western industrial development. But neither can we forget that one aspect of that painful experience in other countries was an emancipation from paternalistic dependence on government or management, a process which, if we can generalize from the "Western" case (which may well not be valid), is felt by many observers to be essential to the creation of a mobile and committed industrial labor force (Bendix, 1956, p. 73).

In fact, however, relatively few workers avoid this experience in Peru because the labor law is very unevenly and inconsistently enforced. The only danger, then, from our point of view is too rigid enforcement, which might result in a "premature stereotyping" of the current system of production, undesirable even in a fully developed industrial economy and disastrous in a partially developed one. The immediate economic consequence in terms of labor costs would be another and quite sufficient argument against such an enforcement. To a certain extent this situation already exists in the textile industry where the work loads of the weavers and spinners are much lower than is found in the United States or England for the same machines.

A major effect of Peru's labor law enforcement in textile mills (but not in the garment shops) has been the sharp reduction since 1955 in the hiring of women. The fact is that if all the laws are enforced it is more expensive to employ women than men, and consequently, women are being shut out of textile factory jobs as well as other, relatively high-paying blue collar occupations. If all of those women were the wives of workers in equally favorable jobs, this forced retirement would be more tolerable, but it is well known that over half of them have no legal husband and only irregular, if any, help from the father of their children. The recently observed high abortion rate among Lima's lower class women is perhaps a reflection of this situation (Hall, 1964, p. 41).

Female labor force participation has been reduced not only in textile factories, but throughout the blue collar labor market. The mechanization of agriculture and the increasingly capital-intensive structure of manufacturing has meant that only tertiary occupations are opening up for women. For lower class women, this means mainly domestic service, street vending, and prostitution. *The urban lower class woman is undoubtedly the most exploited category of worker at this stage in economic development, rather than the proletariat as a whole.*

Beyond foreclosing manual employment opportunities for women, labor and welfare legislation has also served as one factor in fostering an increasingly capital-intensive structure in manufacturing, another factor being the tendency of development loans and currency exchange policies to favor investment in machinery. The result has been a relative decline in manufacturing employment in Peru from 1940 to 1961 from 17.2 to 16.6 percent (Chaplin, 1967, p. 169).

Over all, Peru's labor and welfare legislation has facilitated the recruitment and commitment of a manufacturing labor force – but at the price of institutionalized obstacles to necessary improvements in productivity which must be faced in the near future.

Labor Mobility and Recruitment Practices

Of great interest to all concerned with industrial growth is the question of the social and geographic origins of industrial workers and the process of social and physical mobility necessary in the transition to industrial work.

In Chimbote (in a general sample of all types of workers), I found that a plurality of factory workers today, and an overwhelming majority in the past, made what could be described as the shortest moves possible in the cultural, occupational, and geographic senses. Very few workers even today in the textile factories come from the densely populated rural areas or from mine or plantation work. Most come directly from urbanized areas, either from school or mechanical work. Until the development of other branches of manufacturing, the railroads, docks, and small repair and assembly shops served as transitional occupations for this latter group. The rapidly-increasing number of rural migrants in Lima and Arequipa today are found, as expected, largely in non-industrial "entry occupations," i.e., construction work, domestic service, and the armed forces. (Cf. Bradfield, 1965, p. 69, for similar findings.)

As for the recruitment criteria which determine what types of workers find steady industrial employment, a variety of conflicting and complementary factors are in operation. In terms of the rationality of labor recruitment, we find that no clear, consistent hiring criteria are used by management other than, for example, individual preferences for docile newcomers as opposed to experienced city-bred workers, and most firms let the workers recruit themselves. That is, management either asks respected workers to recommend new recruits or looks over those who show up at the gate (most of whom are told to show up by friends already employed who know when openings are available). One result of this practice is the concentration in various factories of workers from particular kinship groups, birthplaces, and urban neighborhoods. More recently, with newer and more complex machinery and processes, the more "rational" policy of pirating has come into vogue, in which whole crews are bought away from competing firms.[4]

The pattern set by 1940, due to managerial preferences, the types of workers applying, and the effect of turnover and seniority rules, was that new mills began with a labor force composed mainly of women and young men, while older mills had largely older men. Laws restricting the employment of women and children were passed rather early in the 1920's, but only recently have they been so strictly enforced that the percentage of women and adolescents has greatly decreased. Another outstanding feature of the millworker segment of Lima's labor force is its low level of turnover, as Briones and Mejia Valera (1964, p. 34) also noted in their 1962 survey of factory workers in the city.

This extreme stability, in comparison to similar factories in the United States, is a natural reaction to the scarcity of jobs and the relatively high wage level in textiles. In addition, the shortage of housing and poor public transportation tends to hold down intra-urban labor mobility, and the strict seniority provisions insisted upon by the union and generally adhered to by management, make new starts disadvantageous for workers. Moreover, in view of the long-standing preference of most employers for young, inexperienced workers for all but a few mechanical maintenance jobs, the job-seeker over twenty-five may have trouble even beginning at the bottom in a factory.

Optimal Turnover?

It would be theoretically interesting if an optimal level of turnover could be established as a scientific law, but certainly no single rate could possibly be set for all formal organizations, or even for categories limited by size and function, which would maximize all of their legitimate goals, and this says nothing of the methodological problems involved.

There might be, however, an optimal level of turnover for purposes of maximizing the "ideal type" social norms of particular types of industrial organizations. The optimum referred to here is an organizationally-biased one. However, what is good for the organization need not be equally optimal for the entire economy, nor for the national system of social stratification nor the workers as individuals. Probably, a somewhat different level of industrial labor turnover would be most favorable for each of these systems or groups once some set of welfare criteria could be agreed upon. In addition, turnover rates would normally vary for each level and type of position within an organization. My concern here, however, is only with the total turnover of manufacturing production workers.

Kerr (Bakke, 1954, p. 102) and Palmer (Bakke, 1954, p. 111) favor the maximum possible openness in the labor market for the sake of the freedom and welfare of individual workers and the progress of the economy. Blau and Scott (1962, pp. 112, 252), on the other hand, in their study of white collar workers in a welfare agency, deplore high turnover as a sign of low morale for which management is held responsible. Siegel (1953, p. 519), in writing about the general utility of turnover data, also feels that "employers. . .[in the United States]. . .consider low turnover rates as an indicator of efficient operation and good management-labor relations." Ross (1958, p. 903), however, views this change of values as another cycle, noting that "a generation ago, wasteful and destructive turnover was seen as a primary evil. Today it is feared that workers have become badly immobilized."

The long-run decline in the turnover of factory workers in the United States since the 1920's is apparently due (1) to the increasing average size of plant employment (thus opening up more opportunities for internal transfers), (2) seniority provisions together with a rise in the average age of factory workers, (3) increasing positive efforts to lower factory turnover, and (4) possibly, the tendency toward wage equalization among industries at the local level.

Whatever the desired level of turnover may be, the costs of replacing workers is probably not fully appreciated by the average employer. Ullman (1966, pp. 529-30) estimates that the average cost of replacing a factory worker in the United States in recent years is around $500. He also notes that low-wage employers tended to have higher absolute worker replacement costs than high-wage employers, thus reducing somewhat the disparity in their overall labor costs.

I would suggest that during the early transitional stages of industrialization in countries like Peru it may be desirable, as well as inevitable, that a combination of limitations restrict the wage-depressing effects of a labor surplus. The resulting "bias" helps to keep wages above their "true market" level in the urban manufacturing sector where progress is so necessary from an industrial standpoint. The factory workers' status, compared to traditional pre-industrial *or* white-collar occupations, would otherwise be too low. The full effect of the labor surplus which has become normal in currently-underdeveloped countries could, in the absence of market imperfections, drive factory wages below the subsistence level and thus impede economic development (Leibenstein, 1957, p. 91).

Brain Drain

Another type of mobility of growing significance since 1940 has been the increasing number of middle class Peruvians educated abroad. Education in general is the most important means of upward mobility (a good professional education can, of course, also cushion the fall of the son of an ex-provincial "aristocrat"). As the national universities are increasingly democratized, the prestige value of their degrees declines and hence a foreign education becomes even more desirable, aside from its usually much higher quality. Before World War II, the majority of Peruvians studying abroad were upper class. The men tended to go to English or German schools, while the few wealthy women educated abroad (normally only through the secondary level) went to Spain or France. With the closing off of Europe during the Second World War, and the growing importance of the United States in the Peruvian economy, there was a shift to American schools. In addition, the rising entrance requirements and performance standards of the elite American schools meant that the scions of the best Peruvian families could no longer count on being admitted, and their places have increasingly been taken by more talented and ambitious middle class Peruvians.

It was generally expected by all concerned – the students' families, the Peruvian government, and the American foundations providing scholarships – that this new, middle class student group would, of course, return to Peru, where their skills are so greatly needed. What actually happened was what has come to be known all over the under-developed world as the "brain drain," the phenomenon of students from poor countries studying in rich countries and then, having had a taste of the opportunity and affluence to be found there, refusing to return home, or returning only long enough to fulfill the obligations required by scholarship loans and grants. The problem is compounded for the middle class students because they lack the social background and family prestige to achieve the positions in Peru to which, especially given the critical shortage of college-educated personnel, they would realistically be able to aspire *if* the Peruvian economy were governed by more universalistic norms. In addition, students studying abroad may also unlearn and come to reject the *criollo* ("operator") approach to career success and expect to succeed on merit alone, a change in values which renders them unwilling and psychologically unable to play the game – as it must still be played in Peru,[5] or they may simply lose touch with the clique or *patrōn* who might sponsor their careers.

A related question for those not working primarily for the government is whether they will seek employment with a Peruvian or a foreign-owned firm. Each has obstacles to advancement. The national firm is normally a family enterprise giving the best positions to relatives. The foreign firm, for its part, often reserves the top positions for its own countrymen. However, in the latter case there are two countervailing factors. The average total size and relative proportion of higher level positions are larger in foreign firms, and they are also true corporations in a socio-economic sense, and not family enterprises. Moreover, they can be pressured by the government into "nationalizing" their personnel up to the highest local level. Some of those top positions, however, are also particularistic in a "functional" way in that each foreign firm needs a protective wall of local influentials whose only assets need be the right ties to the ruling oligarchy. These positions are, therefore, not open to talented "upstarts."

There is also, unfortunately, relatively little coordination between supply and demand for particular skills. The country may need engineers, but, if twenty-five chemical engineers all graduate and return in a single year, only ten may find acceptable positions in their specialties because the industrial development needed to absorb the others does not yet exist.

Labor Conflict

Along with the pre-1945 world-wide concern with the problem of recruiting and holding industrial workers in less developed countries (today seen as a problem largely for isolated mines and plantations), it seems to have been the popular impression that most labor-management conflict was a battle of the old against the new, of a primitive or non-industrial people defending their "secure," integrated, more aesthetic culture against "devastation" by commercialism and the horrors of factory work. I found, however, as have recent observers in many parts of the world, that the main basis for conflict today is no longer the old against the new, but what is now conventionally known as the revolution of rising expectations or an "over-commitment" to the goals of an industrial society.

One of the oldest types of industrial conflict, the Luddite riots in England, was rare in Peru and apparently absent in textiles. This conflict, the resistance of pre-industrial artisans and craftsmen to the degradation of their status and the market value of their products (Smelser, 1959, p. 249), was avoided in Peru with the destruction, prior to 1900, of organized weavers guilds by an extended period of free and cheap imports of foreign textile goods (Romero, 1943, p. 303). Weaving then "degenerated" into a part-time rural woman's chore – from its old status as a full-time man's profession – well before the growth of Peruvian textile mills. I was unable to find a single former full-time hand-weaver now employed in a textile mill, and I believe this to be the result not only of what might have been their distaste for such work, but also of the apparent elimination of the occupation by years of free trade.

Another source of conflict and absenteeism more common in Peru, especially in rural and small town areas, is the payment of wages so low that workers cannot survive on them, forcing them to regard factory work merely as a source of seasonal employment to obtain goods which only money can buy.

Labor conflict also results from the great social distance between management and labor. This "distance" is not a matter simply of subordination, since such a social relationship was traditional, but of subordination to "strangers," that is, rulers without authority accepted as legitimate, since most of management down to the foreman level is English, Italian, or German. Such managers typically do not fulfill the traditional expectations of paternalistic responsibility, but still demand the traditional subordination (Bendix, 1956, p. 34). Recently, such conflict has also been the result of management's efforts (1) to increase productivity by introducing new machines and reorganizing production, and (2) to reduce labor costs by avoiding the accumulation of many high-seniority workers.

Thus, the proper interpretation of labor-management conflict and other signs of low morale is not simple. It cannot, for example, be assumed that friction *per se* is a sign only of a recalcitrant or "anti-industrial" labor force; it can as often be a symbol of and a primary impetus to industrial development. An examination of productivity and morale – the latter being defined as the absence of strikes or conflict and the positive expression of respect for management – revealed that they are inversely correlated in Peru. The most contented workers, by humanistic criteria, worked in the least efficient mill, (which was the one located on an isolated hacienda), while the most militantly organized "radical" union developed in the mill with one of the highest productivity rates and the highest pay scales (located in the heart of Lima). What "anti-industrial" conflict there is to be found occurs in those mills which currently suffer from work systems "frozen" in an earlier era of lower wages and less commercial competition. The workers' reaction here is not unlike that of American workers fearing automation, with the added problem that there are not enough comparable alternate sources of employment in Peru. It may in fact be the case that the period of sharpest industrial conflict is yet to come. The early recruitment phase is apparently easier than often depicted, but later efforts to increase productivity are likely to be more painful.

We cannot conclude then that workers happily "committed" to their employers are fully socialized industrial workers. In Peru, and presumably in many developing societies, their commitment is usually to a concrete organization and to individual managers, rather than to an abstract acceptance of industrial culture. Thus, one must ask, what sort of management serves as objects of "commitment for the workers?" All too often we find owners and managers more mercantilist than industrial in their actions and beliefs. One of the major obstacles to industrial progress in Peru is the absence of a powerful, cohesive group of "industrialists," men whose primary economic concern is with manufacturing. In many cases, Peruvian textile mills are peripheral activities of men whose major interest is apt to be commerce and real estate speculation. The lack of such an orientation is not necessarily due to ignorance or conservatism, but, rather, to the objective conditions facing manufacturing, which is among the least profitable and most risky enterprises in Peru, given recent economic and legal conditions.

Labor conflict in countries like Peru involves the government at least as much as it does the employers in question. In the United States, labor experts have traditionally deplored labor involvement in politics and underestimated the role of political participation in the success of the movement. In currently-developing areas, however, there seems to be no question that the politicization of labor organizations is both inevitable and necessary for both labor welfare and national economic development (Millen, 1963; Galvin, 1962). In a recent study of Peruvian labor politics, Payne (1965, p. 17), a political scientist, found that urban industrial unions operated quite successfully through "political bargaining" with the national government, as opposed to the preference of American unions for collective bargaining with management and favorable legislation. This tactic, which involves political threats against the president of the country, rather than say, strike threats against employers, escapes the Peruvian structural disadvantages of an oversupplied labor market and relatively undisciplined rank and file union members. Between 1938 and 1961, the success of this method is indicated by the fact that the real income of organized workers in Lima rose much more rapidly than that of the unorganized. In addition, the organized *obreros* (blue collar workers) 1) realized a greater improvement than the unorganized *empleados* (white collar workers), and 2) achieved a rise in their real income even in the face of inflation (Payne, 1965, p. 19).

The "Exploitation" of the Agricultural Sector

In theory, all Peruvian *obreros* are covered by *Seguro Social* (Social Security System), but those in the larger unionized factories of Lima are much more likely actually to enjoy the benefits of those laws. The fact is that Peru's welfare legislation is so advanced that, if it were fully enforced, it would bankrupt the government and the economy. It is, thus, presumably inevitable that the rural and agricultural labor sector in Peru be disfavored in comparison to urban industrial labor (aside from the question of vertical class "exploitation"). Every industrializing country has exploited its agricultural sector in the objective sense that more wealth has been extracted from it than returned to it; Russia, China, and the United States have all capitalized in this manner.

The reasons for this universal "injustice" are worth recalling. Aside from any conscious desire on the part of vested interests deliberately to take advantage of others, there are more basic factors in operation which would suffice even if the economic and political leadership *were* interested in the general welfare. In the first place, persistently high rural fertility in the face of declining mortality means that the mass of the rural population breeds itself into even deeper poverty than it suffered at the onset of modernization. In areas which already have too many people and too little land, even where the land is fairly distributed, the labor market is being flooded with still more workers. This is not to claim that birth control alone would overcome their poverty, for much more basic changes in the social and economic system are also required. Such restraint would, however, greatly help those already overburdened with dependents. In the second place, only productive and efficient workers can effectively claim a rising real income. Such efficiency requires capital and efficient management, factors which the vicious circle of poverty make unavailable to the mass of Indians. It should not be forgotten that economic development also requires the population to become increasingly urban. While Lima is, of course, receiving more migrants than it can fruitfully employ, such a displacement of population is still inevitable; any force which holds more people on the land than can be effectively utilized there is holding them in poverty.

Land reform, in the sense of land redistribution, is central to this discussion. Its value in terms of the labor recruitment problem would be to hold more labor on the land and out of the overburdened cities. It also tends, however, to create a *petit bourgeois* mentality among the newly established peasantry, akin to the case of the Russian kulaks or the French peasants after

Napoleon's land reform, which can offset the political radicalism of the urban proletariat. In Bolivia, land reform reinforced the upward social mobility of the *campesinos* (peasants and other farm workers) and helped to bolster their loyalty to the M.N.R. governmental party after the 1952 revolution. The *campesino* militia served the M.N.R. government as an alternate source of armed support to that of the radical and intransigent miners' militia, and thus land reform helped to stabilize the Bolivian political situation.

In many ways, then, land reform is a deceptively conservative program, one no party line communist should support (Marx, 1898), although many do so. This is ironic in view of the fact that land reform is often seen in Latin America as a subversively radical program. In some ways, of course, it is, but one of its consequences might well be the stabilizing of existing political orders.

Again, if Mexico is used as a model, it becomes clear that land reform does not guarantee higher agricultural productivity, one of its important goals. In Mexico, the *ejidos* have not become a significant source of food for the urban areas, leaving it to the large, commercialized plantations to fill this need.

Land reform, then, viewed dispassionately, can perhaps "buy time" for a government harried by both urban and rural unrest, but ultimately, many persons persuaded to stay on the land, perhaps by land redistribution, will have to migrate to the industrial cities. Even the temporary palliative effects of reform will probably not be realized in Peru because, under the existing law, the sale of land to small farmers is so smothered in red tape and high mortgage payments to the large landowners that relatively little land has actually changed hands. It is likely, to be sure, that many of the new smallholders will default on their payments, and it remains to be seen whether the government will be willing to take the risk of evicting them. Also, possibly even the moderate redistribution now taking place will lead to some of the political, economic, and community organization long overdue among the rural Indians (see the papers by Domike, Huizer, and Barraclough in the present volume), and this may be its most significant long-run consequence.

CONCLUSIONS

In reviewing the history of the development of Peru's textile labor force, it appears that its recruitment was not characterized by many of the problems reputedly chronic in underdeveloped countries. Its gradual growth, largely in urban areas, and its relative protection from purely market-determined working conditions, by law and unionization, seem to be the predominant factors accounting for this ease of recruitment.

As for labor unrest, the predominant type has been "modern" rather than a simple battle of the new against the old. Nor is it the case that management is always more progressive than labor, as is often suggested by U.S. industrial relations specialists. Each side is behaving fairly rationally in terms of objective conditions.

While there is a great discrepancy in Peru between the official labor law and observable behavior, labor legislation has had a great influence on the development of the industrial labor force, at times with unanticipated consequences. The most striking recent effect has been the radical reduction in the proportion of women in blue collar positions.

The real enforcement of labor laws, however limited, has favored the urban industrial workers, leaving the rural workers as the disfavored majority. Land reform as an attempt at social justice *within* the rural sector, and between it and the urban, does not seem very promising. At best it can only "buy time" for a regime committed to a program of rapid urban industrial development.

NOTES

*The field research on which this paper is based was carried out in Peru in 1959 and 1965. See David Chaplin (1967).

1. The majority of foreign observers and many Peruvians seem agreed that a rapid development of manufacturing constitutes the only long-run solution to Peru's current demographic and economic problems. Their reasoning briefly is that the mechanization currently proceeding in the agricultural and mining sectors of the economy will offer little future employment to the rapidly increasing population, while manufacturing and "tertiary" services constitute the only alternative (other than a reduction in the rate of population growth which was not considered). See Pan American Union (1950, 1961), United Nations (1959), and Arthur D. Little, Inc. (1960). As will be explained below, manufacturing opportunities have also been reduced, leaving tertiary occupations the major area of expansion at present.

2. Briones (1963, p. 64) also observed the same ease of "incorporation" in his 1962 study of the Lima labor market.

3. Public Beneficiary Societies set up in the 1830's as an alternative to the church to receive property and manage charitable activities. They are today one of the major landholders in Peru.

4. Until recently, most foremen and managers were therefore forbidden to fraternize with their peers in competitive firms, a practice in keeping with the general climate of *desconfianza* but quite contrary to the early managerial traditions in England from which many of Peru's plant managers come. The "Lancashire System" in England involves a relatively free interchange of ideas between employees from different firms on the lower levels, on both technical and labor problems.

5. Cf. Anthony Leeds, (1964) for an excellent description of the operation of this same prebendary *patronazgo* (patronage) system in Brazil. Ratinoff (1965) generalizes Leeds' findings to all of Latin America. Although, like many of my Latin American colleagues, he manages to maintain an utterly abstract level of discourse throughout without once mentioning a single concrete case of his propositions, I believe that he had Peru and the APRA Party very much in mind.

INFORMAL AUTHOR'S SUMMARY: *CHAPLIN*

My paper deals with a somewhat unintegrated set of empirical findings and interpretations of a specific policy problem. The analysis is derived, first of all, from a study of Peru's textile labor force, about 4,000 workers in thirteen different plants in Lima, Arequipa, and Cuzco, and a survey of existing labor law and collective bargaining practices. I've also done a number of labor market surveys in Lima, going somewhat beyond what economists normally do, that is, investigating working conditions as well as job opportunities and recruitment. In particular, I was interested in various kinds of marginal, tertiary occupations, such as domestic service and prostitution, both being traditional services that have tended to grow in recent years, and are probably a larger percentage of the total labor force now than they have ever been before or ever will be again. These are occupations of last resort. Given a surplus of labor and the absence of any socially meaningful definition of unemployment (Peru unemployment is one percent!), there is no point in being "unemployed" if there is no place to go, and no one bothers to register as such.

The major general model I suggest (it bears also on the Leed's paper) concerns the meaning of the work role during the process of industrialization and modernization, particularly in the cities. What I find particularly interesting is that during the period of great instability between the breakdown of traditional occupations and the institutionalization of industrial occupations the salience of the person's occupation for his total social status declines sharply. This is what leads me to wonder about Leeds' finding that there is a work ethic in *favelas*. It may be there but I doubt that it functions throughout Brazilian society. My own experience is that placing a high value on work and identifying oneself in terms of one's occupation is something that I find Indians, peasants and some factory workers doing in Peru; they use the exact expressions that Leeds mentions, "a good day's work," "he's a good worker," and so on. But, as people become acculturated to the style of urban culture that we find in Lima, they lose this. They become *criollo*. They are more interested in sources of income than in occupations and they take on as many sources of income as possible. Now, what this means is that their occupational identity tends to become blurred and weakened. We can see this in the most extreme form when we meet somebody on a professional level who is likely to carry a number of different calling cards. Which one he pulls out to introduce himself to you depends on how he defines the situation. He may pull out the one that says Professor, or the one that's government official, or the one that gives his private industrial occupation. He may also be in the real estate speculation business or he may pull out his home card, that is, a fairly personal identification.

There is a dilution of the worker's identification with his occupation at this point, and one might generalize this to a model of the way in which occupation changes during the process of modernization from a pre-modern period in which one's overall social status determines one's occupation. For example, until not long ago in Peru, Indians had a caste status (although not as rigid as the East Indian sense), but we can now see that the trend is in the direction of the United States' form of occupational status in which one may identify oneself solely in terms of one's occupation. Between these two periods, we have a situation in which a person's identity is least determined by his occupation. This is especially the case in Lima because, as a person becomes acculturated to the kind of urban culture that Lima has, he mimics middle- and upper-class styles of life which are still leisure-oriented and in which it is quite acceptable not to have a job, but rather, income from any source. In that value system, if one can manage to make a living without having a job, so much the better.

There is also a growing counter-ethic, that one ought to have a recognizable job, but it is difficult to say which ethic is dominant today. It seems probable that the middle-class pattern of having a respectable job is the most common goal, although one is likely to make a strong effort to use one's education to get into the "more desirable" situation which is to have many sources of income and, in effect, retire early. Although they value the leisurely life, especially because of inflation it is difficult to achieve. There is also a shortage of skilled work so that the skilled workers are obliged to take on many sorts of work, not only because they want to make more money and inflation tends to reduce the value of the incomes they do have, but because if they have a modern skill, they will be asked to take on additional jobs. For example, the university professor will be asked to take on consulting work and government work; thus, skilled workers are pulled and pushed into diluting their single, concentrated professional orientation. I would, from my own experience, feel that a work ethic, anything resembling the Protestant Ethic, is to be found in the *lower classes*, and is a rural carry-over, and acculturation into the kind of urban culture Peru has meant the loss of this ethic. Eventually, they may regain it, but in the meanwhile, it is being lost.

Another question which deserves discussion is, "How urban are Latin American cities?" The fact that they are large and densely populated should not make us ecological determinists with the assumption that numbers of people have certain automatic consequences for social structure. I would argue that there are many important ways in which Latin American cities, say, Lima, are not especially urban.

In my paper, I also suggest that many of my arguments can be subsumed under the general argument in favor of urban concentration. The question is important because, if Latin American analysts agree on any one thing, it is that the primate city is a bad thing, stifling the growth of agriculture, causing smaller cities to stagnate and inhibiting economic expansion. Without wanting to sound like a functionalist who always finds a silver lining behind every cloud, it strikes me that the facts of Latin America show that the megalopolis has a number of advantages. I was particularly interested in the problem of a plant location. There is a school of thought which is dominant, for example, in India, which favors decentralizing plants to hold the people "out there." Part of the case for this lies in the rather conservative political orientation which holds that we don't want more people crowding into the cities and making trouble for the government. This thinking says that if we can keep them out there we can control them more easily, and the same kind of thinking now advocates moving the urban universities away from the center of the city and the Presidential Palace in order to reduce this source of trouble.

In the case of plant location, except in the obvious situations in which it is physically impossible to locate the plant in the city – a mine or a plantation operation – it seems to me that the kinds of plants likely to develop in Latin America in the near future, and certainly the consumer goods plants, would logically be located near their markets. Peru has two laws affecting plant location. One favors decentralization and gives plants a ten-year reduction of taxes if they locate at certain specified distances beyond the edge of the cities; unfortunately, the other says that if a plant is more than ten kilometers outside the city, it must provide a school, a church, and a hospital. In other words, it must build a city to go with the factory, which makes it absolutely prohibitive; as a result, there has been very little decentralization of plant facilities.

In addition to having production close to the market, another advantage of having the plant in the city is the availability of a self-selected group of workers who have largely cut their rural ties, thus allowing management to avoid the problem rural plants have of workers shifting back and forth between the factory job and their farms at harvest times and village celebrations, and because of family demands. In this connection, referring still to the notion of ecological determinism as it effects cities, I remain disturbed about the kind of technological determinism that underlies, for example, Manning Nash's (1958) study of the Machine Age Maya. In that book, he concludes that because workers came to the factory and stayed there, they had adjusted to the norms of industrial civilization. He seems to believe that if they are in the factory, the machines are running, and more or less production is taking place, it proves that the kind of community and family life there is, in fact, consistent with the expectations and functional necessities of industrial civilization. I don't believe that it proves any such thing! On the contrary, the local community swallowed the factory and it has, on the basis of evidence Nash didn't look into, the lowest productivity of any factory in Latin America, according to United Nations data. It has received enormous subsidies from the government throughout its life, and it is the only cotton spinning mill in the whole country. The workers adjusted to it because it adjusted to them. It met them more than half-way, and this is what is quite likely to happen to any plant in a rural location. If the plant does not adjust to the rural workers, there will be a great deal of conflict as, for example, in the mining situation where you have modern facilities; in that case, as in the United States, you find the maximum amount of conflict. Thus, the manufacturing plants that attempt to take advantage of cheap labor by going into the rural areas – their usual reason for such locations – find that labor costs much more than they expected.

On the question of legislation, it is common knowledge that the social and labor laws of Latin America are extremely progressive. Much of the credit must go to the International Labor Organization's suggestions on future directions of industrial and social welfare legislation which these countries have adopted in a relatively uncritical manner and which cannot conceivably be enforced because their costs would be so high. If the laws were enforced, it would mean that labor would be taken from a traditional paternalism to welfare paternalism in one jump. Of course, it doesn't actually work out that way because the laws are enforced in the larger factories in the larger cities where fairly strong unions are able to require that the laws be enforced, *at least for them*. The result is a highly favorable situation for the organized urban worker with a job in spite of high rates of unemployment generally. The labor market simply doesn't function clearly, although I would agree with Leeds that the city is the locus of the national labor market. I don't mean, however, that there is a fluid labor market in which people can shift from one job to another easily. The Latin American labor market is balkanized, to use the concept Clark Kerr applied to the United States; the American labor market has many barriers to easy moves between jobs, but there are even more barriers in Latin America. The workers who succeed in getting into the larger factories hang onto their jobs as firmly as possible, and labor turnover in such plants, as supported by my findings in Lima and Santiago, is much lower than in similar plants in Europe and the United States. In the smaller plants and in rural factories, the turnover rates are, on the other hand, extremely high.

One consequence of the enforcement of labor legislation is very interesting. I found that between 1958, when I first began work in Peru, and 1965, there had been a gradual elimination of women from jobs in the large modern plants. Labor legislation in Peru, framed to protect women, protects them so effectively that it makes them more expensive than men in terms of labor costs. Management realizes this, and beginning in 1955, when enforcement of the law began, fewer and fewer women have been hired. In 1965, I found a number of factories which hadn't hired a single woman in eight or nine years, and management reported clearly that it was because of the high fringe costs of maintaining nurseries, giving time off during the workday for nursing mothers and the half-day a week in which women are freed to take infants to the clinic, and the paid full-time leaves required just before and after child-birth. In addition, the unions have been dominated by men who made no effort to prevent this elimination of women.

It may be noted that something very similar happened in England, in the early years of industrialization, as Smelser noted in his study of the textile industry there (1959). As he found, originally whole families were hired and the husband was glad to have his wife and children with him. Later on, however, men began to view this as competition, and not simply as adding to income, and they fought to have them eliminated from the factories. The comparison should not be strained; there has been very little hiring of whole families in Latin American factories at any time.

The elimination of women from the factories is important because it pushes them back into traditional primitive occupations at a time when they most need to have jobs – the number of women with illegitimate children and broken families who have to support their own families is very large. I'm quite certain that this is closely related to the explosion of prostitution, a development which seems to be taking place all over Latin America. In Peru, it is regulated by law, and the women are required to have regular medical examinations. Occasionally, there are raids to cut down the number of streetwalkers, but the brothels are very well organized, and prostitution is illegal only for women under eighteen. (Until recently, the legal age for prostitution was twenty-one, but it has now been lowered to eighteen.)

One final point here, on labor-management relations. My research suggests that, unlike the situation elsewhere, in the Peruvian textile industry there was relatively little labor-management conflict in the early days and recruitment into factory work was not difficult. The amount of conflict is now increasing, and one of the points of conflict has been work loads. Whereas in the United States a textile worker may take care of sixty looms, in Peru until recently workers took care of from four to twelve looms. Under the Odria dictatorship, management was able to increase the work load somewhat, to twenty-four looms per worker. Under another military dictatorship, it is likely that management will again try to increase work loads, but my impression is that this is but a small part of the problem. More important would be the reorganization of firms and the rationalization of the textile industry. There are just too many small and poorly managed firms.

In short, the labor productivity issue remains a major unresolved problem in Peru, and it isn't at all clear how it can be solved.

DISCUSSION

LOPES: I should like to comment on Chaplin's paper, based on my own research. I've studied factories in Brazil, and my findings closely parallel his. My impression is that the ethic of hard work, where it is found, is a carry-over from rural life which disappears rapidly under urban factory conditions. When the worker begins to be an Economic Man, he begins to restrict production. I've found, however, that this is an individual matter, rather than the kind of group restriction of production reported so often for the United States. I found no sign of group restriction in Brazil. Usually, the Brazilian worker restricts production in order to get indemnities and this may happen even where, as in assembly-line work, the wages of other workers are affected. The other workers put no pressure on such workers at all; they just watch their fight against management. The man who slows down production is forcing management to fire him, after two or three years of work, just to collect indemnities, for example, unemployment insurance.

CHAPLIN: At this point, we must really begin to make careful distinctions between one Latin American country and another. Brazil differs from Peru in having a history of much greater paternalism in the development of its labor force, which has been organized from the top down. The Brazilian government manipulates labor unions, collects their dues, pays off the leaders it likes, and so on. The Peruvian workers organized themselves. Their struggle was considerably harder, but it resulted in their unions having greater independence, compared with Brazil. Of course, paternalism has not been entirely abolished in Peru.

LOPES: Your point is difficult to assess. At the factory level, the unions in Brazil have very little influence; they do not exist at the factory or plant level, and are almost "outside" national organizations, rather than organizations of workers in specific plants and industries.

In Brazil, the labor laws were an important factor in modernizing industry in the sense that when industrialists began to pressure to have the laws enforced, the laws effectively undermined the paternalistic organization, especially through their effects on traditional work norms and work ethics.

CHAPLIN: The labor laws, if enforced, make labor more expensive in Peru. But management didn't seem to see this soon enough, and by the time they realized that things were beginning to cost more and that they should modernize and try to eliminate extra workers, it was too late. So the pressure is there, it's true; these laws, theoretically at least, force management to become more efficient, but they do also enforce traditional paternalism in the sense that, although the government promises across-the-board benefits, pensions, and so forth, the owner is personally responsible for giving these benefits. More recently they have reformed this so that there is a workers' pension fund that does not depend on the worker staying in the same factory. Before, you had to stay in that factory, and if you left you would get a separation bonus but lose some of the pension rights. The reform of the retirement fund has opened up the labor market, and, particularly for white collar workers, this is a progressive change. But, before, even if the government had provided the benefits, the individual worker couldn't get them unless the company lawyer supported him. He was still in a paternalistic system. He wouldn't get into the hospital unless the company lawyer got him in, because the hospitals were overcrowded. Therefore, he had to stay in a company with which he had that personal relationship and which would take care of him even if the benefits were not provided by the employer, but by the government. He still couldn't get them unless he was in good standing with the boss.

LOPES: In Brazil, this situation is quite different in several respects. In the situation I studied, for instance, the paternalism was very pronounced, and the owners of the factories really controlled most of the local institutions and most of the employment opportunities. To the extent that labor becomes more expensive, tremendous pressure is put on the labor-management relationship because the owner just cannot afford to be paternalistic any more.

CHAPLIN: Doesn't it take the intercession of the employer to help the worker get those benefits?

LOPES: No. The way the law works creates power positions in the community that are not completely controlled by the local bosses and village chiefs. Thus, the labor law attacks paternalism in two ways. It raises the cost of labor, and it creates alternatives for the less skilled workers. They can go to the owner of the factory when they need help, as they traditionally did; but they can also go to other sources of aid that may have less power, but are more directly linked with the national level.

WHITEFORD: I would like to hear a little more about the matter of attitudes toward work. In recent years a number of studies of rural communities have indicated that the whole stereotyped conception of a person's dedication to his land, the joys and pleasures he derives from growing crops and getting dirt under his fingernails, was a more or less localized thing and certainly not a universal characteristic of the peasant society. Chaplin is saying that people may begin their work career in the factory, but as soon as they are able to move into the middle classes, their concept of work and of what will contribute to their personal enjoyment and status changes. At the same time, isn't Leeds saying that for the people in the *favelas,* there is a pretty definite conception of what is a day's work and pride in craftsmanship?

LEEDS: There's a very grave confusion in the reading of American models into other things, in particular the North European Protestant attitudes where there is an identification of job, occupation, and work. These are, in fact, three separable things and not identical at all. You can have an occupation, you can have a job, you can work. They may, as in the United States, tend to be identical. We tend to identify ourselves occupationally with what also happens to be our job, and we also tend to conceive of this as our work. In Brazil, these are very largely separate things. In fact, particularly in the upper classes, you will rarely talk about your occupation and job, but your work will be very important to you. Aside from the fact that, behaviorally, they all work like hell at all social levels, they really value this and have a pride in it. Sooner or later in any conversation they'll let you know that, in fact, they do work like hell, one way or another, but this is not identified with occupations as such. We tend to say, for example, "My occupation is a riveter in a factory." This gives one identity. The Brazilians are not interested in the fact that you're a riveter in a factory, but that you *do work* is a different thing. It's not important that the fellow is a riveter; it's irrelevant. For example, people may have multiple occupations, or multiple jobs, or maybe a single occupation and a number of jobs, or perhaps a single job in which they do several occupational kinds of things. But all this involves a tremendous amount of work, and the total activity is what they're concerned with, the work of doing things and getting things done, that is, the total productivity.

The primary thing, I think, is a man's productivity and creativity, but not that he is necessarily identified with a specific type of job. Furthermore, there is a parallel here to certain parts of the United States. I've worked in factories in the United States, and I'd say that many of the kinds of workers I've worked with don't identify with their specific occupation. I've worked with riveters who couldn't care less that they were riveters. They might say they were factory workers. They didn't have a particular work ethic at all.

WHITEFORD: There are two parts to my question. One is that individuals may take pride in being hard workers, in doing a good day's job. But, this doesn't necessarily mean that they derive any personal pleasure out of being riveters *per se*. This may just be the means to an end.

LEEDS: And it doesn't give an identity as such.

WHITEFORD: Right!

LEEDS: I think the identity question is rather critical. In other words, part of what I'm saying is that there are more sources of identity than occupation, and to say otherwise is to read American experience into these affairs.

CHAPLIN: I think we have a major disagreement here in the way we use models of other societies. I'm not trying to make the Latin American people behave in our way, but we do have to have a frame of reference. I'm saying, let's see *whether* they behave our way. Maybe they don't, but at least it gives us a way of looking at their behavior. Their work ethic is not focused on what we would call occupation. Leeds would argue that they have a work ethic that is focused somewhere else. How do you measure the behavioral consequences of their work ethic except by the way they perform what we call their occupation? By the fact that they're tired at the end of a day? How do you know the person has a work ethic if it is not focused on his occupation (other than the verbal way in which he says he admires people who work hard)? What does he do that you can observe that shows he has a work ethic, if it isn't focused on his occupation?

LEEDS: He invests in his house.

CHAPLIN: Yes, but if he works hard at his occupation, then there is a work ethic.

STANTON: He may not have an occupation in the sense that what he is doing this month is what he did last month. But whatever opportunity comes up, he tries to take it and work hard at it. What is the difference?

CHAPLIN: I think there's the difference. It is very true that the middle class is working like hell. They are spending an awful lot of energy. They're not really doing a good job for anybody at anything, but they are spending an awful lot of energy. A bank clerk is so tired at the bank because he drives a taxi at night, and he doesn't do a good job at that because he has accidents.

WHITEFORD: But he is working hard. He doesn't like it; he would much rather not be working so hard.

STANTON: That's another question, whether you're enjoying it while working hard.

PEARSE: Whiteford's question is interesting because there is a difference in the form of socialization. With people who work in agricultural communities, especially on family farms, the young man starts work with his father at about six or seven years of age. I guess that's where the socialization takes place. I should imagine that the approval of his devotion to work comes from the father. Presumably in the industrial situation, the reference group is a different one. It's not inside the father or family at all. It doesn't necessarily get through to the child in the socialization process. It starts as he begins to work or in some other circumstances. I think there is a noticeable difference in attitude between people who work within a family group and are socialized because they observe the mother and father, and those who are not present for those work activities.

LEEDS: Not only for the family, but for the whole community. Part of the verbal message as well as the behavioral message is not that they work in the factory at a specific job, but that they invest in housing and improvements. Work becomes a means to an end instead of, as in the American definition, becoming the end itself.

CHAPLIN: I would agree that they work hard at consuming.

DOMIKE: The conception of the importance of a work ethic is certainly derived from the American model or European model. I would like to point out that this may not be the critical variable, or even a very important variable, in determining productivity in a developing society. The work ethic is not so important there. If you're working hard at something that's unproductive because the structure of the factory situation, in this case, does not permit you to be very productive, why should you love your work?

CHAPLIN: I've said that management is mainly responsible for low productivity.

DOMIKE: My point is perhaps an extension rather than a contradiction of yours. The work ethic may not be a worthwhile variable to be concerned with when you are trying to understand the process of industrialization.

FIELD: Do you mean that it doesn't matter how the worker feels about his work?

DOMIKE: It may not make that much difference!

CHAPLIN: You could make him want to work harder, and it wouldn't help. They do expend an awful lot of energy, but they don't produce. The reason for that is the structure of the system. Therefore, in land reform, when farmers are given title to their land, they begin working very hard, and in the *barriadas* squatters who can get a title to a piece of property begin pouring their money and time into fixing up the house. If they don't get the title they don't put the labor in because it wouldn't make sense. They're likely to lose the value of their work.

BLAUT: Let me introduce the skepticism of the geographer who is not really a social scientist. There is a strange parallel between what is being said here about work in the factory and the kinds of things that have been said over the last twenty-five years about work in the peasant farm. We start out with a United States' model saying that if we put the factory down in Arequipa, we can just begin turning things out as though it were Elmtown. Then, we turn around and say, "Ah! But there's something mysterious holding back the productivity of these workers. They have all these looms, but can't or won't tend more than a few of them." Perhaps there's a third stage, where, without introducing hidden variables like the work ethic, you begin to find a certain functional interconnection among the parts of the system. For example, you may discover that the worker cannot tend forty looms because a certain tool that he needs to keep the things moving isn't there, or the oil isn't there, or the cotton is piling up. Basically, the way he operates in that situation is as efficient, in a strictly economic and technological sense, as is possible, given the nature of the system. This raises broader questions. What are the class relations between management and workers? This is the first point I want to make.

The second is that we've not paid enough attention to the factor of time. A work ethic comes over time. Pearse mentioned socialization as being relevant; he's talking in generational terms. Stanton mentioned something about people holding a job for a month and then having to turn to another job, which would probably involve having a different occupation. In other words, a man is working, but he is actually working either at a number of occupations at the same time (because he's not sure that any one of them will keep him alive, or he's not sure that any one will continue to pay), or he works at one and then loses that job. I can't see an ethic developing under those circumstances. You might have to have a man working for ten years as a riveter before he'll identify himself as a riveter. I don't think you'll find this type of steady employment at any class level in underdeveloped countries. I knew one man in Indonesia who had ten different jobs. He was basically, and wanted to be called, a university professor, and he supplemented his income at nine other jobs, four of which were illegal. But in that context, nobody objected because he had to stay alive.

CHAPLIN: The fact is, it would be very disfunctional and incorrect to say that we're going to improve productivity by giving pep talks so the worker will work harder.

FIELD: What about skill training? If the tool is missing, how is the worker involved in getting that tool, or doesn't it work that way? What about ingenuity, that whole set of things we sometimes think of as going with workmanship?

CHAPLIN: The reason management is in this bind on work load is that years ago, when they set the work loads up, labor was so cheap that they could get away with it. Or they were using a different kind of loom, one that looks rather similar to the present one, but actually did need more attention. They set the standards then. Since then, they have introduced new looms, many more of which can be managed more automatically. But the work standards are now set by law and will be hard to change. I think the work ethic is that people are willing to work hard if they can just change the structure of the work situation. Then the work ethic will focus on the occupation. But the structure doesn't allow it yet.

LASKIN: I don't understand the kind of criticism that is leveled academically at Chaplin's use of what we call an American model. I think the problem is that it's labeled as an American model. I feel the bias against using such a model is a more dangerous one that the bias injected by using it. We're studying industrialization and urbanization. Our cases of the most industrialized and urbanized systems happen to be the United States and the countries in Western Europe. If we're going to study traditional cases in traditional places where industry and urbanization might exist, then we have the right to hypothesize that the conditions concomitant with those which we find in more extreme or advanced cases might exist in newer forms. And just the knowledge that they don't exist, or exist differently, provides the basis for a comparative model. It is probably a very valuable working tool as compared to going into a situation blind, which suggests objectivity but really involves only a greater degree of ignorance.

CHAPLIN: There is a problem of generalizing from North American experience, that you confuse the particular with the general. That is to say, a unique institution arises in the American economy, for example, collective bargaining. There is no reason that other societies resolve labor-management relationships in our style of collective bargaining, and they won't do it. They believe in highly political unions (and this still distresses the AFL-CIO). In a general sense, there are labor-management relations in all countries, and there are typical issues that will be fairly universal.

BLAUT: This business of models is very important. If you criticize someone for using the American model, you're not criticizing him politically. The adjective, heuristic is relevant. The use of an American model or a Hottentot model by a social scientist makes no difference, providing he's a Hottentot in the latter case, because it implies that he has linguistic categories, perceptual categories, and a set of implicit theories that he will pull out almost automatically to apply to the particular situation. I grant you that going in absolutely naive is ridiculous and impossible. On the other hand, if you start out saying this is the best model around, and we'll use it as far as it will go, you will ignore very important variables. This is certainly true in the case of peasant farming. I'm sure it's also true in the analysis of factory workers. In terms of peasant workers, you see them using a tool and automatically say, "Inefficient: It doesn't fit my model. My model says a hoe must have a long handle." Your conclusion is automatic, by virtue of all the trappings that the model carries with it, the lenses through which you see the world, the theories that you are ready to apply to a particular case, the evaluations that you make without even realizing that you're making them. You simply distort the situation to fit the model. You cannot help doing so. There comes a point where you have to say, "Get rid of the models and start over. I'm going to avoid using the American model even though it seems useful in certain circumstances. I must start over and try to create a new one." This is precisely what we're trying to do with peasant agriculture now because the American model or any other model that we had available to us, including the non-economic anthropological model, turned out to distort the situation very badly.

CHAPLIN: I'm not calling for the use of the American model; I'm saying, use generalized social theory which have been derived from other societies, including the United States. You're setting up a straw man by saying the American model includes such highly specific points as the length of the hoe handles, and of course, if you're going to generalize like that, you will make mistakes.

BLAUT: Let me ask a specific question. When you went into that factory and counted the number of looms that a man was working, did you look for the ancillary tools? Did you look for the grades of oil needed to keep the machines working? Did you test whether a larger number of looms per worker would have somehow upset the output of the factory, or done something else? In a very simple technological sense, I'm not saying this makes it more basic; I'm trying to say that the application of the American model to a textile mill in Peru very likely prevents you from seeing variables that are quite critical in determining the productivity of the Peruvian worker. This would certainly be true if you were looking at a plantation worker or a peasant farmer.

LASKIN: Just as it would be absurd to suggest that in applying the model, one should look for exactly the same details that exist in the situation from which the model was derived, it is equally silly for someone to go down to Peru, and say, "I'm going to do a study – what's this?" As soon as you say that it is a factory, you are implying a great many things about it, and directing your own interests. Presumably you're supposed to look at this thing and say, "My goodness, What can this possibly be? I haven't the vaguest idea." That's also absurd. The methodology of social science is to be able to abstract from the empirical information that you have a correct model or a conceptual scheme, and try to see the variations and similarities in larger arrays of empirical situations. And the same thing applies to studying factories within the United States.

BLAUT: The same thing does not apply to factories in the United States! That's my whole point. There comes a point of cultural difference where you simply have to consciously say that it's better not to explain the situation than to start out with a set of distorting lenses that will give you the wrong answer, which is worse than no answer at all.

LASKIN: Wouldn't you agree, then, that this whole discussion has been misnamed by even using the terms "urbanization" and "industrialization," when such terms may distort what's going on in the rest of the world?

BLAUT: No! What I'm saying is that you have really linguistically to test out the denotation of the terms you use before you apply them. The kinds of models we're talking about here have built-in language, built-in concepts. I'm not at all anti-theoretic; I'm all for theory. I'm against naked empiricism in the sense that you're using one body of theory thoughtlessly, mindlessly, and are trying to apply it to something it doesn't apply to. It's better not to explain the phenomena at all.

WHITEFORD: I feel the same way as Blaut except for one thing. I agree with what you said about the unconscious models, but you can't get rid of them, you're always carrying them around in your mind. I think you're much safer, as Chaplin was, to work with a conscious model. At least you know what your assumptions are. You're testing assumptions that you've stated, and theoretically, at least, have written down. So they're subject to testing. The unconscious ones are the ones that are dangerous.

LEEDS: No, I think there are as many unconscious ones as the conscious ones you're talking about. This word, "productivity," for example, is used with the amount of work turned out per worker as the main concept involved. There are other conceptions of productivity that do not revolve specifically around work, productivity in interpersonal relations, for example, and which are also absolutely critical in the factory situation. There are other ends to be gained here which are productive and are exchangeable kinds of things. The moment that you introduce the usual definition, you prevent yourself from seeing them. I think that Chaplin failed to see this, and failed to see some of the integrations in Peruvian society.

NEEDLER: This is ridiculous!

CHAPLIN: They've got to improve productivity in our terms, or they've had it; that's it! If Latin America is going to develop, they're going to improve productivity as we see it.

LEEDS: You're applying American standards.

CHAPLIN: Absolutely!

NEEDLER: Aside from knowing about interpersonal relations in the factory, it would be nice to know if the factory is making money.

LEEDS: I'm not preventing you from asking whether the factory is making money.

NEEDLER: But you're criticizing Chaplin for trying to ask that question.

LEEDS: No, because he fails to relate the system of the factory to the whole society. I'm saying that there are other ends which are gained by the way workers relate to the factory and the factory relates to the workers. These are not being looked at in Chaplin's paper.

BIBLIOGRAPHY

Bendix, Reinhard

1956 *Work and Authority in Industry,* New York: John Wiley and Sons.

Blau, Peter M. and W. Richard Scott

1962 *Formal Organizations.* San Francisco: Chandler Publishing Company.

Bradfield, Stillman

1965 "Some Occupational Aspects of Migration," *Economic Development and Cultural Change,* Vol. XIV, No. 1, Oct.

Briones, Guillermo

1963 "Movilidad occupacional y mercado de trabajo en el Perú," *América Latina,* Vol. VI, No. 3, (July-Sept.).

Briones, Guillermo and Jose Mejia Valera

1964 *El obrero industrial,* Instituto de Investigaciones Sociologicas, Universidad Nacional Mayor de San Marcos, Lima.

Chaplin, David

1967 *The Peruvian Industrial Labor Force,* Princeton University Press.

Economic Commission for Latin America

1959 *The Industrial Development of Peru,* United Nations, Mexico, D.F.

Galvin, Miles E.

1962 *Unionism in Latin America,* Bulletin 45, School of Industrial and Labor Relations, Cornell University, Ithaca, New York.

Hall, Francoise

1964 "Investigación sobre los problemas de la interrupción del embarazo," *Servicio Social* (La Escuela de Servico Social del Peru), Vol. XXI, No. 19, (December).

Haour, Roger

1959 *Estudio sobre la modernización de la industria textil en el Perú,* United Nations Office of Technical Assistance, Lima, Peru.

Kerr, Clark

1954 "The Balkanization of Labor Markets," *In* E. Wright Bakke *et. al, Labor Mobility and Economic Opportunity,* New York: John Wiley and Sons.

Leeds, Anthony

1964 "Brazilian Careers and Social Structure: An Evolutionary Model and Case History," *American Anthropologist,* Vol. 66, No. 6, Part 1, December.

Leibenstein, Harvey

1957 "The Theory of Underemployment in Backward Countries," *Journal of Political Economy,* April.

Little, Arthur D. Inc.

1960 *A Program for the Industrial Development of Peru,* Cambridge, Mass.

Lizarrage, Jesũs Veliz

1957 *El Perũ y la cultura occidental,* Instituto de Investigaciones Sociales del Peru, Lima.

Marx, Karl

The Eighteenth Brumaire of Louis Napoleon, New York: International Publishers.

Millen, Bruce H.

1963 *The Political Role of Labor in Developing Countries,* Washington, D.C.: The Brookings Institution.

Moore, Wilbert

1959 *Industrialization and Labor,* Ithaca: Cornell University Press.

Palmer, Gladys

1954 "Social Values in Labor Mobility," *In* E.W. Bakke, *et al. Labor Mobility and Economic Opportunity.* New York: John Wiley and Sons.

Pan American Union

1950 *The Peruvian Economy,* Washington.

1961 *Informe sobre la integración económica y social del Peru Central,* Washington.

Payne, James L.

1965 *Labor and Politics in Peru.* New Haven: Yale University Press.

Ratinoff, Luis

1965 "Las clases medias en América Latina," *Revista Paraquaua de Sociologia,* Año 2, No. 4, Sept.-Dec.

Romero, Emilio

1943 *El pensamiento económico latino americano,* Fondo de Cultura Económica, Mexico.

Ross, Arthur M.

1958 "Do We Have a New Industrial Feudalism?" *American Economic Review,* Vol. 48, No. 5, December, pp. 903-920.

Siegal, Jeanette G.

1953 "The Measurement of Labor Turnover," *Monthly Labor Review,* May.

Smelser, Neil

1959 *Social Change in the Industrial Revolution,* Chicago: University of Chicago Press.

Ullman, Joseph C.

1966 "Using Turnover Data to Improve Wage Surveys," *Personnel Journal,* Vol. 45, No. 9, October.

United Nations

1951 *Labor Productivity of the Cotton Textile Industry in Five Latin American Countries,* United Nations, Dep't of Economic and Social Affairs, New York.

1959 *Analyses and Projections of Economic Development: VI – The Industrial Development of Peru,* Mexico City.

URBANIZATION AND THE INCORPORATION OF THE PEASANT

Andrew Pearse

I shall be concerned here with the relations between urbanization and the structural-cultural changes connected with Land Reform and rural development. "Urban" refers rather promiscuously to many different kinds of phenomena which are like one another in one respect (having to do with cities), but are difficult to group together in any sort of conceptual unity at a higher level of sociological generality. Perhaps better sense can be made of the phenomena by trying to find some explanatory principles about the persistent motors of the contemporary process of change in the agrarian sector, and that is what I am attempting. My observations are confined mainly to the peasant or smallholder rather than the estate sector, that is to say, to the rural population in which livelihood is gained by each family for itself by working the land to which it has rights of access, and most of my analysis will focus on Latin America.

The smallholder population has been characterized especially by its marginality which is almost universal despite marked ethnic, historical, and geographical differences. Moreover, within the agrarian structure itself, the estate has been the prevalent form of economic organization, and the occurrence of large zones occupied by smallholders usually signifies the non-existence or the decay of land and market conditions in which the great estate could prosper. Thus, the quality and location of the smallholders' lands are marginal and offer an indifferent basis for a competitive market agriculture because they are poor, unwatered, and hilly, because they are too small to allow much beyond family subsistence, and because they are too distant from a suitable market for their products. They are also marginal in the sense that the juridical institutions, elaborated for the regulation of large holdings, offer instruments which are much too unwieldy or otherwise unsuited for the regulation of small properties, and consequently give way to custom and illegality. Further, the smallholder is marginal in the sense that his participation in the general social system has been that of a dependent, powerless element, disposed of by decisions of others, isolated from the circuit of ideas current in the society by illiteracy, rudimentary transport systems, and cultural differences, and contractually inferior in his market relations. Finally, where he has been confined to "Indian" status, language and other cultural differences have furthered his exclusion.

Whatever his local situation may be, one of his obvious social functions in the national system during the last hundred years has been that of providing a labor reserve for the occasional or seasonal needs of the estates and the mines. Such relations exist, *within countries*, for example, between peasants in Northeastern Brazil and the estates of São Paulo, and between the Sierra peasants of Guatemala and the lowland plantations; and *across frontiers*, between the peasants of Chiloé and the sheep-raising *estacias* of Patagonia, and between the smallholders of the Santanders and the coffee farmers of Western Venezuela.

In the modern period, that is to say, since the end of World War I, the modernizing urban center of the society have been caught up in an accelerating process of penetration of these marginal sectors, exhibiting a drive toward the full incorporation of all such territories and peoples into the national society.

The motive force of this drive toward incorporation of rural populations originates in the centrifugal expansiveness of the national and international market-system which seeks out even marginal sellers of raw-materials and cheap labor; it draws further strength from the new place of the electoral system in the assignment of power, the natural expansiveness of institutions, and a generally positive attitude in the larger society toward the need for technological, social, and economic development, and to "achievement" as a value. The great alterations taking place in agrarian structure, and in the values and behavior of country people, must be seen as elements in a complicated process whereby the rural social and economic systems respond to these exogenous pressures.

The incorporative drive requires the intensification of interaction between the rural communities and the urban centers of the great society, made possible by improved transport and the circulation between country and town of people, ideas, and manufactured goods. It implies the direct attachment of local production, exchange, and consumption to the national market system (market incorporation), and the establishment, alongside of local customary institutions and traditional markets, of standard national institutions (institutional incorporation). It results in modifications and transformations of values and the cultural goals which are in harmony with them, and in modifications and transformations of the social structure of the rural neighborhoods and market areas, and of the structural relations between them and the larger society.

Models based on a chronological continuum running from isolated communities meeting most of their own economic needs to communities fully integrated in a national and international market system with modernized means of production are misleading. During the historic period in Latin America, there have alway been communities of families each with functioning productive organizations linked directly to consumers; but co-existing with them there have been isolated groups maintaining themselves with a minimum of exchange relations with local and national markets. However, for historical reasons, the market linkage of communities of small producers working in relative independence (as also of estates in which small producers were organized under compulsion) has been intermittent rather than continuous. The rise and decline of heavily populated mining centers, the development of new forms of transport, and periods of excessive demand in the metropolis for a particular natural product have been typical stimuli of market relations.

The present period is characterized by the rapid growth of cities, rising population, the general extension of transport, bring cheap, manufactured consumer goods and agricultural elements of production to the rural zones in exchange for money, and a much greater and more consistent demand for agricultural products. But, incorporation into the larger market system is partial, and does not lead to an evenly distributed economic development involving increased productivity, income, and capital formation.

The consequences of the incorporative drive depend on its strength and the internal configuration of the rural community. There is considerable evidence of the negative reactions such communities show to penetration by communications networks and offers of commercial relations, especially communities which have institutionalized a solidary system of collective defense against the larger society, including the defense of many elements of a local colonial subculture. Nevertheless, in the present paper we are dealing with the processes of change which are set off by such penetration.

Local semi-autarchic economic systems, in which direct exchange of labor and a variety of goods keeps the circulation of money to a minimum, are upset by the coming of cheap manufactured goods and the diffusion of machinery. Manufacture for home consumption, and informal arrangements for the exchange of labor fall into disuse. Money increases in importance, for the purchase of manufactured and processed necessities. As a consequence, there is an increase in the relative importance of commerce, transport, and credit, and of those who manage and control them. In general, total production does not increase, since both additional labor and technical inputs require cash or credit which are not available to the majority. The younger men are less willing to meet their obligation to work for their fathers in exchange for domestic subsistence, and there is more temporary migration for wage work, as well as permanent migration toward centers of urban and industrial employment. Thus, there is less labor available locally at busy times. Failing a really lucrative cash crop, the more accessible markets do not offer a secure and substantial return which could make possible a radical improvement in the local economy, and most families are obliged to cling to subsistence agriculture for security. The labor-force available is devoted to securing a harvest of cereal or potatoes which will provide for the basic food requirements of the family, plus other items the sale of which will provide the cash necessary for subsistence purchases the year 'round. A further obstacle to the commercial development of the smallholder's economy is the marketing mechanism. Because of the contractual inferiority of the peasant and the usual concentration of three commercial functions in the hands of single individuals (purchaser of produce, supplier of credit, and vendor of consumption goods), any surpluses developed by the little economy tend to be transferred to the middleman rather than remain available for reinvestment.

Full incorporation into the market would require the establishment of competitive commercial farms, which implies certain additions to the peasants' assets of land, labor, and traditional technique, for instance, access to credit, knowledge of improved methods of production, and the addition of some powered machines. It also would seem to imply a very difficult social transformation, namely, the abandonment of a life guided by a network of community rights and obligations, and its replacement by economically motivated activities in which neighbors and kin are manipulated like any other input. The traditional gearing of productive roles to family relationships must be modified by the submission of the latter to commercial exigencies.

Under these conditions, the commercial agriculturalist is not likely to emerge directly from the peasantry, since the accumulation of the qualifications for success, namely, technical know-how, credit, and commercial ability, can only be made during a period following escape from an occupational status which carries with it continual dedication to manual labor, and from a social status which carries with it a network of particularistic obligations within the community and contractual inferiority in relations with the market. The commercial farmer may be the peasant migrant who returns from an industrial or commerical occupation to lands already in the possession of his family, or which he acquires. He may be an outsider attracted by the productive and commercial opportunities of a community which are not perceived or not realizable by its members. Or, he may be a member of the peasant community who has been able to establish himself in commerce or transport, and has been exposed to urban socialization without necessarily living in the town. The outsider already lives within a circuit of ideas in which market intelligence and improved methods have currency, and he retains contact with this circuit even if he now lives in the rural community, though his rural neighbors are not necessarily able to "plug in" to it. And his economic behavior suffers little restraint or control by this community, since he retains his urban reference group. The other two types of modernizers will adopt free, competitive, economic behavior in proportion to the decline of their community obligations and the growth of their identification with town reference groups and other modernizers.

An alternate mode of change may be seen in which no commercial farmers emerge within the peasants' holdings, but in which entrepreneurs providing modern inputs associate with the peasant, raising his productivity but securing his dependence and taking the lion's share of his surpluses. In effect, the lot of the traditional peasant is tied to the decline in the relative importance of the factors of land and (unpowered) labor in the productive process, and the relative devaluation of recompense in respect of them.

The drive toward incorporation brings to rural neighborhoods and market areas a set of formally organized institutions (some a part of the state apparatus and some not) which are characterized by national standardization, conformity to urban cultural norms and developmental aims (such as schooling, public health, agricultural development, the provision of credit, and the education of adults), and mobilization of peasants in community organizations, as voters, in political associations, and in social and sports clubs. While market incorporation is a blind process in which individual agents and groups pursuing economic ends provide the motor, institutional incorporation contains a coherent goal, and is to some extent an instrument deliberately used by the state to fit the lagging peripheral subcultures into their prescribed roles in the national economy and society, though the degree of intentionality should not be exaggerated, however prominent are the explicit aims. Institutional incorporation offers partial alternatives and palliatives to the dilemmas of commercialization.

Education can be expected to diversify skills and prepare country people for easier acceptance of innovation. It undoubtedly facilitates the integration of migrants into the cities. The process of acculturation which accompanies institutional incorporation and the intensification of interaction with the larger society, diminishing the cultural differences between town and country people, also removes one of the props on which the contractual inferiority of the peasant is based. The implantation of the national institutions, organized at least formally on the basis of "secondary" relationships and standard norms, provides experience in leadership and membership in organizations through which local pressures may be exercised and local demands presented.

Development agencies offering credit and technical services can be expected to provide some alternatives to local monopolies. Co-operatives may lead to the strengthening of bargaining positions, and political participation may gain some attention for peasant interests.

The incorporative drive, accompanied as it is by an intensification of communication and the exchange of goods, persons, and ideas between the rural neighborhoods and the urban centers, puts on display, as it were, a series of alternative behaviors and orientations which may be adopted by the peasants. If they are adopted, they replace elements of the traditional local and particular subculture with elements of a national, standard, contemporary (though not necessarily "modern") urban culture, but at the same a new kind of dependence of rural social organization on the urban center is established.

The obsolescence of the local economic institutions which grow up around subsistence is accompanied by the decline of other social institutions belonging exclusively to the neighborhood, and a loss of self-containment and self-sufficiency. Exogamy becomes more general, and local leadership diminishes in prestige and effectiveness. The new institutions offer apparently more efficient means to the fulfillment of social goals. But, the status of the peasant in these new institutions is inevitably a dependent one since their management requires urban skills (just as entrepreneurship does), and the greater the scope of the decision to be made, the more remote and metropolitan is the locus of decision-making.

The forces operating to incorporate the smallholder sector into the national economy are differential in their effects, and lead to the counterposing of two groups, the new entrepreneurs and the traditional peasants. The entrepreneurs and the other groups in the rural neighborhood who have experienced the urban world and, also, are not dependent upon their own manual labor applied to the land seek to differentiate themselves socially from the remaining traditional peasantry. This is made possible by the increase in intensity of communications with the urban centers.

A new rural middle stratum begins to acquire identity, associating with the middle strata of the market town, and adopting behaviors and symbols taken from urban life. The values of the new rural middle strata are urban-oriented and sustained by urban reference-groups. Agricultural work and investment are justified by urban rewards. "Objective" justifications are found for the rejection of many traditional norms and disrespect for the traditional peasantry.

The expansion of the middle strata and the induction of the new institutions occur at the same time. It follows that the middle strata welcome the opportunity of validating their status by moving into the leading roles of the new institutions. This may mean that the use of the institution to demonstrate prestige or to exercise power may predominate over its dedication to its formal purposes. It almost certainly means the appropriation of the institution to the ends of this sector. Thus, the replacement of the traditional, peculiar, and local institution-set by the modern, standardized, and national institution-set is accompanied by the taking-over of the new authority-roles by the emergent middle strata.

With the growing importance of the national institutions and the decline of the local ones, the local solidarity based on a tightly-knit network of loyalties and obligations gives way to emancipation from local control, to the increasing isolation of the nuclear family within the neighborhood, and at the same time, to an increase in controls exercised directly over the community from the distant urban centers. The importance of the neighborhood as a community declines. The characteristic, unique status of the traditional rural person is replaced by the enjoyment of different levels of status in different sub-systems. There is a tendency toward differentiation and multiplication of social as well as economic roles. Action sequences which have been valued because they fulfilled the tradition are now valued as means to economic ends.

The traditional peasant's change of status is subtle and gradual, and is likely to be initiated when the pressure of the market economy renders the instrumental, technical, economic, and institutional means belonging to the subsistence system inadequate. Substitutes are sought, and in the new phase, attempts are made to reach and enjoy goals by the use of new techniques, changed productive and market relations, and the adoption of roles in the new national institutions.

The adoption of new techniques may sometimes take place without important social consequences, provided they are instrumental in reaching the desired goals, but the abandonment of the subsistence elements of the economy and the local institutions, and their complete delivery to the commercial system and the national institutions, is fraught with far-reaching consequences since both exact stern conditions. To play the role of agricultural entrepreneur in the new system requires technical and bureaucratic ability and access to credit on a considerable scale, assets which very few of the traditional peasantry are likely to possess individually or to dispose of jointly by collective action. The majority must be expected to suffer progressive decapitalization and more and more to assume the role of wage-laborer, either locally, in other farming areas, or in the cities.

In the incorporation process, there is a substitution of new institutional roles for old. The traditional local institutions allocated roles according to local criteria and a status system with a local apex based on local realities, such as the kinship situation, control of resources essential to the functioning of a subsistence economy, and special knowledge of lore and custom. The new national institutions are profoundly and systematically hierarchical, having their apex situated in the national capital (or beyond it, in Rome, Washington, or Moscow), and each one is a "status sub-system" in which the individual status is derived from bureaucratic and schooled skills (which have not hitherto been available to rural people), and the amount of power enjoyed in the general social system, in regard to which the peasant is inevitably placed at the lowest point in the scale. Thus, the new institutions, although they may aspire formally to equity in the distribution of rights in the new society, nevertheless offer to the peasant essentially dependent roles whose norms have not been adapted to local conditions. Under these circumstances, their performance is very likely to be "inadequate."

The new dependence of the traditional peasantry on the bureaucracies of the new institutions and the controllers of transport and the market takes the place of the former patterns of dominance exercised by local bosses, such as *caciques,* priests, and the big landowners of neighboring estates. The personal ascendence of the latter is replaced by the attachment of the peasants to specific organizations as clients.

Thus, the penetration of the rural areas by commercial relations and new institutions may be seen as a flow of action from the center to the periphery of the society, making for incorporation, but the reactions to it are varied and result in contrasting rates and forms of incorporation. It can be conceived of as the catalyst of a whole set of forces latent within the local, rural structure. Despite the differences between one situation and another, three general dimensions of change can be conceptualized, as seen from the point of view of the destiny of the peasant and his communities:

In the economic dimension – movement from family-bound production toward productive enterprises largely dependent on industrial inputs.

In the structural dimension – movement from membership in a neighborhood community marked by "structural peninsularity" toward membership in a national class-society.

In the cultural dimension – movement from territorially-defined cultural variety toward national cultural homogeneity modified by subcultural class-differentiation.

For traditional country and market-town people, change in each of these dimensions implies decisions leading to the free or forced alteration of behaviors, usages, forms of economic activity, and techniques, the acceptance of rules about rights and duties pertaining to the new relationships, and participation or deliberate abstention from participation in one or another of the institutions.

What generally operative principles can be adduced to explain why the traditional peasant decides to change his way of life? The answer seems to be that the alternative to changing his behavior is a deterioration of his already-poor condition as a result of the obsolescence of traditional techniques and institutions. At the same time, new means become available to replace them, and new goals come within the range, first, of his aspirations, and then of his expectations. This phase marks the passage from a static to a dynamic situation since the new "facilities," which offer an infinitely wider range of goals than were hitherto available, must be competed for. Competition for the appropriation of new facilities now takes place, but their distribution is different because the competitors are unequally equipped for the struggle. Not all facilities are scarce. Primary schooling is not a scarce facility; secondary schooling is. Land, labor, and traditional agricultural skills are widely held by the peasantry, while the "industrial inputs," credit, and bargaining power are scarce facilities. Economic differentiation is amplified in accordance with each family's potential for appropriating facilities. Those with the fewest facilities tend to provide labor-power, those with the most, entrepreneurial performance. What begins as a quantitative difference becomes a qualitative one.

A third stage can be discerned in which the two differentiated groups, at odds over the price of labor, access to land, and the monopolization of scarce facilities, take on the conformation of social classes, each embracing common symbols, seeking organized strength, and making common cause on a national scale. The new dynamic consists of the competition and conflict between classes, and the struggle for social ascent from one class to another.

The observable trends in rural living referred to as *urbanization* are, according to my system of prejudices, by-products of the process which follows a positive reaction to institutional and commercial penetration. "Townishness" is a coincidental rather than essential characteristic of the incorporative drive, at least from a sociological point of view, and our polar concepts are *national-local* rather than *urban-rural*.

In conclusion, Land Reform is an historic episode, and development programs are typical elements in the incorporative drive. Thus, the analysis of the relation between Land Reform and urbanization must be carried out within the framework of the foregoing incorporation model.

INFORMAL AUTHOR'S SUMMARY: PEARSE

My paper was written as a result of my experience in a good many neighborhoods of small peasants, and represents an attempt to find some central concepts and hypotheses for a general approach to social change in peasant areas, by which I mean areas of family agriculturalists. Actually, the communities to be studied represent a fairly wide variation from the point of view of their ecology, their situation with regard to the larger society, and their ethnic make-up. If you use the concept of modernization, for instance, you would have to say that Bolivia and Peru are at different points, while Canada, for example, represents still another point in a road which seems to be followed as the industrialization of a society hits the small agricultural producer. Thus, my paper is an attempt to develop some concepts which will be useful in explaining this process of change.

I should point out that I am speaking about only one part of the agricultural sector, that part which consists of land groups of family producers, rather than multi-family enterprises. I think it is possible to make a fairly clear distinction between these two systems. In my paper, I stress that the main stream in Latin America has been the seigneurial type of organization, with the smallholders marginal in many senses. The really operative point is that they are able to occur and persist where market relations do not develop; where market relations develop, they tend to disappear. When markets dry up, they tend to reappear. This point is overgeneralized, but worthy of discussion, and it's a principle I should be willing to defend.

Now, I'm taking the worm's-eye view in the sense that I'm attempting to look at a national problem from the point of view of the peasant. This, in a way, simplifies my task because I am able to find something which I can take for granted, namely, that whatever may have been the oscillations of market relations in the past, the intensifying of industrial development and the rapid growth of the nation have created a situation in the last twenty years in which the agricultural population is undergoing unceasing penetration from the urban sectors. Therefore, a constant that one can assume to exist is the drive toward incorporation, whether in commerical and economic terms, that is, buyers looking for goods and employers looking for laborers, or in terms of international charity organizations looking for recipients of parcels, politicians looking for clients, or government organizations looking for the possibility of ever-more posts to be filled, for example, in rural schools and post offices. This is an undeniable movement which everyone with Latin

American research experience is aware of. Conceptually, I've broken this down into commercial penetration and institutional penetration, noting also, that with these two forms of penetration, there is a continual intensification of communications between people living in the small and hitherto more isolated communities, whether in terms of ideas or the movement of people and goods.

Commercial penetration depends upon communication. It implies – as a dynamic principle which may be useful in explaining rural change – the intervention of market relations into a subsistence system. It typically comes about through the offering of cheap manufactured goods, which leads to the upsetting of the subsistence form. Many occupations become redundant; they are no longer pursued. Money becomes more important.

Incidentally, I should like to explain what I mean by "subsistence" agriculture. I mean situations in which families using their own land and labor produce in order to consume; this does not exclude market relations, but it means a way of looking at market relations. In a recent visit to a community, we were rather impressed by the contrast between the peasants who had three or four cows and used them for savings (when they needed to buy something, they sold a cow), and others who had a good eye for cows and, although they did not have many more cows, were businessmen, *comerciantes,* who went looking for thin cows they could fatten up. The latter were trying to accumulate capital.

One key to this situation which is often overlooked is the tendency for so many of the experts to speak about underemployment in the traditional agrarian sector; but the problem that the peasant will tell you about is not that, but rather the lack of labor *when he needs it*. That doesn't mean it isn't abundant; the point is, rather, that the younger members of the family come to want money for consumer goods, which means that they will not remain on the family farm, working for father and for neighbors on an exchange basis in the customary style. Thus, the unmarried, landless, younger ones tend to move out, and there is, in fact, a *functional* labor shortage in subsistence agriculture.

On the other side, that is, on the idea of institutional penetration, we find that new, national institutions are implanted in the rural situation, and they open up a series of alternatives which the peasant may adopt as a substitute for the malfunctioning subsistence system. The subsistence system no longer works, in particular, because the peasant can no longer get labor from his neighbors when he needs it.

The next stage after the beginnings of institutional penetration is a condition of differentiation. This is where sociological analysis tends to part rapidly from that of the administrator and promoter; the more one looks at it, the more one becomes convinced that the situation which has been produced is full of conflict and difficulty. In the new situation, one can't simply expect the efficient use of the new facilities introduced, say, by government, but something quite different. The scale of possibilities changes greatly, and a differentiation of productive role-sets takes place amongst the peasants. The old role-set was owner or usufructuary, manager, and laborer, all together. Now, you have a separation of property, and possibly management, from labor. I suspect that the critical element in whether you are going to be able to use the new facilities and become an entrepreneur, or are just going to improvise and do the best you can, continuing in a subsistence system, is the question of whether you have to invest YOUR labor in your enterprise. In the rural community, a line begins to be drawn between those who have to labor and those who are able to withdraw from laboring, and have others labor for them. When I speak of "labor," I mean the traditional usage. Driving a truck, for example, may also be called labor, but it is of a different kind, with a different economic value in the society.

To generalize the process, the factors of land and labor in the economic enterprise have an ever-decreasing value in terms of the total set of inputs in the productive enterprise. Thus, what takes place is an economic differentiation which leads to social differentiation in the rural areas as an alliance grows between the rural people who become entrepreneurs and the town people; these people look to the town as their reference group. The problem here is that your new institutions which offer a whole set of new roles (as presidents of committees, for example) appear just at the moment when there is a tendency toward differentiation amongst the rural people. Those who are developing entrepreneurially, and trying to break away from the peasant culture, are able to take control of the new institutions; for example, they become the Committees of the cooperatives which were set up to help the small peasants to develop bargaining power. Perhaps that's why such Committees almost never work.

In essence, I have attempted to conceptualize a process of social change, taking for granted an expansive quality in the national society. In terms of problems of urbanization, this line of analysis may also be useful in explaining what keeps people in agriculture and thus slows down the rates of rural-urban migration.

REALISTIC MODELS OF PEASANT FARMING

James M. Blaut

This paper will be addressed, not to the development of agricultural societies, but, rather, to the development of those who are concerned with such societies. In other words, I'd like to discuss the confrontation between development experts and peasants; in essence, the title of my remarks might be, "The Analysis of the Peasant Farm by Urbanized Aliens."

At the end of World War II, the so-called Age of Development began. Before that, very few researchers were interested in peasants or peasant societies. Since that time, a series of models of the peasant farm has appeared. After a period of use, or misuse, of each model, we discover that it doesn't work, scrap it, and develop another one. In broad terms, I would identify three phases. The first one involved taking certain reasonably live specimens out of our grab-bag of ideas about society in general and applying them to unfamiliar situations. For example, the concept of a farm *per se* was taken directly from the American context, revised a bit and turned into a model for peasant agriculture. It was superimposed upon the peasant setting under the unspoken agreement that we would act *as though* peasant farms clearly work by principles which we know to be relevant to American farming. Fortunately for the researchers, the very convenient phrase "all other things being equal" could always be brought in to explain why the model didn't work. In other words, when our conceptual models failed, we would say, "We knew all along that there were differences, but all we can do is work with the tools we have, the ones developed in Western Europe and the United States; if they don't work, it's because all other things are NOT equal." I'm tempted to call this the "tropicalizing" approach to theory-building. It resembles taking a raincoat produced for mid-latitude climates and modifying it slightly to apply to the tropics; it will undoubtedly prove to be uncomfortable, suggesting that what we need is not slight modifications, but a completely new raincoat suited to tropical weather.

This is not to say that the first model was not plausible. It did, after all, employ the findings of anthropologists, reasoning that tropical farmers could not be so alien as to resist all the blandishments that we, the developers and reformers, could offer in the form of capital, extension work, agricultural education, and so on. We further assumed that if only the programs were made massive enough, we could eventually force this model on the real-life situation. The results obtained proved to be very limited indeed, and highly local. Thus, within a decade after the Age of Development began, we began to notice that, in fact, food supplies were getting worse in some places. At that point, some of us scrapped the first kind of model and began to build a second kind.

The new model made use of variables which had previously been ignored or assumed to operate randomly under the *ceteris parabus* clause; for example, the value system, the kinship system, and community leadership. Instead of saying that, in the elementary sense, peasants all over the world are certainly farmers who, though they may differ from country to country, have many characteristics in common, there was a tendency to withdraw to what amounts to a *non-economic* model in which "mysteries" are substituted for variables. This might not have worked out so badly if it had been left to the scientists who would eventually have tested the model, but, unfortunately, the administrators who manage the scientists took over the model, and a whole new atmosphere soon surrounded development programs, based on the theory that the peasant farm is so mysterious and such a non-economic system that, in fact, it must be treated as one of the mysteries of life which should be ignored; in concrete terms, this amounted to administrative decisions to invest in other things. It was assumed that the peasant farm was not just slow-moving, but that it could not be moved at all. If that is true, it would seem a waste of money to invest in peasant agriculture.

This reasoning led to a search for alternatives; for example, by-passing agricultural investment altogether, and investing everything in industrialization in the hope that by some process based on an unbalanced economy, the agricultural sector would dissolve into the modern sector. Another alternative, would be investment in large-scale farming, or if family farms are necessary having them under the control of administrators as in colonization projects. Or, if we decide that we dislike the feudal form of farming organization common in Latin America, we may still try to invest in large farms in the belief that they, at least, have a chance for economic survival. All of these programs basically by-pass the peasant farm, and they were encouraged by the "anti-model" which says that peasant farmers do not respond to what we in developed countries think of as the normal stimuli to change. Unfortunately, this second approach has proved to be only slightly more successful than the first, and we have also come to realize that not only do the small farmers and farm laborers constitute more than half of the populations of Latin American countries, but also generate a large proportion of the total national product, something that is overlooked in the large part of the literature which assumes that subsistence farming makes no significant contribution to national production.

What is now happening is that we are paying more attention to modern anthropologists, "modern" in the sense that they no longer tell us that every culture is so different that no way can be found to fit them into the same model. Today, social scientists are beginning to build a new model of the relations between small groups and resources in which the content of particular beliefs and techniques is emphasized less than such general categories as cognition of the environment and boundary processes. We are now beginning to look for a model of the peasant farm which differs significantly from the two models noted above, and is neither a copy of the "developed country" model nor assumes a form of alien culture which bears no relation to what we know about farms in developed countries.

The new, third model requires much more analysis than I can give it here. It requires at the outset the re-evaluation of some of our most familiar terms, for example, "subsistence agriculture." The old idea that there is a sharp break between commercial and subsistence farming, with the commercial farm the one with which we are familiar and the subsistence farm a "bundle of mysteries" which does not respond to market forces, is now being revised. Sociologists in Western countries have come to pay more attention to the non-economic variables underlying economic behavior; by the same token, the economists, anthropologists, and geographers in looking at subsistence systems are beginning to discover that the motives in subsistence production are not so very different from those which motivate commercial production. We are also getting some hard data to suggest that subsistence farms are not as isolated as we had supposed, and that they probably market, on the average, half or more of their produce, although they may not purchase large amounts of inputs. It is also being recognized that there is no clear division between the traditional subsistence production and modern, commercial production; the division seems to be largely a reflection of the number of restrictions which tend to prevent the subsistence farmer from moving fully into the commercial sector.

In addition, new questions are being asked about the efficiency of peasant agriculture. The experts are beginning to look at such farms as ecological, land-using systems, and finding that, given the set of constraints, which do not lie largely within the farm or even within the value system of the farmer but in the milieu, the peasant farm is a very skillfully-integrated entity. In economic terms, any major shift by the individual farmer in his allocation of resources would not make sense given the existing constraints; in geographic *and* economic terms, we find that the productivity of labor is essentially maximized and the methods of conserving soil tend, given the constraints again, to be quite efficient. The tendency among planners is to focus more and more on those constraints which are societal, and less and less to ask what can be done in the way of educating the peasant farmer or trying to motivate him to change. Our attention is turned now to questions of what can be done about the market system or the class structure of the region; that is, factors in the milieu, rather than about the peasant and his behavior and values. One further question concerns the so-called ignorance of peasant farmers; one striking finding in research is that it is absolutely essential to our scientific analysis of the peasant as an ecological unit to make a distinction between the kinds of technical skills a farmer has or knows about and the technology he applies. We now know that there is a wide gap between these two. Thus, in most areas, the thing that would probably produce the least return on investment would be extension programs trying to teach the peasants about farming. We find, instead, that the cognitive element, what the peasant knows, is not used because conditions in the social system prevent him from using it. We find that farmers do not apply particular practices for very good reasons; the reason may be, for example, that if they invest in fertilizer, the risks of their losing are high; that is, they may face greatly increased problems of marketing the additional produce at reasonable prices. What I'm suggesting, in general, is that we're beginning to evolve a new model of farmers in developing societies, one which gives to the farmer what is due him in terms of his skills and concentrates on the society as a whole as the nut which must be cracked in order to organize agrarian development.

Essentially, what I've done here is suggest that it is becoming more and more difficult to find large-scale examples of what we usually call traditional, isolated farming. I want to note, however, that this particular model can be carried too far if one goes off into the ecstacies of theories about the dependent status of peasant farmers, something which much of the recent anthropological literature does! It is obviously a mistake to think of peasants as "laborers in the rural area" without any degree of incorporation into national systems, without any rights in land-use and tenure, any expectancy of permanence; if we were to believe that, we would have lost sight of reality. What we are dealing with is an open system, not an absolutely closed traditional unit, nor on the other hand, even where farmers have to give up half their produce to the *hacendado,* are we justified in speaking purely about "factories in the field." In brief, peasant farming *does exist as an entity.*

DISCUSSION

DOMIKE: One of the most important topics raised here concerns the transformation of traditional agriculture. The question finds us still struggling to provide a comprehensive description of what agriculture is as an occupation and a way of life, and struggling even more with the problem of finding the most effective means of modernizing agriculture in the less-developed countries and understanding the social effects of various changes. Pearse has concerned himself largely with problems of smallholder communities, while Blaut has spoken about the plantation kind of economy or what Pearse refers to as "estate agriculture." We shall certainly need to consider the different requirements of agrarian reform and reconstruction in these two types of rural economy.

LOPES: Blaut has made the point that the peasant subsistence system must be seen as part of a larger social and economic system, rather than in isolation, and I would agree. I would add that both the *hacienda* and the peasant smallholder systems must also be seen as combinations of farming and manufacturing activity, although the latter is frequently at the handicraft level. At the subsistence level, many of the inputs into farming are hand-made or performed by hand. The modernization process consists of introducing a much more complex division of labor in which, for example, the production of farm tools becomes more specialized, and many farmers stop making their own equipment and begin to buy or trade for them. An important research question concerns the permanence of this more elaborate division of labor. My impression is that the process is often reversible; when the market is good, farmers spend less time on this sort of manufacturing craftsmanship and more on crop production, and when the market declines, they revert to making what they need by hand again. It would be interesting to know when modernization is and is not permanent. The example that comes to mind is in the southern part of Brazil, the Rio-São-Paulo area, where the plantation system for producing coffee took over from a previous subsistence agriculture system. This represented modernization of a kind, in that production was much more specialized and efficient. However, when coffee production began moving west, there was a revival of smallholder farming, some of it at the subsistence level, supplying food for the urban markets. However, the previous handicraft skills were not revived, and these farmers now depend on the factories, mostly located in urban areas, for tools and other inputs.

BLAUT: In order to discuss this properly, we need at least two separate models for Latin America. In one case, there was a pre-existing peasant form which a conquest state had essentially wiped out in favor of a European "feudal" system. When a shift takes place from smallholder to plantation farming, there is almost always a total loss of handicraft skills. What isn't clear is whether, where plantations are broken up into smallholdings, the farmers learn or re-learn the crafts necessary for making tools, equipment, and personal articles, or remain dependent upon trading and commercial markets.

LEEDS: What Lopes describes as an oscillation between subsistence and plantation agriculture is deceptive because he has, in fact, described an evolutionary situation, that is, a subsistence type of agriculture supplanted by coffee, and in turn supplanted by what looks like the previous form of subsistence agriculture, but is in fact oriented entirely differently in the total institutional structure of the culture. You never get a complete reversion to a previous system because, for example, in the intermediate situation all the folkcraft is lost, and such things can never be reconstructed suddenly and out of nothing. These things are lost permanently. Once certain relationships – social, cultural, technological – are lost in a shift, say, from subsistence to latifundian agriculture, they are lost permanently, and they are never revived even with a shift back to smaller farm units.

PEARSE: I think that we have to try to visualize the situation in which there is large-scale commercial farm and, alongside of it, vestiges of smallholder farming. In some cases, a man will farm his own plot of land and also work seasonally on the nearby *hacienda* or in a factory even at some distance from his home. This situation is likely to persist indefinitely.

LEEDS: That's undoubtedly true, but the point is that such smallholders are very different from those we find in full-blown peasant societies.

BLAUT: These questions come up all the time when we find ourselves in the role of advisors on agricultural development. Until very recently, most of us assumed that the Western model of agricultural development could and should be applied all over the world, and we advised peasant areas to take up extension services and hybrid corn. I think that we came to reject that model not so much because the condition of the peasant changed (there hasn't been that much change), or because our knowledge of rural areas became more sophisticated, but rather because of the institutionalization of development itself. Development programs have been taken over by the elites of the various countries, and the international development agencies have come to have very close ties with those elites. This has led to a frequently-unnoticed accommodation of development philosophies to the political and social *status quo* in these countries, symbolized, for example, by the fact that architects, engineers, and businessmen tend to move into leadership roles. People who wanted to maintain the *status quo* and had backgrounds in urban professions found it comfortable to say that the peasant farmer should just be ignored, and to develop theories to rationalize that view.

LEEDS: If you're saying that none of the models of peasant culture presently available is much good, I'd agree with you. The models have been improved, but it's still true that there isn't much resemblance between even our best models of peasant societies and what you see when you actually go out and look at real peasants. One of the problems is that you don't usually find smallholder and large-scale farming operating independently in an area, but rather, the subsistence farming will be tied into commercial operations. In the cocoa area of Bahia, where I spent a year, I found that the plantation workers were also carrying on subsistence farming on their own plots. They are wage workers, and not subsistence peasants at all in any traditional sense.

PEARSE: The question of the availability of rural labor has been raised here several times, chiefly centering on the apparent discrepancy between statements about rural unemployment and the low productivity of farm labor on the one hand, and the shortage of labor on the other. This is really a question of timing. Under the subsistence system, much of the year there is a good deal of routine, economically-unproductive activity, but when the sowing and plowing actually take place, all of the available labor power is put to work. A week ago, I was talking to a group of small peasants who are about twenty-eight kilometers from a very poor town with poor transportation facilities. They figured out that they need about twenty-six to thirty quintals of wheat for their subsistence, that is, to keep in the house and have, and this was very important to their security. This has tended to go up as they become more dependent on the local market for their needs. Producing this amount of wheat requires nearly two hectares of land and about sixty-five days of labor with oxen. They complained to me that if they had had one or two more people to work their land during the short time they have for plowing and harvesting, they could have produced more and gotten more land into production.

BARRACLOUGH: There is no question that under present forms of farm organization, there is often a labor surplus during most of the year and a shortage at peak periods, but this is not inevitable. My office has developed hundreds of specific farm plans in which we have used present technology, present capital, and present farming techniques, but changed the organization of the farm and, to some extent, what is grown, and have greatly increased the income from the farms on which these plans have been tried. The point is that the labor can be used differently and more efficiently.

FIELD: My impression is that farm labor is highly redundant in many underdeveloped countries, not in the sense that much of the labor force is idle, but rather that the work is unproductive. Pearse has pointed out how it is possible to have a surplus of labor at the same time that those who need labor can't get it, and his explanation is that they can't pay for it, either in cash or in labor time returned through a cooperative arrangement between families. The question nevertheless remains of how the rural population gets enough to eat if it is unemployed, or so unproductive. More, precisely, why is the price of labor not driven down to the point at which peasant farmers can get the labor they need?

BARRACLOUGH: Many years ago, Keynes disproved the theory that a labor surplus drives wages down to the subsistence level.

BLAUT: Supporting Pearse's argument, I might cite some good studies, one on Jamaica by M. G. Smith, where you have the admission that there is labor redundancy in some seasons and a shortage in others, and this type of analysis has been carried forward to the point at which it is shown that as population density increases without technical changes in agriculture, there will be more and more seasonal unemployment.

BARRACLOUGH: Let me offer some concrete examples. First, an extreme case of labor surplus. I spent a morning watching about forty-five people harvesting a half-hectare of potatoes. They had already been at it for three days. I was brought up on a farm on which we would harvest that many potatoes on a Saturday morning. But, someone there explained to me that the use of all those workers was a distributive process; it was the only way available to divide the product without fighting about it, and everyone was allowed to pick a part of the crop. This is not an uncommon example.

In Chile, on the farms which have been expropriated, we have some studies now of labor use. Whereas previously the peasants worked very small plots of land and gave some labor to the large landowners, they were now able to plow and plant much larger pieces of land. Production had increased at least 400 percent, and the use of labor had doubled because the land and labor were being used much more efficiently.

In Cuba and Puerto Rico, which are different but have some characteristics in common, you have real labor shortages at harvest time, but this does not contradict what I said before. In both cases, there were fundamental changes in the economic structure. In the Puerto Rican situation, there was an out-migration of many workers to New York, but also agriculture has become very much integrated into an industrial economy. In the Cuban case, the government deliberately used planning to create many new jobs in public works and industry. In both cases, it required major structural changes to reduce the rural under-employment. Unless one is willing to make these changes, the labor surplus problem is going to be with us for a long, long time.

STANTON: There is an interesting contrast between Hawaii and Puerto Rico. In Hawaii, sugar production is much more mechanized, and the development of other industries has made possible the virtual elimination of seasonal unemployment; the Puerto Rican sugar industry is much less mechanized. Part of the explanation is that the organization of Hawaiian sugar workers into unions stimulated management to introduce mechanization wherever possible. In Puerto Rico, where there wasn't the same unionization of sugar workers, and therefore, less pressure on management to reduce seasonal variations, some of the capital that might have gone into farm machinery has been invested in industry instead. Despite the shortage of labor in the cane cutting season, most laborers now tend to be older men, with very few of the younger men. The younger Puerto Ricans would rather be unemployed than take a job that lasts four months.

I don't think that it's uneconomical to operate that way, that is, to make do with less mechanization in sugar, in terms of world sugar prices. However, it may be more profitable and less risky to invest in other industries.

BARRACLOUGH: There are many institutional arrangements possible in developing countries and each one has its own particular level of labor demand, with its own pressure on the rural population to migrate, seasonally or permanently, to urban areas or to other rural areas. Basically, assuming that economic development does take place, there are two ways in which the rural population can share in the rewards. One would be that the demand for labor would increase so much that wages would go up; I'm saying that this won't happen for a long time, if at all. The other is that, through structural change and political reorganization, the workers and peasants can organize to demand a larger share of personal and farm income.

CHAPLIN: Domike, among others, has written about the importance in the development process of keeping as much as possible of the rural population on the land. There are very real problems which accompany rural-urban migrations; it puts an added burden on the modern sector and depresses its rate of growth because of the necessity of providing at least minimum services and social overhead capital, and it is likely to increase political instability. In other words, rural development has benefits beyond the increase of food production.

BLAUT: You are quite right in saying that there has been much talk about the importance of keeping the farm population in the rural areas, but I don't know of any plan that has succeeded in doing that.

BARRACLOUGH: We do know that the exodus from farm areas can definitely be slowed down by agrarian reform, as it has, for example, in Chile, and the same thing has happened elsewhere. It won't *stop* out-migration, but its ability to slow down the movement is crucial, especially until fertility rates can be reduced.

When you consider the actual process of economic development in Western Europe, you find that there was agrarian reform in some countries, but not in others. For example, you certainly didn't find it in France or England (in the sense in which the term is used with reference to Latin America). Nevertheless, the presence or absence of agrarian reform has a great influence on what the society looks like during development, including its political character.

STANTON: I quite agree, but I raise the issue because many of the plans for the economic development, say, of Latin American countries, which are coming out of the United States assume as desirable such things as the strengthening of the family farm. This was relevant and important in American history, but is probably much less significant or useful in other parts of the world.

STANTON: It's true that much of the agrarian reform effort is directed toward keeping people in the rural areas, but there's no question that we need at least a seepage of labor into the cities and towns. That was certainly necessary in Europe and the United States as part of the long term growth of industry. In the short run, of course, such serious problems as *barriadas* are included in the cost, but in the long run, there has to be substantial rural-urban migration.

BARRACLOUGH: One of the interesting questions concerns the extent to which landlords, prior to agrarian reform, try to keep their *peones* on the land, but afterwards make efforts to expel them. A good case can be made, using Mexico as an example, that the *ejidos* served as a kind of cold storage reservoir of labor that could be released in a somewhat more orderly fashion. We see this everywhere now in Latin America. Any modernization or unionization of the *haciendas* leads to the expulsion of labor.

DOMIKE: This raises the point that there is a definite difference between the smallholders and the estates in the way in which they hold labor. The smallholder absorbs the labor that is not attracted elsewhere or can't get out; the ones who get out, of course, are the able-bodied who can get to the city and survive there for a while. In a sense, then, the smallholders have the role of holding the labor that isn't attracted away. On the other hand, the estates take very little responsibility for this. Except in the most paternalistic settings, they don't take on the role of absorbing labor as a matter of family responsibility. Therefore, one cannot speak of agriculture as having a uniform pattern of labor absorption. This mistake led to some of our difficulties earlier in the discussion; that is, we were treating the various forms of agricultural organization as though they were all the same. Even noting just these two patterns, the smallholder and the *hacienda,* should make us wary of easy generalizations. In general, agrarian reform is, in fact, intended to stop or slow down the rate of out-migration during the period in which, presumably, steps are going to be taken to build up the industrial base.

PEARSE: It must be emphasized that land reform works quite differently in different places, and it might be well to consider three examples of different stages in the operation of land reform. The first concerns Bolivia, where the market relations to the city involve the farmers' taking their produce directly to the city and marketing it there. Land reform broke this marketing link completely, and within a short time, the peasantry had to improvise new kinds of markets. What resulted was small, local markets which amounted to an interesting form of urbanization. In Bolivia now, you'll see peasants building towns, usually on the edge of the old *hacienda* lands, which may amount to twenty, thirty, or forty two-story houses. They are doing this mainly in order to catch the transport to the market, and also because previously they had been forbidden to enter the society culturally; for example, they were told to go on wearing peasant clothes. Now that they are permitted to enter the society, this town-building is also a way in which they become "civilized."

If we go to a smallholding area in Chile, we find that supporting services come in to help with marketing, and we also find buses coming in on a large scale. The produce is no longer going to the local market at all, but in all cases I've seen lately, it takes the long jump to the regional markets. Instead of being linked to the local town, the peasant now goes once, twice, three times a month in a bus to the large town with population of 50,000 or more. In the third example, if you look at the marketing structure which has been effected by the land reform of the *haciendas,* you'll find a much higher level in the process we've been discussing, in that the peasant is in alliance with a bureaucracy of specialists who operate marketing through a national organization where decisions are made right at the center, where prices are fixed, and so on. It seems to me that it's no good trying to talk about land reform and retention of labor unless we take into account the fundamental variable of the penetration of urban markets into rural areas on which my paper focuses.

BLAUT: That doesn't quite answer my question. It seems to me that we may need a model (many anthropologists have insisted on this) of the "unmodern" *hacienda* system. In terms of the European example, it is clear that the peons were prevented from going into the city until the system began to collapse. Now, when you have capitalization of land, the sort of thing that happened in Argentina, which seems in many ways to imitate the process that took place in England, just the opposite takes place. There is a shift in the calculations of the *hacendado,* and he now wants to get rid of the excess labor, and rationalize his operation. If the unmodern *hacienda* is reformed, will there necessarily be a release of labor as part as the process of change?

CHAPLIN: You get the release in the second stage of the land reform. In the first stage, the small farmers try to hold their land, but then a reconcentration of land ownership begins inevitably, as some farmers are more successful than others. I would also guess that reform has a tendency to increase fertility as people marry earlier because they have land of their own. The process of population growth defeats the division of land. Some do better than others and buy them out, and one sometimes sees legal battle in which land reform agencies try to prevent the peasants from selling their land, in order to keep them on the land or to protect them from being victimized. On the other hand, many of the peasants want to sell their land so that they can clear out and go to the city; thus, those who remain have larger pieces of land and can operate more efficiently. This "recollectivization" of land seems bound to occur. The plots of land distributed prove to be too small, some farmers show more managerial ability then others, and so forth. Even if this process takes place, it can be valuable if the government has made good use of this period of time, and planned it so that those who leave the land have places in the towns and cities which are prepared to receive them.

IV

ISSUES IN URBANIZATION

Urbanization, the growth of city populations in absolute numbers AND in relation to the total society and the spread of secular, scientific, and materialistic values, is a universal phenomenon, a characteristic of modern times which seems to proceed by its own irresistible dynamics.Its pace reflects rising rates of natural increase in the cities (the result largely of improving health conditions), the pull of rural populations toward the cities for jobs, welfare services, and social mobility opportunities, and the push, because of hunger, land shortages, and traditional oppression, from the countryside. In short, ours is the Age of the Urban Revolution. Part IV treats some of the issues.

Historically, social scientists first approached urbanization in the Third World by comparing it with what appear to be similar changes experienced earlier by the advanced countries, those which long ago moved into self-sustaining economic growth, but this has recently come under more and more furious attack as a view through badly distorted lenses. The critics are troubled most by two assumptions, (1) that the rural backgrounds and continuing rural ties of many urban residents set them apart as a category completely separate from the city-born populations, and (2) that the favelas and barrios of Latin America, the poorest urban quarters, made up often of squatters and recent arrivals from the country, have the same characteristics of personal isolation and social disorganization claimed, say, for American slums. That there is a measure of truth to these generalizations is accepted here in the essay by political scientist, Martin Needler. However, it is the attempt to counter them that provides one of the main themes of the highly personal account by the husband-and-wife team of Elizabeth and Anthony Leeds of their experience in the "squatments," (to use the term they prefer), of Rio de Janeiro and Lima.

The Leeds's arguments are instructive in several ways. First of all, they approach their data in terms not of the universal models of slum and transitional areas which tend to be derived from European and American evidence, but in their own context, that is, as they fit into the particular political and economic structure. This leads them to see that what appears to the outsider (and the social scientist using the models found in American textbooks in Urban Sociology) as unproductive and often absurd behavior, for example, buying a refrigerator for a hovel that lacks even running water, can be a sane attempt to cope with a difficult environment when it is used to make ices for sale. Further, rather than take the word of "informed" Rio residents that the people "down there" in the favelas live like animals, the

Leedses lived in several of them and found a surprising amount of organization and adaptation to the poverty, confusion, inequality, and lack of opportunity of the city at large.

What requires attention about Latin American squatments, aside from the necessity of refuting the common mythology, is the question of why the myths are so pervasive and so readily believed. The three-fold lesson here applies equally to the United States and Latin America; people believe the mythology of poor and lower class neighborboods because they WANT TO BELIEVE IT, because they are seeing with the selective perception of middle class eyes, and because they have little or no conception of the total social system within which they and the slum-dwellers live. People with diplomas and secure jobs see those living in tar paper shacks as combining bad habits and lack of ambition, and have difficulty believing that in Brazil (or, for that matter, in the United States) there may simply not be enough jobs or decent housing units to go around. Perhaps they will be even more disturbed by the Leed's evidence that many people, including some with ample means to live elsewhere, live in favelas by choice. It is another question, of course, whether the culture of the squatment can be defended in its own right or only as rational adaptation to bitter necessity.

The Leeds's essay provides a wealth of evidence on such topics as the characteristics of rural-urban migrants and the processes of adapting to urban living. What stands out is how much more complex reality is than simple models and categories would suggest. None of the usual definitions in the social science literature seems to survive empirical test. The rural population, whose migration provides much of the urban growth, is made up not only of isolated and primitive farmers and hunters, but also of people living in large villages and market towns, some who have lived in cities, worked abroad, served in the army, others with relatives, friends, and business connections in the city, and many with skills in business, repair, and personal services which are also useful in the city. The squatment population is not made up only of society's failures, but also of people (often newly arrived in the city) preparing for jobs that will eventually enable them to improve their favela housing or move out, fully-employed people responding to the pressures of rampant inflation and the suffocating red tape that surrounds land ownership and construction, and people who can afford to live elsewhere but enjoy the freedom and prestige they have in the neighborhood. Similar examples could easily be multiplied from the Leeds's analysis.

From the point of view of social theory, the Leeds's essay is disconcerting. Their evidence casts serious doubt on many of the generalizations in the literature about the universal hopelessness and lack of organization of transitional and low-income neighborhoods; in their place, it offers what might be called an indeterminate, social systems model in which one can only evaluate behavior in terms of societal context. Unquestionably, describing behavior in its specific setting is indispensible to fully understanding it, but it provides little basis for prediction and theory. What they do, rather, is force our attention TOWARD the structural problems – social, economic, and political – of the larger society, and AWAY from value and psychological explanations. This is in contrast to Needler's analysis of Mexican urbanizations which concludes "that Mexico will continue to find its greatest obstacle to the achievement of full and stable political development in the problem of developing and strengthening democratic CIVIC ATTITUDES. . . . It is likely that ATTITIDES engendered by the life-style of the urban poor are dysfunctional for political modernization." (Emphasis added: AJF)

The two essays in this section disagree in other respects, as well. For example, Needler suggests that the intensive political activity and interest of the Rio favelados, reported by the Leedses, is by no means typical of Latin American shantytowns. He argues that, while there is always some unrest and revolutionary potential among the urban poor, it is more common for them to show little involvement in politics, particularly in countries such as Mexico which have a single, dominant political party; the Mexican Partido Revolucionario Institucional maintains its hold over the shantytown residents by playing the familiar roles of political machines in the United States. What is important here is the contrast in views about the significance of machine politics and client-patron relationships. Who manipulates whom, and who benefits? What alternatives are open to the lower class city dweller, in the specific setting? How do the political attitudes and actions of shantytown residents affect the process of modernization and development?

The topics treated in this section do not exhaust the problems of urban change in the Third World, but they do represent some of the most fundamental issues in urban research. This is especially true of the Leeds's insistence that the root problem of the Latin American slum resident is not rural orientation, anti-work and anti-schooling values, non-political outlook, or unwillingness to organize, for these are often a grossly distorted picture of him. They suggest, instead, that the sources of the problem lie in the inefficiencies, inequalities, and corruption of the larger society, the slum's societal context. To define the larger problem in this way is not, of course, to solve it, but it has the useful function of guiding us toward more sophisticated and, hence, potentially more productive planning and research.

BRAZIL AND THE MYTH OF URBAN RURALITY: URBAN EXPERIENCE, WORK, AND VALUES IN "SQUATMENTS" OF RIO DE JANEIRO AND LIMA[1]

Anthony and Elizabeth Leeds

I. Introduction

The prevailing myths held by citizens of the capitals and other cities of both Brazil and Peru about squatter settlements – favelas and barriadas[2] – assert, on one hand, that the residents are highly rural in social organization and values and unskilled in and unfamiliar with city ways, even though essentially forward-looking and wanting to improve themselves, or, on the other, that they are people who do not wish to work, are assassins, thieves, marginals, and prostitutes, and are present-minded with little care for the future. Both consider the favelas separate and isolated from the larger society, "enclaves within the city," a kind of rural or criminal cyst in the body politic of the metropole. "Scientific" justification of these views has even been discovered recently in the writings of a variety of social scientists, some of whose major works, like *The Children of Sanchez,* are being circulated in Portuguese and Spanish translations in the respective countries.[3] The rural background and the improvidence of the favela poor are supposed to have been shown, too, in the allegedly autobiographical book of Carolina Maria de Jesus (1962) which was avidly, but most uncritically, read by Brazilians.[4]

Regarding these mythic elements, A. Leeds has already dealt extensively with the question of present-mindedness (1966b). E. Leeds' paper (1966) on political integration and Morocco's on carnival groups (1966) effectively deal with the myth of the isolated enclave. Modesto (1966) trenchantly deals with the multiple of webs of cause, of which favelas are an expression. Even Pearse (cf. 1957:245; 1962) clearly indicates, in a general way, the erroneousness of such notions as "marginality" and isolation by his discussion of the relationship of favela residents to the labor market, although he builds in, *as assumption*, that the urban institutions are strange and foreign to the favela residents, and, hence, that the latter must be essentially rural. He seeks to set forth the "relacoes estabelecidas pelas familias com *pessoas e instituicoes estranhas ao groupo de parentesco* [na] sua integracao efetiva na sociedade urbana" (1957: 245, emphasis ours). Mangin (1967a) and Turner (1967) have listed exactly parallel elements of this myth for the barriadas of Lima and, in much the same phrasings as we shall set forth here, have been indicating its fundamental falsehood. It seems to us that the data for Puerto Rico, Chile, and Venezuela also show its untruth.[5]

Our aim in this paper is to show the essentially urban character of the experience and values of favela and barriada residents. Doing so intrinsically contradicts the myth of rurality and present-mindedness, and converts Pearse's implicit assumptions into explicitly verifiable propositions – for both countries – ones which we hope to show to be essentially false.[6] It should be noted that the assumption-turned-proposition contains independently verifiable assertions: (a) that the urban persons and institutions are foreign to the populations in question; (b) that these populations have, in some way, not been integrated effectively into the urban society.

Before turning to our own data, we wish to make two methodological and theoretical observations. First, a word about the term "integration". It is currently being used in a vast literature on developing societies in a value-determined manner to mean, in essence, "our," i.e., an American, "Western," "democratic," "price-making market," kind of integration (cf. Pearse, 1957; it is also clearly set forth in Needler, 1967, and Chaplin, 1966, without using the word). By implication, other societies are non-, un-, or disintegrated. On the theoretical, methodological, and observational grounds, this so-commonly but unconsciously held view is nonsensical because it necessarily implies, *logically,* that such societies as Medieval society, irrigation societies, oriental despotisms, "traditional" societies, archaic societies, "under-developed" societies, and even the anthropologists' dearly-beloved primitive societies are non-, un-, or disintegrated. Such views are preposterous in terms of any generalized, viable societal theory whatever. It becomes plain that we must begin to think of qualitatively different forms of integration, whether as ideal types, as empirically-oriented structural models, as evolutionary forms, or any combination of these (see Leeds, 1964a). Social scientists should direct intensive effort at understanding these integrational forms, *in their own terms,* as viable forms independent of the American or "Western" models.

A conclusion to be drawn from these observations is that one should empirically seek or theoretically predict the form of integration of favelas and barriadas with the rest of the society, rather than start with the theoretically implausible assumption of the non-, un-, or disintegration of these entities.

Second, as follows from the above, squatter settlements cannot empirically or theoretically be understood unless they are looked at in detail as parts of a larger system and as products of the operation of the system. Specifically, we – as well as those who have done field work in the barriadas – have learned, largely from empirical experience rather than from theory,[7] that neither favelas nor barriadas can be properly understood without understanding a whole range of other socio-residential types concurrently, since movements into, between, and from favelas or barriadas constitute part of the process of favela-barriada development, rural-urban migrations, and the urbanizing of non-urban persons, and so on. According to Matos Mar (interview, Sept. 4, 1967) and according to our review of virtually the entire literature on housing in Rio (and elsewhere in Brazil), no studies exist for Lima or Rio on these other residential types except Patch's (1961). Generally, they are unknown except through Oscar Lewis' work on *vecindades* in Mexico. The best materials we have for Rio and Lima are impressionistic because they are based only on brief forays into these other housing types.[8] Consequently, all pictures of the social structure and social process involved are, to date, incomplete, whether for Argentina, Brazil, Chile, Columbia, Guatemala, Mexico, Nicaragua, or Peru – the Latin American countries in which the most extensive studies of such phenomena have been undertaken.[9]

II. Urban Experience of Squatters

We turn first to the conception of 'urban' to be used in this discussion. One component of the urban phenomenon, which may be designated 'the urban ethos,' has been dealt with in detail by Harris (1956) and A. Leeds (1957, Chs. 6 and 7) for towns of 1,500 and 3,500 respectively, in the interior of Brazil. Both authors are in vigorous agreement about the essentially and strongly urban ideology even of small towns in Brazil, especially if they are administrative centers. Both authors base their arguments on generally accepted notions about the urban phenomenon held by such authorities as Mumford, Wirth, and others. A. Leeds further argues that even the latifundia so commonly occurring in both Brazil and Peru are urban in organization and orientation, that is, essentially industrial systems oriented toward city markets, activities, and interests.

A second component is the localized, complex inter-relationship of a large number of qualitatively different technical, social, administrative, political, and other specializations (cf. Leeds, 1965). A third component we wish to include is the sheer physical apparatus of the city: public utilities, communications systems, transportation, congeries of different building types, etc.

It is with respect to urban characteristics such as these that the residents of favelas and barriadas must be examined if one is to make a valid assessment of the nature of their social experience and values. Before the question of their rurality of urbanity can be discussed soundly, it is essential to have available some minimal sociology of the place of origin of the residents. Most surveys have simply asked the name of the place of origin which has then been arbitrarily classed as urban or rural according to more or less personal criteria of the investigator – always one from large urban centers and generally with little or no experience of the "interior," as, with implicit dispraise, it is called in Brazil, even by social scientists. In that country, to ask the name of the place of origin is most inadequate because, unlike the United States, the name of the municipal (county) administrative seat (the *sede*, which is juridically a *cidade* (city), regardless of size, possessing all the basic agencies of government and administration) and the rural sections of the *municipio* are identical. One cannot tell from the response, giving only the name of the place, what the respondent's experience is, what sorts of institutional contexts he had known, or what sorts of values he has been exposed to.

A second problem has been lucidly set forth by Browning and his associates (1967, also Browning and Feindt, 1967): that migrants who come to a city as babies, or even children, have, in prior studies, been called natives of their place of birth, rather than of their place of socialization. The latter, from most social science points-of-view, is the more significant information. Browning *et al* (1967) therefore distinguished these data in their questionnaires in Monterey, Mexico. We hope to be able to do the same, but because our own survey data are not yet tallied, impressions with regard to Rio's favelas must, for now, suffice in this matter.

Logically, from the point of view of a metropole like Rio – disregarding migration from cities towards rural areas (insignificant in Brazil), back-and-return migration, and metropolis-to-metropolis or intra-metropolis migration – fifteen types of cityward migration are conceivable, where the following locations are possible as starting and/or finishing points: the rural hinterland (R), village (V), town (T), city (C), metropolis (M). R → M migration alone allows for eight permutations, if all, some, or no intermediate stops are calculated. V → M allows for four permutations. If, following the characteristics of 'urban' given above or the Brazilian juridical definition, one defines the "town" as the minimal urbal level, then out of the fifteen possible combinations, only three (R → V → M; R → M; V → M) do not have either a town or a city as intermediate steps.

In fact, all fifteen types and, in addition, the inter- and intra-metropolitan types of migration, plus combinations of the latter with the above fifteen, are found to have been patterns of migration of residents in both favelas and barriadas. Therefore, it is not surprising that truly rural migrants in Rio favelas are so few. What is surprising is how very few there are. Our guess is that they constitute no more than five percent of the population of the favelas.

But these figures do not tell all because they still give no indication of the sociology of the places of provenience. Thus, one may ask a man, "Where are you from?" Answer: "From Sant' Antonio de Padua." Q. "But, from the city itself?" A: "No, from the *roca* (fields)." Q. "But, were you actually out there hoeing (*trabalhando na enchada*)?" A: "Yes." Q. "What did you raise?" A: "Well, we raised rice, corn, beans, eggs, coffee, and made manioc flour." Q. "Did you eat it all?" A: "Hell, no, we sold it in town." Q: "For cash? How often did you go in?" A: "Every week. We lived in town for a while before we moved out to the *roca*;" or, another A: "We took stuff in all the time. I know how to cut hair, too, so I used to set up shop on the edge of town – we got customers on their way in and out of town."

Conversations such as this are typical. The respondent labored on a farm, sold in the money market, was familiar with commercial transactions, with the urban ambience, and with urban institutions – police, bureaucrats, licensing, trade, exchange, traffic flow, and transportation. He did not come unknowing and unprepared for large city life.

But even these considerations are, in a way, spurious. Implicitly, they assume the persistence and relative unchangeability of so-called rural values. In the literature, this assumption pervades the treatment not only of rural migrants to the city, but of virtually all matters having to do with ruralia. The city-born observers all seem to be convinced of "the idiocy of rural life." A more sophisticated and generalized phrasing of the same notion is that ideological aspects change more slowly, or "lag" behind, change in technology or social behavior.

Interviews with the few people we identified as having come specifically from rural village areas of Brazil or Portugal directly contradict these assumptions more often than they confirm them. In a number of cases, the person in question appears to have adapted exceedingly rapidly to the urban and favela ambience and grasped vigorously at what it offered. Thus, for example, the "rural" president of one favela association who had gotten training in electrical work, plumbing, and other construction skills had carried out a clever embezzlement once in office and stayed in a full term, to boot and had invested in land in the State of Rio de Janeiro where land values are appreciating rapidly.

One is led to suspect that the so-called "rural values" include a good many values and *savoirs faires* such as "peasant shrewdness" (cf. Bierstedt, 1967, p. 89) which are highly adaptive in urban settings especially when dealing with urbanites who are not familiar with these "peasant" values or ways of doing things. Even the so-called paternalistic mode of relationship, said to be characteristic of the Brazilian ruralite, can be used in highly adaptive ways for counter – exploitation of the system in the urban area – by milking a *patrao* ('boss' or 'patron'), a social service agency, a welfare body, a church or women's group, a Peace Corps, a US-Aid, anthropologists, and others.

Alternatively, it seems evident that new immigrants to the city change *some things* very rapidly, indeed, and although it may not be the innermost core of their value being, the tasks, the standards, the interests, the goals, the enjoyments, especially of the men, transform rapidly into fully urban ones. Almost without exception, if one asks them if they want to return to their place of origin, the answer is no. Reasons given range from the vague, "It's good there, but better here," to quite specific answers about the more desirable conditions of work, livability, and things to do and see in the city. (See below). Only some of the women, more closely tied to the house, struggling with the daily drudgery, and without the compensations of the bright lights or the hurly-burly of the town, sometimes speak of wanting to go back to the quiet, homey place they came from.

The Urban Born

So much for the ruralities; let us turn to the extreme contrast – the urban-born favela or barriada residents. In Rio, these constitute a high percentage of the favela population. Pearse's uncited source for 1948 (1958) gives twenty percent of the sample population as born in Rio. He notes, however, that Esqueleto (Skeleton), the favela in question, was newly-growing, while the older favelas averaged thirty-eight percent Rio-born. We do not know, of course, how many came to Esqueleto as children and were, consequently, socialized in Rio, their "place of socialization", Browning and Feindt's second category (1967). It must be remembered that the respondents were adults. If a head-count were made of the persons born in Rio, the percentage would probably be higher, because most of the children would be Cariocas (born in Rio city). The *Estudos Cariocas* (Estado de Guanabara, 1965, Vol 5)[10] permits one to calculate the following percentages:

	Percentage born in Guanabara	
Age	Favela	Non-favela
All Ages	51.4	59.1
0 - 19	81.4	84.5
20 - 49	23.8	45.6
50 plus	14.3	31.7

These figures are, of course, for persons *born,* not enculturated in Rio de Janeiro. It is striking that the percentage differences between favela and non-favela among the city's young people are negligible. The group, 20-49, which contains a large number of the persons of Pearse's sample, is still only 23.8 percent Carioca compared to Pearse's twenty percent. The category of 0-19 years old embraces 49.3 percent and 40.0 percent respectively of the total favela and non-favela population, a fact reflected in the percentages, between 50 and 60 of both favela and non-favela people born in Guanabara.

In an older favela we studied in the summer of 1967, Tuiuti, talking only to adults, perhaps forty percent or more were Cariocas, i.e., a higher percentage than the average for favelas in general. Quite a number of these, perhaps five to ten percent of the total population, were second and third generation in the favela itself, a situation not paralleled in the Lima barriadas, most of which have appeared since World War II. All the rest of the forty percent had migrated into the favela from various parts of the city where they or their city is paralleled in Lima. In the latter case, too, many of the migrants from other parts of the city were born in the city (interviews with residents of barriada Leticia, Wpt. 1967, cf. Mangin, 1967a).

This fact is of utmost importance because, first, these are urbanites whose entry into squatter settlements is an adjustment to life in an *urban* setting and is distinctively an *urban* choice. In general, this indicates, once more, that the favela or barriada is a phenomenon strictly of urban areas, not of rural ones, where, in any case, no parallels are found (cf. Mangin, 1967b, p. 80).

Second, it demands that the pressures which push people out of the authorized parts of the city into unauthorized settlements be studied in order to understand the favela development properly (cf. Modesto, 1966).

Third, it means that there is a permanent core of native urbanites, long-term residents in the favelas, around whom later migrants aggregate. The data suggest that many of those who migrate from the authorized city to the favelas or barriadas are the more enterprising, those who are more aware of urban economic, social, political, and administrative facts and policies (cf. Turner, 1966b); that some of those who migrate are doing so to preserve or improve their social and economic situation under the regnant difficulties of the Brazilian economy and social system.

In most of the interviews of our survey of 1967 and all of those carried out in February and in the summer of 1968, we obtained the places of origin of the residents. We have already noted that a sizable percentage of the adults was born in Tuiuti itself, while another considerable percentage was born in

TABLE 1 – URBANIZATION OF FAVELA RESIDENTS' TOWN OF ORIGIN ABSOLUTE GROWTH AND CHANGES IN COUNTY–COUNTY SEAT RATIOS (IN THOUSANDS)

Name of Municipio		1950 Mun	1950 Seat	1950 Seat %	1960 Mun	1960 Seat	1960 Seat %	Growth 1950-1960 Mun %	Growth 1950-1960 Seat %
Sao Joao de Meriti,	RJ	77	44	57.34	192	103	53.6	149.4	134
Duque de Caxias,	RJ	94	75	79.64	244	173	70.9	159.6	131
Nova Iguacu,	RJ	146	59	40.16	359	135	37.6	145.9	129
Sao Goncalo,	RJ	129	21	16.22	248	64	25.8	108.4	205
Niteroi,	RJ	190	175	91.79	245	229	93.9	28.9	30
Pocos de Caldas,	MG	26	20	76.19	39	32	82.0	150.0	60
Juiz de Fora,	MG	129	87	67.25	182	124	67.6	41.0	43
Leopoldina,	MG	41	11	26.94	46	18	39.1	12.2	64
Cataguases,	MG	34	13	38.40	42	21	50.0	23.5	61
Muriae,	MG	49	12	24.13	53	23	53.4	8.6	92
Carangola,	MG	43	9	21.91	35	12	34.3	–18.6	33
Aimores,	MG	38	9	25.71	41	11	26.8	7.3	22
Teofilo Otoni,	MG	88	20	22.97	129	41	39.5	46.6	105
Linhares,	MG	30	3	10.24	65	9	13.8	116.7	200
Vitoria,	ES	53	51	97.70	85	83	97.6	60.4	63
Cachoeira de Itapemirim,	ES	82	25	29.94	92	39	42.4	12.2	56
Itaperuna,	RJ	76	9	11.89	78	18	23.0	2.6	100
Miracema,	RJ	19	7	37.04	21	12	56.6	10.5	71
Santo Antonio de Padua,	RJ	38	4	11.08	32	9	28.1	–16.0	125
Campos,	RJ	241	63	26.32	292	90	30.8	21.2	43
Macae,	RJ	53	11	20.36	59	20	33.9–	11.4	82
Nova Friburgo,	RJ	49	29	60.10	70	50	85.9	42.9	72
Cabo Frio,	RJ	17	7	40.40	27	13	48.1	58.8	91
Sao Paulo,	SP	2,228	2,042	91.66	3,825	3,165	82.7	71.7	53
Salvador,	Ba.	424	396	93.36	656	631	96.2	59.4	60
Recife,	Pe.	534	522	97.75	797	789	98.7	49.2	51
Joao Pessca	Pa.	121	91	75.17	155	136	87.7	28.1	49
Fortaleza,	Ce.	280	213	76.26	515	355	68.9	83.9	66

SOURCES: Instituto Brasileiro, 1951, 1963; "Populacao Brasileira em 1960."

ABBREVIATIONS: RJ – Rio de Janeiro State; MG – Minas Gerais State; ES – Espirito Santo; Ba. – Bahia; Ce. – Ceara; Pa. – Paraiba; Pe. – Pernambuco; SP – Sao Paulo

NOTES: As a rule, municipal seat growth far exceeds the percentage growth in the *municipio* as a whole, even where the latter has been great. In two cases the percentage growth has been large (in one, an addition of 125% of the 1950 population!) while the total population of the *municipio* has *decreased*! Only in the suburbs of Rio have the *municipio* population growth rates exceeded that of the seat – the municipal hinterland filling out in the zone of influence of the metropolis.

The order of listing the towns is in a great circle about Rio, starting with its immediate suburbs on both sides of the bay, working northwest, then east, and again to the south towards Rio, thus grouping the towns somewhat by ecological area.

the city of Rio outside favelas and moved in later. We spoke with persons who had come from the state capitals of Sao Paulo (very few), Vitoria, Salvador, Recife, Joao Pessoa, and Fortaleza, as well as from the large suburban independent cities in the State of Rio de Janeiro, immediately contiguous with and, in fact, sociologically part of the city of Rio de Janeiro, though administratively outside the State of Guanabara. These suburban centers are Duque de Caxias, Nova Iguacu, Sao Joao de Meriti and, across the bay, Niteroi, capital of the State of Rio and Sao Goncalo (See Table I).

In addition, a very large percentage came from the county seats of *municipios* in the states of Rio de Janeiro, Minas Gerais, and Espirito Santo (see Table I). An apparently smaller percentage came from towns and villages in the hinterlands of municipal seats and, as we remarked above, a very small percentage come directly from fully rural areas (see Peattie, p.13).

In connection with these observations, it should be noted that all of these cities, towns, and villages are themselves growing, sometimes very rapidly, (see Table I) and becoming measurably more urban, judging by the indicators of urbanism listed earlier. In other words, migrants from all places except the most stagnant backland villages and rural areas have continuously been experiencing the urbanization process before they ever left their points of origin.

With respect to the urbanness of favela residents, three other issues related to the problem of place of origin and place of enculturation must be considered: a) the varieties of entry into, and establishment in, the city and the question of receptor centers; b) the occupational history of the favela resident prior to his residence in the favela; and c) the factors operating to select persons to enter the favelas from within the city. We turn first to the routes of entry into the city.

Routes of Entry into the City

The entire question of entry into the city has, to our knowledge, not been studied at all for Rio. Our comments, therefore, rest mainly on impressions gleaned from thousands of conversations with hundreds of people in many favelas. For Lima, the question of receptor centers has been discussed at some length (Mangin, 1967a, b, c; Turner, 1963). The data for both cities seem to be parallel, but the manner of entry in Rio is much less neatly defined than in Lima.

In both cities, one of the main routes of entry for the migrant poor[11] is by way of areas of old, decayed housing or housing apparently built for proletarian residence, e.g. (see Fig. 8), the *corticos, cabecas de porco,* the *avenidas* built on *lotes proletarios* ('proletarian lots'), and decayed residences in Rio, and the *callejones,* the *corralones,* the *viviendas continuas,* and the decayed mansions of Lima. In Rio, there appears to be considerable moving around from one to another of such residential types by a large proportion of the immigrants until they settle down, move up, or move out to the favelas, for very few appear ever to return, or at least return permanently, to the "rural" area or even their non-rural point of origin outside the metropolis.

In Rio, we know many such persons. Miguel Genio, for example, came from Rio Grande do Norte as a young man, son of a lawyer in an interior town. He learned the watchmaker's craft while still living, first, in a more run-down part of Copacabana, the elite playground; then, in another *bairro* of the city. Finally he moved to favela Jacarezinho (Little Alligator). He did not like Copacabana or Tijuca (mostly an upper-middle class residential area) but said "Eu adoro Jacarezinho." And he does! He lives there making his living as a watch repairman, goes to night school studying law, has been involved in the mainstream of favela politics, owns his own house. Others we know entered the city through more proletarian sections of the town "proper" like Olaria and Ramos, but later moved to the favela.

However, in the favelas of Rio, we also encountered a goodly number of persons who had come directly from some point of origin outside the city. This was especially true of Northeasterners from the state of Paraiba[12] whose later migrants often appeared to be family segments or friends of the earlier migrant groups and would move to the same house or location as the latter. Thus, there are pockets of Paraibanos ("cabecas chatas") in various favelas, e.g., in one of the subdivisions of Tuiuti called, interestingly enough, "Mineiro," because of the large number of persons born in Minas Gerais living in another part of that same subdivision.

Nevertheless, it should be noted that there appear to be no persistent and highly focal receptor centers such as have been reported for tribal immigrants in African cities (cf. Epstein, 1967, p. 280). The Rio and, apparently, the Lima pattern is for persons to disperse into centers which, through time, vary in number and location in the city depending on prior migrations, sources of present migrations, housing and other conditions in the receptor areas, conditions of the local job-markets, administrative policies affecting housing, work, or transportation.

We know virtually nothing about the migratory stops of one special category, the foreign favela dwellers, born almost exclusively in Portugal, because we failed, in general, to ask much about their places of origin. Most of the handful of Portuguese-born in Tuiuti were brought up in Rio or had lived in Rio since arrival. Most Portuguese are active in commerce in the favelas, some having made a very good thing out of it, indeed. Some (mainly men) are artisans. Those raising crops at the top of favela Salgueiro 'Willowtree' were peasants in the old country before they came to Rio a half-century earlier. Others half-dream of going back, except that their realism tells them there is not much to go back to; it is better in Brazil, although, some will tell you, we did not expect "this," meaning living in the favelas.

Brief mention should be made of some interesting cases of migration. One is the case of the owner of a store and eighteen apartments in favela Tuiuti. About 1916, his grandfather bought and titled the land on which the buildings stand. He had financial difficulties, and so decided to try his hand at farming. He therefore bought a plantation in the State of Rio, to which he moved. Though born in the city of urban parents, the present owner of the favela property was raised on the plantation from his first year on, not moving back to the city until he was a young man, after his grandfather died. He then took up the property and developed it. This is an extreme case of back-and-forth migration, one which would probably be listed as "rural migrant" in simple statistical enumeration. We have a number of cases of persons born, say, in Cabo Frio, who spent their childhood in Rio or came there as young people for a number of years, then returned to Cabo Frio for a period, either on a prolonged visit or to search for a possible alternative to life in Rio. Eventually, they returned to Rio, finding the life in Cabo Frio too confining, economically deprived, or otherwise unsatisfactory. Some of these, too, although largely enculturated as big-city dwellers, may be picked up on simplistic census counts as rural migrants. Finally, we discovered a lady born in Tuiuti who as a two-year old moved to Spain with her Spanish parents and lived there until she was seventeen. She then returned to Rio, lived outside the favela for a couple of years, finally moving back into Tuiuti to the lot her parents had bought and titled more than half a century earlier (about 1912) of which she is now owner.

All-in-all, these cases simply illustrate that the range of experience of residents of favelas is quite broad (cf. Peattie's mention of Chinese, Lebanese, and Arabs living in her bairro, pp. 12, 13), sometimes including several kinds of settlement from village to metropolis, many types of housing and residence units, all kinds of legal papers,[13] and even considerable international experience.

In this latter connection, it is to be noted that the area comprised by the states of Minas Gerais, Espirito Santo, Rio de Janeiro, and Guanabara – the area supplying 78.5 percent of the residents of the favelas of Rio[14] – is largely coterminous with the induction zone of Brazil's First Army, whose center for military training is Rio de Janeiro. All eighteen-year-old men are subject to one year's military service, which, being in Rio does several things. It contributes to the migration into the metropole; it enculturates into a larger institutional structure whose central locus is not only the city but in this case the cosmopolitan and urbane Rio de Janeiro; it breaks down localism and regionalism; it often assists in giving specialized training to persons who later return to civilian life and become skilled specialists; and, on occasion, it even gives an international experience to some.

Thus, our friend Socrates had spent some months in Santo Domingo in the Brazilian army contingent and a few weeks in Viet Nam with an Army group looking over the possibilities of Brazilian participation. Socrates was from a small town in Ceara where his family owned a cattle ranch and carried on an (illicit) business in mineral water sales. Socrates himself had worked for the *Jornal do Brasil* (a major newspaper) as a typist before he turned to being a green-grocer and chicken-seller in a favela because he could make more money by this both licit and illicit operation (see Schultz, 1966).

We also met persons who had served in the Navy and the merchant marine. A number of these had visited various parts of the world, a surprising proportion of the older ones having been in battle in Italy with the Brazilian Expeditionary Force in World War II. These experiences are remembered vividly (see Guilherme, Ms., Ch. 4). Others have traveled to New York, Philadelphia, and other American ports where they learned a little English and sometimes a lot about racial discrimination. These experiences, too, are remembered vividly.

In sum, various military and, in Brazil, paramilitary services (like the police and the fire department) contribute to the migration patterns, to the intensification of urban and cross-cultural experiences, and to the urban enculturation of persons, some of whom come to reside more or less permanently in favelas.

Prior Occupational Experience

We turn next to the question of occupational experience prior to entry into the favela. Again, no systematic data exist on this for Rio; we can, at present, only report our impressions. First, it must be pointed out that the range of occupations found among favela residents as a whole encompasses the entire range of status levels or evaluative categories (so often called 'class' in the literature) delineated by Hutchinson and his colleagues (1960, p. 30ff) for the Brazilian occupational stratification system. However, the range varies with the size of the favela. It is only in large and complex favelas such as

Jacarezinho, with 70-80,000 people, or Rocinha with, perhaps, 30-40,000, that one finds lawyers, doctors, dentists, ministers, engineers, responsible public functionaries, or the like, who fall into Hutchinson's categories A and B at the top of the scale.

In Tuiuti, with perhaps 7,000 people, these top two levels – the professionals – are absent, though an accountant (level B) lives there (see below). Clerks, secretaries, expert dressmakers, lower level functionaries, including firemen, military police, detectives, regular police, and the like, constitute representatives of levels C and D, which are not clearly distinguished in the favelas (see variant on Hutchinson's scheme, *ibid.*, p. 77). Highly skilled artisans such as goldsmiths, lowest level public functionaries – including some firemen and civil guards and the like – and craftsmen such as cabinet makers and carpenters comprise level E (with some overlap with Hutchinson's D). Here, too, are the skilled workers – in the textile, yarn, string, can, pocket-book, rum, elevator, plaster, and marble-cutting factories in the surrounding industrial area. Here, too, would be the chauffeurs, taxi, truck and bus drivers, mechanics; skilled construction workers, waiters; etc. In level F, the lowest level, are the unskilled and semi-skilled workers: stevedors, ship-yard workers, janitors, night guards, dishwashers, domestic workers, and the like. At the very bottom of the scale, but not properly in a separate category, are the unemployed, marginally and irregularly employed, and crass criminal elements (the more refined criminal elements should probably be assigned to the different evaluative levels according to their skills, their training in criminal and civil activities, and their social ties; unfortunately, standard sociological techniques do not lend themselves to studying stratification in this "mirror-image" or "reverse" segment of society, nor to relating its stratification system to that of the "obverse" segment).

In a very small favela like Xepa ("Left-overs" or "Garbage") or Ruth Ferreira, the tendency is for only representatives of levels F at the bottom, and E, to be found. Xepa even has few of the upper elements of F, while Ruth Ferreira has many of level E, e.g., bus drivers, factory workers, and night guards, and some of D (see Peattie, p. 12).

As far as we now know, there is no clear correlation among migration, length of residence in the favela, and the level attained in the occupational stratification; that is, both immigrants and native-born seem to be more or less equally distributed on the scale. Naturally, those born in the favela have acquired their occupations while residents in the favela. A number of the goldsmiths of Tuiuti, for example, were born there. In other words, entry into that occupational level, in a skilled urban craft, was not barred by favela residency. At the same time, some of the immigrants, too, have entered occupations of these types. The accountant living in Tuiuti arrived from a small town in the interior when he was seventeen and has sufficiently mastered the "strange" and "foreign" urban institutions to maintain two offices, become a part-time detective, thereby getting himself access to all the football games at the Maracana ("the world's largest") Stadium, solve legal problems such as business licensing for people in the favela, and maintain four households, three of them each with one of his three wives who collectively, by 1967, had blessed him with eleven children with whom he is to be seen driving around, of a Sunday, in his sea-green Mercedes-Benz.

At the same time, some of those born in the city, in the favela, or in various kinds of places outside Rio, occupy the lowest rungs of the occupational stratification scale: unskilled workers, unskilled criminals, domestic workers, and the rest.

With respect to location in the urban occupational stratification system, it appears that an important determinant is the person's prior work experience. Many informants had had a variety of work and occupational experiences before coming to the city, let alone the favelas. People from agrarian parts of the country had, even when working primarily as farmers or farm labor, had secondary occupations such as barbering, small store keeping, and market selling. Others had worked primarily in the towns, without farm work experience at all, as clerks, masons, bricklayers, electricians, truck drivers, secretaries, or domestic workers. Both of these work contexts involve experience with money, exchange, taxes and imposts, licensing, minor officialdom, official papers of all kinds, communications, transportation, more or less sophisticated tools, and so on.

Two things may be said about such prior work experiences. First, the contexts of these experiences involve exposure to a whole series of positions, institutions, and behaviors which are urban in content and ethos. Second, a great many occupations and activities found in the small towns and even in some "rural" areas are common to the larger work market in the cities of so-called under-developed countries; a large part of that market consists of work for which curricularized training (see A. Leeds, 1964a, p. 1325ff) are at a minimum or non-existent but which are nonetheless specialties for which experience is relevant in a competitive market situation. The articulation of the work market with the labor force is itself uncurricularized and in flux,[15] though highly institutionalized. In short, for virtually all migrants to the city who end up in the favelas, the prior work experience gives them experience of urban ways and preadapts them to the intensified expression of these ways in the metropolis.

Factors Operating to Select for Favela Living

Finally we consider the factors which operate to select persons out of the total urban population for life in favelas. The reasons may be conceptally examined in terms of a kind of continuum.

true marginality stress economizing taste

By 'true marginality' we refer to situations in which persons operate effectively neither in the legal nor the extra- or illegal (criminal) economy of the city, but are pushed out of all of these. For example, during a severe depression of the labor market such as has developed in Brazil since the *golpe* of 1964, the more sporadic and uncurricularized forms of labor have been the hardest hit; that is, the more marginal labor supply which in reasonable times, scrapes by, was pushed willy-nilly into true marginality. The crime rates rose all over Rio for all kinds of crimes, especially those which are characteristically carried out by individuals acting alone and in stress; thefts, assaults, battery, robbery with murder. Others beg, live on handouts, vegetate somehow.

'Stress' refers, on the one hand, to situations which may resemble those producing true marginality, but in which the personnel involved is in better circumstances to deal with them or, on the other hand, to situations and events which are sudden and unpredictable, e.g., death, job loss, sickness, accident, and so on, or, though predictable, involve a major change of life circumstances, e.g., marriage or the birth of a baby.

By 'economizing', we refer to situations in which persons have more or less stable but limited resources which they must allocate among various ends according to choices based on their hierarchy of values (see last section). Obviously, any stress will produce an acute need to economize in the sense defined here, but we prefer to treat such situations under 'stress'.

By 'taste' we refer to cases like that of the watchmaker mentioned above who lived in the favela because he liked it, not because of any need.

It is illuminating to watch slum-dwellers, residents of "lower middle-class" housing areas, and favela residents change positions along this scale under varied conditions. In such changes, favelas play a most important part. For a great many, the favelas may represent a refuge area in two senses; in that of being a place where one may escape, relieve, or minimize stress, thereby returning one's living patterns to a state of "normal" economizing, and in that of being a place where one can survive by various marginal procedures including, in some cases, living off the land, carrying on peripheral crime, being kept and other forms of prostitution or semi-prostitution, and, generally, by minimizing external stress and threat. For others, the favela can be part of a person's or family's economizing among a number of values, especially where long-term goals are sought, while maintaining the house-holding system in as nearly stable a condition as possible, or even improving it. These comments apply to the barriadas of Lima as well (cf. Mangin, 1967b). Finally, as has been said, some people *like* to live in favelas. Movement may be in either direction on the scale: movement to favelas is *not* identical with moving down the scale. Many cases prove the contrary.

A. *Taste*

Let us look at a few typical cases. Those of the watchmaker and the accountant have already been cited. Both of them live by preference in favelas. They like it there. There is an atmosphere of freedom (see last section) from the trammels of the business "middle-class" and elite worlds "down below" or "out there" (*la embaixo, la fora*), which these people enjoy. They feel they can have the good things the city has to offer, yet freedom and comfort, too. They can also have a great deal of influence among their co-residents, engage in favela politicking, have a degree of social recognition and prestige. They can participate in all kinds of activities outside the favela such as business, politics, religion, schooling, recreating, and soccer.

Old Orlando Ferreira, too, lives in the favela by preference. He has a diploma in architectural drawing and he taught school. In his middle years, he became interested in *quimbanda* (one of the forms of Brazilian Afro-Catholic cults) for which living in the favela gave him more freedom and a more congenial atmosphere. Also, he can enjoy his common-law marriage to his second wife in peace and without social censure.

Cases such as these can be multiplied by the score. They involve people with perception of the conditions and qualities of urban life and of its possibilities which can, to some extent, be fashioned to their desires. They are people who take a certain command both of their own lives and of their surroundings, exercise choice, are explicit in their appreciation of a degree of liberty, and yet, are fully dealing with urban institutions to which they are no strangers.

The taste for living there is not restricted to the reasonably well-off in the favela, but is most clearly seen among them because they are not *compelled* to live there. Others, too, enjoy living there and seem to do so largely by preference, although not living in the favela might, in some cases, create stress for them. They, too, like the favela, though they may complain about wretched housing, the expense of food, and so on. Often the favela life lets them live in extended family enclaves or networks or in home-town, or at least home-state, neighborhoods (a behavior not necessarily rural, as so many commentators seem to think, but quite characteristic, for example, of rustic Bostonians, New Yorkers – the Northeasterners in metropolitan Austin, Texas).

Also notable among many of the people is a strong aesthetic appreciation of the landscape, as in Tuiuti, which has some of the most magnificent views in all Rio. The residents speak of the natural and man-made aspects of this landscape with a certain awe. The washerwoman, D. Yaya, was such a person. She was second generation on Tuiuti hill; her husband had been a semi-skilled worker in a furniture factory before it went bankrupt some years before. He was still trying to collect indemnity for his layoff and, meanwhile, was earning less-than-minimum salary in some job, while she earned extra money by part-time work as a domestic and by *"lavando para fora"* ('taking in wash'). These people live next door to Yaya's mother in a small neighborhood where a considerable amount of neighborly activity occurs.[16] Yaya and her husband spent much time looking at the landscape when not busy doing other things, and Yaya spoke contemplatively of it, its beauty, and their enjoyment of it, made possible by their living on the hillside of Tuiuti.

B. *Economizing*

The use of the favela as a place to live in order to economize is exemplified by innumerable cases. In general, residents of favelas, by virtue of being squatters, are "homeowners" who have built their own houses – whether shacks, chalets, or *palacetes* ('mansions', 'little palaces') – or renters who pay relatively low rents (although this pattern has begun to change with the increasing scarcity of space in older, denser, and more desirable favelas). In a great number of favelas, especially ones on the mountain sides and hills, it is possible to raise fruits, vegetables, pigs, and chickens in a kind of specialized urban farming which permits creating economic values that can be directly consumed, exchanged, sold or, in the form of pigs, used as a form of storage which itself, while growing, makes use of local resources: garbage heaps, grasses, roots, human feces, etc.[17]

As a specific example of economizing, Orlando Munhoz chose to live in Jacarezinho where he had come as a boy from the city, *la fora,* where his mother lived at the time we knew him. He made this choice because the rent was low and the cost minimal for the breakfast and supper supplied by the landlady downstairs. By living this way, he achieved several goals. The economizing goal was that of saving a large part of the salary from his job as chief of the accounting division of the Rio Stock Exchange. Had he not lived in the favela, he would have had to spend most of his salary. Instead, he invested it, against the time of his marriage which took place while we were there, in the house he built near his future in-laws' home in the city proper. He and his fiancee did a large part of the work on this eminently "middle-class" house, thus saving on costs, in turn, investing these savings in household and other goods. The other goals were his participation in favela politics and his running of a soccer-cum-social club in Jacarezinho, both of which contributed greatly to his prestige and to his following (cf.Galijart, 1964). He was the most influential person in the council of street representatives of Jacarezinho.

Joao, for a long time, did not live in a favela, while working for an American agency. Though his pay of three minimum salaries was higher than that of the great majority of the Brazilian labor force, it was still tight when confronted with the costly alternatives of city rents, a good education for his four children, maintaining a certain standard of living, or others. He opted for the good education for his children, seeing in the long run, greater security for them and for himself in education. He, therefore, moved to a favela so that he could economize on rent costs and allocate his resources in what he felt were more important directions. It will be noted that in this choice there is at least an implicit analysis and understanding of how the city society works, and in it, he is attempting to maximize rewards for his family transgenerationally.

C. *Stress*

Helio was born in the city proper. He became a skilled factory worker, but was involuntarily and permanently retired by the Industrial Workers Social Service Institute (I.A.P.I.) when, at age thirty-one, an accident broke his legs. He received a sum for workmen's compensation. Calculating his resources and costs in the short and long run, he decided that his best course was to buy a cheap house, really a shack, in favela Jacarezinho since, even without improvements, it would appreciate in value while providing him a tax-and-rent-free place to live, and this appreciation would be proportional to the ever-present Brazilian inflation rates. Furthermore, it was conceivable that, with time, he might be able to improve the house, which would either increase its value or make it tradable for another house in a better (more valuable) location. Later his family – mother and sister and their respective spouses – moved into the favela, creating among them a series of interlocking holdings in water and sewage systems and in the houses themselves. One of the sisters, recently marrying and moving out of the favela, has sold her interests to the rest of the family. All of these calculations and operations show a keen familiarity with city – in fact, national – institutions and a clear ability to cope with them. The case also illustrates the relationship, on our continuum, between a situation of acute stress and one of economizing in order to maintain a certain pattern of living and even, in the long run, to maximize gains. He has since, through a complex series of swaps and favors, acquired an almost luxurious house.

D. *Marginalization*

Space permits us only one example, a case in which a family attempted economizing but was pushed to the edge of marginality by a series of stresses. The husband had immigrated, apparently from a truly rural hinterland of a small town in Espirito Santo some time before his wife. He found unskilled work in the industrial area of Ramos, a part of Rio, having set up a wattle-and-daub house in the favela Nova Brasilia. Once on the job, he sent for his wife and children. For a while the wife worked as a domestic so that they had two incomes. With the scanty sums of money they could scrape from this income, they invested in a few bottles of *cachaca* (a kind of rum), wine, soft drinks, and some condiments, trying to start a *botequim* ('hole-in-the-wall store'). They hoped that this little *botequim* would develop, in part for the profits, but in part too, because the wife felt she could no longer be away from the children who were growing up without direction and alone. Their capital, however, was not enough to build up the business. Thus whatever income it brought in was absorbed by the family as a replacement for the wife's former income from domestic work. This was the situation when the first of a series of stresses occurred. The husband fell ill. Though he improved, he never fully recovered (as is so commonly the case among the working poor in Brazil), and then successively fell ill of one thing after another for months. He found it progressively more difficult to find work (the labor market was also contracting), so that, by the last time we saw these people, he had been out of work for almost two months and was lying at home sick, more or less permanently incapacitated. The wife had to sell what little stock there was and seek domestic employment in a work market already glutted because of the general economic depression. The house was in decay, the children ragged and ill, and household care virtually nonexistent.

The causes of marginalization, in this case, do not appear to be rurality and unfamiliarity with city ways, but a combination of structural and accidental (stress) features acting in concert. The structural features include the man's low position on the scales of education and training (a pan-Brazilian characteristic); his isolation, as a newcomer, from the job placement networks; the malfunctioning of the Social Welfare Institutions; the sagging economy, a result of national conditions; the lack – again because they were newcomers and their part of the favela was only recently settled – of what might be called "support-in-crisis" groups which provide a kind of informal insurance mechanism in times of crises, especially the extended family, neighbors, a *rapaziada* ("the gang"), a patron-client dyad, or *compadres*. In such structural circumstances, stress situations became unmanageable for the individuals under stress, leading to marginalization and, sometimes, death.

Cases are innumerable. But they are histories, not only of the country-born, but also of the town-born, sophisticates and unsophisticates alike. In all cases, structural and accidental features combine in much the way that our more or less prototypic case just illustrated. The structural or institutional features are those common to all Brazil and characteristic of the structure of the Brazilian economy, polity, and administrative organization, or, more inclusively, of the structure of the society of which these institutions are facets (cf. Frank, 1967; Leeds, 1964).[18] These structural incapacities seem to have their analogues in Peru, if our reading of Patch's article (1961) is correct. The tremendous efforts expended by Patch's informant – who, after years of struggle, perhaps makes it – and by others of his *callejon* who fail, and some of the details of the struggle, suggest quite the same sorts of structural impediments to the working poor, rural or urban, in Peru.

It must be emphasized that the opposite type of case also occurs very frequently; persons as rural as the husband and wife just described make good in the metropolitan milieu. In fact, the family for which we have the most documentation is one of this sort. Suffice it to say that, over time, they have built a house in Jacarezinho worth today NCr$10,000 (while the dollar was worth NCr$2.70/US$1 and minimum salary was at NCr$105/month); have a radio, television, electric sewing machine, refrigerator, phonograph, electric lights, several bathrooms, running water; have assisted, by loans, labor exchange, and other services, in building up their son-in-law's land, house, store, inventories worth at NCr$40,000,000; are in the process of helping another son-in-law increase his wealth in the same manner by providing a rent-free house while his store is rebuilt, baby sitting, building pieces of furniture for the store, and so on.

Urban Experience Inside the Squatment

To conclude this section, we wish briefly to discuss the urban experience of residents in the favela or barriada itself. The myth holds (cf. Mangin, 1967a) in its extreme form, that the squatter settlement is "the rural slum within the city" or "the run-down rural *bairro* in the city" (respectively Bonilla, 1961, 1962).[19] In our opinion, on the basis of a number of man-years of living in favelas, intimate knowledge both by ethnography and questionnaire survey of a half-dozen favelas, visits (ranging from a few hours to repeated trips) to another forty-five favelas, and studies by Mangin, Matos Mar, and Turner of Peruvian barriadas and Peattie of a Venezuelan *barrio,* especially in regard to their settlement histories, associational life, occupational patterns, and political outlooks, these views are, in general, fundamentally false. Both favelas and barriadas, as a rule, are highly political places (as, incidentally, are the interior towns of Brazil; cf. Harris, 1956; Leeds, 1957, Ch. 5). They are doubly political in that they often have very elaborate political relations with politicians and agencies outside the favela.[20] The larger the favela, the more this seems to be so. In Rio, the extreme example is, of course, Jacarezinho, with perhaps 70,000-80,000 people. As E. Leeds (1966) has pointed out, these people are intimately involved in state politics, while state administrative agencies are involved in a whole series of favela parties, factions, or other groupings both in behalf of various state administrative persons and in their own behalf by extracting rewards from these latter. The state administrators and agencies, which are involved in a whole series of favela parties, factions, or other groupings, all use the technocratic-bureaucratic offices as "neutral" fronts for their highly unneutral party interests. The favela residents are aware of this and play upon it. After all, Jacarezinho has an electorate of perhaps 30,000-40,000 (although party and agency overestimates put it at as much as 50,000-80,000)[21] and that is enough to swing the entire Regional Administration or electoral district.

In addition, Jacarezinho now provides enough rewards internally to make political life intense. Control of the electric light system yields rich possibilities of graft, about a dozen patronage jobs, and a powerful position to hand out favors to electric power customers, favors to be returned on call. Control over the light system also puts one structurally in contact with a series of external administrative agencies like Rio Light, the State Light Commission (C.E.E.), the Regional Administration, unofficially the Military, the various now-legally-extinct political parties, the non-extinct new political parties created by fiat two or three years ago by the Brazilian military government, and so on. It may be pointed out that, besides this barrage of urban experiences, the sheer installation and administration of as extensive and complicated a lighting system as that in Jacarezinho – about 10,000 houses – is itself a significant urban management experience.

It will be argued that this sort of thing is very recent. In fact, the C.E.E. types of organization are recent, but, as has been shown elsewhere (A. Leeds, E. Leeds and D. Morocco), the C.E.E. power systems are only the most recent form of a long development of light systems, the earlier forms of which were networks privately managed by favela entrepreneurs for individual profits, while certain later forms, legalized by the decree called Portaria 2 about 1956, often took on cooperative forms as well as individual profit-making. Incidentially, cooperative water systems, as in Borel and Jacarezinho, go back for many years (see Wygand, 1966).

Some organized favelas, like Guararapes, have recently moved in the direction of becoming communal landholders. Guararapes purchased the land on which it stands from a private owner. It had developed a cooperative not only to purchase the land, but to urbanize (i.e., "install urban facilities in") it, create training centers to raise income through specialization of its youthful labor so that the cooperative could be maintained, building substantial housing for its members, and so on. Similar plans are afoot in favela Coroa (Crown) and others. Jacarezinho's leaders have often spoken of the idea of buying the land it stands on, but it is now government land, and, thus, an almost insoluble problem exists since the government sees the solution only in terms of selling individual lots for private ownership by residents, necessitating ripping down the whole favela. The ostensible reason for this is to conform to national and state lot-size law. A less overtly-stated reason is that the COHAB (Popular Housing Authority: Companhia de Habitacao Popular) will take in the money from such sales (to finance other projects), a sizable fortune, although it only paid about US$8,000 for the immense tract (about 125 acres) of potentially prime residential and industrial land in the middle of the city.

In Peru, such large-scale planning and management has been part of the barriada experience from the beginning. The invasions themselves were often planned. Once invaded, the areas of invasion were laid out in streets and plazas, water, sewer, and light supplies were planned, and school and other service areas delimited. The barriadas, as social entities, were often large-scale corporate managerial bodies creating clearly-urban neighborhoods, some of which have recently been officialized as parts of the city of Lima (cf. Turner, 1963; Mangin, 1967a; Turner, 1967; interviews, Sept. 1968).

Furthermore, Rio's favelas have had a long history of associational activity. The Uniao de Trabalhadores Favelados (The Favelaized Workers' Union, or Unity – UTF) was originally set up by a lawyer (Margarino Torres), of the ex-P.T.B. (Brazilian Labor Party), of the, then, Federal District (now Guanabara State), in cooperation with favela leaders between 1946 and 1948. Only favela Borel's branch of the original UTF remains today, but it is a highly political organization (cf. Schultz, 1966) which has successfully led the residents to defeat two attempts and one threat (about 1948, 1954 and 1966 respectively) to evict the favela; has used – and outlived – at least one major community development agency (cf. Leeds, 1966a); has founded a health post with an extensive membership; has set up a cooperative funeral fund; and has constructed an all-favela water supply whose four administrative subdivisions (*'sociedades'*), each with its mimeographed statutes, are responsible to it. The officers of the association, all residents of Borel, include one man who is a member of a labor union, another who owns butcher shops both inside and outside the favela, another who is a sergeant in the military police, another who is a non-commissioned officer in the army – all of them with close ties to institutions outside the favelas, including the highly urban labor unions.

Most of the favela associations extant today are of more recent date, not because all the favela residents suddenly urbanized in 1961 and 1962, but because the discriminative political and administrative pressures against favela residents were not only lifted, but governmental action was purposely undertaken to create associations and full citizenship for all residents of Rio. This was started in 1960 (when Carlos Lacerda's government initiated the new State of Guanabara) by the then Directorate of Social Services under Jose Arthur Rios. This effort included supplying legal information and lawyers, otherwise extremely difficult for the working poor to come by since, in general, lawyers identify their own interests with the political and social elites of the country (cf. Naro, 1966), not with the problems of the lower class. Legal information, we have found, is extraordinarily hard, even for lawyers, to excavate. In other words, when a number of class-maintaining barriers are breached or circumvented, the favela residents suddenly develop all the urban characteristics which the rural-stereotyped investigators – who have never examined the structural situation in which favelas exist – find lacking among the "backland rustics" who compose the favela population.[22]

The Lima barriadas are perhaps even further evolved in this respect. They began in large-scale, coordinated, associational activity, often connected with some political official. Many members had had considerable prior experience in home-town associations (cf. Mangin, 1964, 1965), shifting to membership in the barriada associations as the barriadas emerged. The home-town associations function in part to enculturate and urbanize the Peruvian upland peasantry (cf. Cate, 1962, 1963, 1967 for parallels in Brazil), which differ in language and culture from that part of Peruvian society in which the urbanization process is taking place. The barriada associations are not only administrative agencies for the barriadas (the largest of which today has about 50,000 people), but also agencies for bargaining with the federal and municipal governments; as key nodes in political relations with the surrounding society; and as internal political systems which, untypically for Peru, have carried on annual elections among the entire population of the barriada for officials (Mangin, 1967c).

What we have said about favelas and barriadas as, in themselves, loci of urban experience, and of city political, administrative, and associational activity, can also be said for the economic, recreational, religious, and social life. We cannot go into these here but refer the reader to Leeds (1966), Leeds, Leeds and Morocco (1966), Morocco (1966), Schultz (1966), Cate (1962, 1963).[23]

No adequate treatment has yet been given of favela social organization. What has been written is exclusively about family. Little or no attention has been given to the following aspects of the social order (and the links or identities with the same elements outside the favela) all of which we found inside the favelas: stratification, elites, cliques, networks *(turmas, rapaziadas, garotadas, meninadas, panelinhas),* neighbor groups, ambiences, social clubs and other associations (e.g. combos), patron-client dyads of many types, career mechanisms (see Leeds, 1964a), etc., and those social factors which contribute to the partial sense of community observed in favelas.

In brief, the favelas are shot through with all the forms of organization common to the including society; most of the operations of these types of organization are analogues of those outside unless something about the structural situation of the favelas with respect to the matrix society prevents this from being so. If the including, matrix society is urban, then, too, is the favela urban and, in most important respects, continuous with it. For now, we can only assert these conclusions; full documentation will appear later. Meanwhile, it would be profitable for the reader to study the paper by Helio Modesto (1966).

III. Urban Values

In this final section of the paper, we turn to the urban values of favela residents. Many of these have been alluded to in preceding sections, but it is well to refer to them again here, in the context of a general discussion of values.

First, among most favela residents, especially the men, a generalized preference for the city is expressed. The country is backward, sad, paralyzed, without any special attractions as country or living place. Except for some women, most people say, when asked, that they do not want to go back. Why? Because it is better here. Life is better, one feels better, economically it is better, it is not *atrasado* or *parado* ('backward' or 'at a standstill), etc. In other words, the city atmosphere and environment are, in an inchoate, almost sensory way, felt to be desirable and, for those familiar with the rural areas, the more desirable.

Specific features of the urban situation are valued. The broad and varied job market is valued in terms of "opportunity," the possibilities of earning money through work to live better. For those coming from the interior, the life of the *roca* (the 'rural area'), the life on Mother Earth was not so endearing as to overcome their negative feeling about its ever-increasing economic rigors or about being sharecroppers, wage laborers, or even smallholders-in-debt. It was no longer worthwhile even if it was still possible. So they cleared out to the city which, even in its present economic distress, is better than the country. There is, for both the migrant and the city-born working poor, always some opportunity, some possibility of keeping oneself economically alive, at worst, and, at best, one may earn well and learn to earn better still. Many can get special training on the job, in the SENAI or SENAC (Servico Nacional de Aprendizagem Industrial and Servico Nacional de Aprendizagem Comercial, respectively the Industrial and Commercial Training Services), in vocational schools, and even in small shops. Some of the welfare organizations and community development programs also occasionally have training projects.

Even for the man who has been out of work for a long time, who has been sick on welfare, for example, the city is still the place of opportunity, of possibilities. The lack of work, the inability to get cured so he can work, is laid (often correctly) to the "malfunction" of the federal government, the Social Welfare Institutes, and other institutions. In other words, contradictions between his values regarding the city as a place of economic opportunity and his actual situation do not push him "back" to rural values, but rather, to quite sophisticated and astute ("urban") analyses of the social structure of his urban and national society.

Related to this set of values are the values both for education in itself and for the specific educational opportunities available in towns and cities.[24] To virtually all Brazilians, education – perhaps represented best in the honorific 'doutor', i.e., any college graduate – is an ultimate and intrinsic good. John Turner, in a questionnaire applied to barriada residents in Lima, found that the position of school teacher was given, in a majority of cases, more prestige than other occupational categories such as doctor, priest, policeman, business man, etc. (unpublished data). This value is itself a product of the urban civilization of the Iberian peninsula and has always been part of the urban ethos of Brazil, now generalized to all "classes" and sectors of the population and given importance by all the prevalent means of mass communication.

The specific educational opportunities include public and parochial primary, secondary, and higher institutions of learning, vocational schools, specialized public training facilities like the SENAI and SENAC mentioned above, a plethora of small private schools and others. No one has yet done a census of schools in the favelas, but some favela residents have recognized the need and market for private schools inside the favelas. Thus, in Jacarezinho, we know of at least half-a-dozen schools, two or three of them reasonably good, though very short of equipment and books. One of the largest has a trained teacher. She teaches about 180 children a day in three shifts. Thus, many favela residents who, for a variety of reasons, have difficulties (such as cost of uniforms, major avenues to cross, distance, etc.) in sending children to state or parochial schools, greatly value schools inside the favelas. More and more, as the discriminatory pressures from outside have lessened, favela residents have sent their children to secondary school and even to college, so that, in another decade or so, a considerable stratum of professionals will be found in larger and wealthier favelas.

The favela inhabitants also value other kinds of institutional opportunities of the city. It is really irrelevant whether they were born into them, as it were, as urban-born persons, or learned of them after migrating to Rio or other cities. Either way, they are valued, even when harshly criticized as its frequently the case. We refer especially to the "Institutos" – the federal institutes of social welfare – which ideally provide sickness payments, retirement pay, family payments, widow's support, medical care, maternity care, and so on. Why they malfunction so grandiosely is not for analysis here. Nevertheless, even given the actual "malfunctioning," they still provide the promise and reality of a measure of security against stress and unpredictable crisis, a certain additional control over a difficult and fickle environment. In fact, the global payments by the Institutes comprise a very considerable percentage of the total income of the entire working class of a city like Rio. However "uneconomic" such a system may seem to productivity-minded economists, under the conditions of the Brazilian national economy and its stage of development, this global expenditure of payments *is* economic for the working poor who must cope with that particular form of capitalist economy.

On the whole, also, the labor syndicates are valued, though by a much more limited number of inhabitants; we heard no complaints about them from favela dwellers. Structurally weak as the syndicates have been and, after the coup of 1964, more than ever are, over the long run they had been strengthening, improving their bargaining position vis-a-vis industry in the tripartite play of syndicate-industry-federal government which, by law, is always involved in the bargaining situation. The increasing strength of unions has meant better working conditions, better salaries, greater safety, and increased fringe benefits. There have been a number of efforts to link favela interests with syndicate organization, e.g., the favela-dwelling syndicate officials who ran for office in the Rocinha favela association election of 1966, the president of the UTF of Borel who was a union official, and the effort to tie the "urbanization" action program of FAFEG (Federation of Associations of Favelas in the State of Guanabara – itself a notably urban phenomenon!) with the metallurgical workers union after the awesome rains of January, 1966.

These last points focus attention on the highly urban values for political participation on the part of favela residents. Brazilians, in general, and almost all Brazilian town-city-or-metropolis dwellers, are inherently interested in the polity, its operations, and the machinations of persons in it. Most favela residents we spoke to – at all economic levels and backgrounds – are keenly cognizant of what is happening inside the favela and, especially since the advent of the transistor radio, often extraordinarily well-informed about, and acute in their analyses of, what is occurring in the matrix polity. In fact, we would assert, out of hand, that their views of the political structures and processes of Brazil basically provide better models of the Brazilian political realities than those one gets from most sophisticated native, and certainly almost any foreign, observers. Their political and social action is taken in terms of these perspectives.

A great many favela residents are not only interested in, but value actual participation in political matters of all sorts. Along with the professional politicians and administrators of the Brazilian polity, the favela residents are the most subtle and conniving politicians we have ever met anywhere, far and away more politically-minded in all senses than the American population as a whole, and quite incomparable to any equivalent categories of people in it. Politics is a game, a recreation, a system of rewards, an enjoyment of power, a road to economic mobility, a path to social mobility, and a commitment to some set of interests. The game of politics is extremely complex, moving at many levels, through manifold modes of expression (cf. Leeds, 1964b), by multiple paths of interpersonal relationships. Only those who have been tossed around in the surface swirls of the favela political ocean or have dived in deeply can have an inkling of how really political these people are and how the system is operated. As an outsider, even participating, observing, and resident in the favela over as long a period of time as a year or two, one gets more or less full glimpses of only segments of the system and its events. Some of the most important clues always seem to lead one to arcane mysteries.

We have already mentioned above the positive values for work. In general, we found that favela people value work as an end in itself – presumably as part of the central Christian value towards work (cf. Tilgher, 1930). Work is a proper state of being, whereas idleness and inactivity, especially if imposed and particularly under exigent circumstances, produce expressions of discomfort, denigration, impatience, or anger. Work – the activity of doing something productive – is often used to evaluate the worth of others (ele e *muito trabalhodor, ela trabalha muito*: 'he is very much a worker', 'she's a hard worker'). Work, as a rule, is to be enjoyed *(gosto de trabalhar,* 'I like to work'), to be productive of goods and values, to be creative. Work is, of course, also valued as a means towards ultimate values or goals – to the Good Life, to the desired social position. On the whole, the content of these ultimate ends is urban in character, as we have been stressing.

The city is valued as the place of work *par excellence.* The work of the countryside is inherently narrow and constricting for the Brazilian. More pragmatically, the work of the country does not serve well as a means to the ends that he, as an urban dweller and even as many a country dweller (cf. Leeds, 1957, ch. 7) holds dear. The city provides variety of work, work opportunity, and work rewards; it provides the paths to his ultimate values.

It should be noted that we are talking of the values of favela inhabitants, not of their factual observations and analysis of the work situation, although they see the latter clearly enough, often with extreme bitterness and intense criticism. They are eminently realists in their assessment of their life conditions.

The city is valued because it gives a wide range of possibilities for upward economic mobility. The central values are for bettered standards of living, regularity of food and medical supply, capability of enjoying recreational facilities, and so on. The value is not necessarily to move into some other evaluative level, stratum, or class (cf. Mayntz, 1967, and A. Leeds, 1967b) of the society, but often, simply to lead a full and comfortable life within the existing known framework.

In passing, it may be noted that the anthropologist is in the peculiar position of being something of a participant in, and always an observer of, structurally quite differentiated nodes and trans-nodal bodies (cf. Leeds, 1967), whether these are assorted horizontally, vertically, or in no particular arrangement. Thus, he has multiple vantage points, or varied understandings of, or thoroughly relativistic experience in, the societal structure as a whole, which he can come to see as no other person can. Thus, for example, A. Leeds experienced smalltown Brazilian life, plantation life, a limited amount of peasant life (Leeds, 1957), observed urban-national cliques (1964a), lived and participated in urban "lower-class" life (1966b, 1966c; with E. Leeds and Morocco, 1966), and has had long contact with various branches of the intellectual elite. He has had little or no contact with the military or the church (except in the School of Social Work in Rio) in Brazil. Because of having some entry into these different locations of the society, he has learned petit bourgeois, "left" intellectual, "center" intellectual, and public administrators' views of the "lower classes," the working poor, and the "favelado." From the latter three, we both have learned "favelado-eye" points of view of the "upper" layers. It is not our purpose here to describe all these points of view, but simply to set forth several considerations.

First, the favela residents, in general, have no idea of what the life of the grand bourgeoisie, the intellectual elites, the upper echelon military or church, or even of much of the petit bourgeoisie and most of the bureaucracy is like. They have no way of learning these life patterns, the specialized inner core of values that differentiates each category from the others, the tasks and meanings involved in their jobs and the jobs of their friends, the content and channels of their communications (cf. Leeds, 1964a). The nearest approach to favela residents' experience of them is in the women's work as domestics in their houses, but this represents only a small segment of the lives of those categories of people and is that segment which is most like the favela residents' own life of cooking, eating, dishwashing, cleaning, and so on. What the domestic learns from this is "better" standards of living, not channels of upward mobility. What is verbally expressed as value is usually the former, not the latter; essentially, the "mobility" conceived of is, for the most part, a continuing expansion of what they have now, not a change of state.

Some favela residents dream of moving into the city proper when they can enjoy the kind of housing and city services that persons of the "middle-class" do. To some extent, this is a rejection of the favela and their co-residents there, a vague looking-away from and "upward," but the content of the "upward" consists mainly of the outer trappings of what is evaluated as higher position in the society. On the other hand, one also finds some explicit disparagement of the *gran-finos* (the 'lap-of-luxury people') or the *ricos* or, with highly sophisticated persons, of the *"clase media"* itself.

The "upward mobility" desires tend more to be in particular spheres. A common one is to rise in the hierarchy of political offices, the underlying value being for mobility into positions of personal power and influence for oneself and, perhaps, for a few friends and cohorts, but not for mobility into positions in a different class, stratum, or status level. It is primarily a desire for positional mobility along a chain of positions which is seen, desired, and valued. Another aspiration is for professional training as a doctor, lawyer or, with perhaps more frequency than either of those, some kind of engineer. Such ambitions are not so much in terms of a class or the like, but in terms of a position, its prestige, the *work* that can be done as that sort of professional, the service that can be rendered one's own people, e.g., favela residents.

Plainly, these aspirations are highly urban values. They are increasingly realizable, not so much because there are more positions open or because educational facilities have increased or democratized, but, rather, because discrimination against favela residents has decreased and because favela residents have evolved, finding more ways to circumvent the barriers.

Favela residents have a strong positive value for organization in itself, despite the common notions that Brazilians do not like organization, preferring highly personalized individualistic relationships, and that they do not organize well. The value for organization seems reflected, at least in a rhetorical, formalistic way, in the concern for the law, for the *estatuto* and the *regulamento* (articles and by-laws), of and for procedure. In a favela, as an association drew up its constitution, it was much concerned that the instrument be fitted to the specific conditions of the favela in question so that the formal organizational channels be present and be appropriate to real states of existence.

There are, besides, a number of interests which are served by organization, especially of voluntary organizations. Thus, soccer, a central concern of all Brazilians, generates much organization in the favela. A favela of the size of Tuiuti has three or four soccer clubs, each with its own equipment, its unique uniforms, usually with a club house, and with its schedule of games with teams from the same and other favelas and from outside. Some of the clubs belong to federations of clubs. Members are proud, not merely of their football playing, but of the quality of organization and management itself.

Samba is as pervasive an interest as soccer and has an actual range and intricacy of organization probably greatly exceeding that of soccer. Morocco has given an account of this (1966; cf. Cate, 1962, 1963, 1964). Samba interests become formalized in the organization of *escolas* ('schools') *de samba, blocos* ('blocs') *de samba* and *cordoes* ('strings'), as well as in social clubs, *festas,* and so on. The *escolas* and *blocos de samba* are complexly linked to major textile, beer, and soft drinks industries, to the very large-scale business of the numbers rackets, to the tourist trade, to the Department of Tourism of the state government, even to the state and private welfare agencies and schools, possibly also to prostitution rings, real estate interests, and *macumba* (Afro-Catholic cults). To grasp the ramifications of organization of the samba groups, one must needs have attended innumerable meetings of the directory of an *escola de samba,* watched the fights for power therein, watched *coups d'etat* going on, learned of the swindles, watched the organizing of the rehearsals, the annual show, and the parties. One must have watched the *escola de samba* represented in the Federation of *escolas de samba* and in the supposed Confederation, as well as in their dealings with representatives of the State. One needs to have seen the popping in and out of candidates, deputies, and State officials (like Lutero Vargas, son of Getulio, at Jacarezinho and Mangeira and Governor Negrao de Lima and the Secretary of Social Welfare of the State of Guanabara, Hortencia Abranches, also at Mangueira) at *escola de samba* rehearsals, ceremonies, and *festas.*

It is not merely the samba and its proper execution that are valued, but the organizing itself is, at least verbally, conceived of as a good thing, a thing which will bring benefits to the favela as a whole, a thing which gives (through samba, it is true) a moral guidance to youth, a proper place for recreation, an *ambiente familiar* ('family atmosphere'). That this does not correspond very closely to reality is beside the point. These are the overtly expressed values. Even for covert interests, such as graft and political careerism, organization itself is also a good thing.

Organization can help give morality – emphasized even more markedly perhaps in the strong Protestant sects in the favelas, help give security, help provide the channels to a variety of ends. One of the severest criticisms that can be made of a favela is "*falta uniao aqui*" (loosely, 'we can't get organized here!').

The entire concern with organization and both the value and the factual content of organization in Rio favelas strikes us as eminently urban and directly contradictory to the picture of favelas as organized, almost exclusively, on family ties (Bonilla, Pearse, *et al.*) and strikingly different from the picture afforded us for *callejones* in Peru (see Patch) and *vecindades* in Mexico (see Lewis). It is to be noted in this connection that the *escolas de samba,* dating back forty to fifty years in their present form and preceded by older forms of carnival groups, have, until recently, been associated almost totally with favelas. It is only with the evolution of the favelas themselves and their urban surroundings that some of the *escolas* have moved to the edges of favelas and then, a few, to the city proper. Others more recently have been founded outside the favelas but drawing primarily on favela personnel, e.g., the Bloco Cacique de Ramos.

Another set of clearly urban-oriented values concerns the broad cultural possibilities of the city. In general, having many things to do is a good state of being (cf. Harris, 1956; Leeds, 1957). The *movimento* of the town and especially the city includes movies, clubs, all kinds of recreation; in most of the major cities, beaches, *futebol* games, religious programs, circuses, even theater for some. In the many things to do and among the broader cultural possibilities may be included, too, the radio with its myriad programs, the TV, the various newspapers and magazines, reading materials, the various kinds of training mentioned earlier, even learning foreign languages, especially English. Perhaps a characteristic expression of this set of values is the private party given at someone's house by a young person for other young persons. Many such parties have come to be called a "hai-fai" (hi-fi) because L-P records of the Beatles (English) or the Bitles (Brazilian) or any number of Brazilian groups imitating British and American folk rock bands (to which one frugs, monkeys, etc.), on one hand, or, on the other, a live combo from the favela provide music. Drinks – vodka, rum, *cachaca,* even scotch *nacional* ('made in Brazil'), and soft drinks are served and the party goes on until four or six in the morning. People are dressed in the latest fads and fashions of the mini-skirt, the wrap-around, or what-have-you, familiar from the TV programs watched on the TV sets they own or from the fashion magazines they buy (see Peattie, p. 24).

For a number of people we do not doubt that the value for crime and its rewards are high. For some, it is seen as an alternative, more desirable than the struggle to find, keep, and survive on regular work in the city under difficult conditions of a vicissitudinous labor market and without job skills. Crime in the city is a complex set of activities with its specialists, its trained and untrained workers, its managerial personnel, its moguls, its sanction systems, and its labor market. We know little about crime in Rio except for interviews with several numbers "racketeers" and friendship with several criminals.[25]

One of these, Rio-born Emilio, was, in his quiet way, a force for order and organization in Tuiuti. He was concerned that the favela be organized right and operate well. He was always much concerned with samba and with the organizational welfare of the Gremio Recreativo Escola de Samba Paraiso de Tuiuti. Aside from these interests, he ran a gambling card game and was undoubtedly a marijuana-pusher. For him, these were legitimate activities – there were consumers and interested participants – nothing, we suspect, that he saw as any more moral or immoral than other activities of the business world. He knew, of course, that society defined such activities, and certainly killing a man, as crimes, and he knew about courts and the penal code and Statute 59 regarding vagrancy (if one does not carry an identity card). But these were outside him and the world he enjoyed and valued – his card game, his marijuana business, the defense – yea unto death (and there were deaths while we lived there) – of those interests and his family, friends, and neighbors. The content of his values and his knowledge impressed us as being essentially urban.

Finally, a value permeating the favela is that of freedom – freedom both from and to. Favela residents are quite aware of the social restraints of bourgeois and bureaucratic society outside the favela – they see it in clothing, appearance, formalities of address, language, the poses, and so on – an infinity of cues which identify the others, the outsiders, the "classes" (cf. Leeds, 1964a). The favela provides a refuge from the rhetoric and hollowness, the formality and constraints of the poorly understood "middle-classes" and "elites," *la embaixo*. This taking refuge reinforces the absence of desire for upward mobility to "middle" or "upper" class status, though not for the material advantages attached thereto.

Values regarding freedom from "middle" class constraints appear in many contexts. One day after we had been living in Tuiuti for some time, we were called into a little bar by people we did not know though they later became our best friends in Tuiuti. Almost immediately the conversation turned to *giria* ('slang'). *"O senhor conhece nossa giria?"* ('Do you know our slang?') No, I did not. There followed a half-hour of instruction in favela slang terms. I asked if they used these words *la embaixo*. Maria Antonia said no. I asked why. She said, *"Por vexame!"* ('For shame'). Her meaning was not that they would feel embarrassed, so much as that the language has no place there and they, too, therefore, would have no place "down there." The language of the favela slang is an impropriety to the stiff and stolid middle class which defines its users as *brutos, assassinos, ladroes* ('thieves') *maconheiros* ('pot-smokers') *malandros* ('no-goods').

On the hill, they are free to use this language, rich, funny, ironic, allusive, and largely incomprehensible to outsiders. With it, they can mock the system that presents so many *encrencas* ('monkey-wrenches in the works') and hardships. Some of it appears now and then in the sambas which favela residents write (based, be it noted, on subjects researched in the library!) and which the rest of the city listens and dances to. They enjoy the language, they enjoy its use, and they are able to sit back as *observers* of the language, with sophistication.

On the hill, there is also a much greater freedom as to choice and permanency of relationships, with notably less attention to their formalities. For many, the legal act of marriage is not terribly important, especially if the person has experienced one marriage and found it wanting. The freedom to get married in the *"igreha verde"* ("the verdant church", i.e., to establish a common-law-marriage , metaphorically "in the bushes") to honeymoon in the *hotel das estrelas* ('the hotel of the stars' i.e., 'outdoors') to set up or at least try out a decent life outside the niceties and proprieties – and costs and difficulties – of formal weddings and marriage, are definitely valued. It is valued as humane in a society that does not yet have divorce. Generally we feel that favela residents see and value a greater freedom to establish relationships and freedom in the quality of those relationships – openness, directness, non-instrumentality – than they see in relationships outside the favela.

The pervading concern for freedom, for choice in relationships, for circumventing the traditional bonds, for finding structural situations and social enclaves in which one can enjoy such freedom strikes us as the essence of urbanism.

In closing, we quote a song sung by several little girls jumping rope in Tuiuti, the day after the gubernatorial elections of 1966. The Establishment, which had evicted favelas and sent their residents thirty miles out of town to Alliance for Progress "levittowns" away from the work markets and city amenities and costly and time-consuming of access, had put up Flexa Ribeiro as candidate. He is the brother-in-law of Carlos Lacerda, the then-incumbent governor of the State of Guanabara, leader of the Establishment in the State and preeminent participant in the coup d'etat of 1964 which brought the hated Castel-Branco Government and its economically devastating policies to power. Negrao de Lima was his opponent. Negrao, ex-ambassador to Portugal, former prefect of the Federal District, now Guanabara, was favored by favela residents because he *was* opposition, though they expected little from him, knowing his record. The verse indicates the political acuity of the ten-year olds, the mockery, a bit of the use of language, the freedom of comment on Tuiuti hill:

Lacerda morreu	Lacerda is dead
Pricisa caixao	He needs a coffin
Flexa' ta de luto	Flexa is in mourning
Negrao e campiao	Negrao is champion

NOTES

1. The data of this paper are derived, for Rio de Janeiro, from eighteen months of field work in the favelas and, for Lima, from articles by and extensive conversation with Mangin and Turner, two lengthy interviews with Jose Matos Mar, several visits to barriadas, two months of research for Turner by E. Leeds, dealing with comparisons between the two. The terms "favela", "barraida", and "favelado" (favela resident) will be used as if they were English

words, without *underlining*. The generic terms for the type of phenomenon under discussion, like Abrams "squatment" and "squatterdom", are unsatisfactory because of the barbarities to the English language and because the implications of the root, "squatting," are frequently misleading. Abrams has suggested 'squatter settlements', but it has the same difficulty of being misleading and is unwieldy, but by far the most accurate denotatively. In general we shall use the native terms except where a generic term is more useful. [Note: At the authors' request, this manuscript is being published almost exactly as it was submitted, with no more than the barest minimum of editing. AJF]

2. Similar settlements are called *callampas* in Chile, *turgurios* in Colombia, ranchos in Venezuela, etc., etc. Data emerging from these countries suggest that what we found in Brazil and Peru is paralleled there.

3. Unfortunately, Oscar Lewis has given us virtually no urban sociology of the entities he is dealing with in Mexico City. They do not appear to be the equivalents of favelas and barriadas, but rather of *callejones* and *corticos* (see below), about both of which virtually nothing is known. However, Lewis appears to be saying things similar to what he has said about the *vecindades,* also about Puerto Rican entities which appear to the equivalents of the favelas (cf. Lewis, 1966a); Bonilla (1961) is also cited regularly. The much more careful and insightful papers of Pearse are virtually never cited in general discussion. Even Pearse (1958, 1962), however, makes errors of emphasis, as, for example, on the importance of familism, because he fails to keep in mind that (a) familism is important throughout Brazilian society, not exclusively in favelas, and, (b) familism plays a much more restricted role in proportion to the total number and variety of forms of interaction than he represents.

Note the following passages from Goldrich (1965:368), based primarily on O. Lewis and on Carolina de Jesus (1962): "Margin (sic) orientation is probably promoted by the tendency of the Latin American urban poor to hold no regular job but a set of irregular jobs, or to move from job to job, as a "labor nomad." If one fails to identify oneself on the basis of a rather integrated occupational role, then one may well be less likely to develop a stable orientation toward politics based on one's occupational status, a factor that would retard the development of a sense of group or class consciousness and a set of interests related to it". Or again, "It has been noted by Lewis and others who have dealt with the culture of poverty that under pressure of deprivation slum dwellers have little ability to defer gratification, and exhibit a sense of fatalism and resignation. Thus the favelados are reported to respond to political compaigns with hope and relative enthusiasm, because candidates come through the favelas distributing food or clothing or money – it is perhaps the only time politicians exhibit any interest in these people at all. But except for such infrequent occasions, living is so close to the edge of disaster than an orientation toward the future is not likely to develop – – The electoral process is unlikely to have meaning for the impoverished because its very nature is gradualist and abstract and . . . the poor are unlikely to perceive constitutionalism as a whole as having a relation to their lives" (p. 369).

4. Several cautions should be observed in reading Carolina Maria de Jesus; (a) The book has clearly been heavily edited by its discoverer, a journalist; (b) we consider it quite possible that the whole book was not, in fact, written by Carolina; (c) the book plainly served in the career operations of the journalist (cf. Leeds, 1964a); (d) Carolina is certainly most uncharacteristic of the couple of thousand favela residents of Rio we know, as we show here, although it is conceivable that the population of Sao Paulo's favelas is different. It *is* true that Sao Paulo's favelas are smaller and poorer than those of Rio.

5. Cf. Caplow, et al., (1964) and G. Lewis (1967). Migration of Puerto Ricans to New York in itself indicates a concern for the future, work, improved standards of living, a search for opportunities, a mobility of various sorts, as well as a degree of information about conditions beyond the island. Similar concerns – not characteristic of the alleged culture of poverty – are reflected in an article in the *San Juan Star,* November 4, 1967, which, under the title "La Perla Group Starts Repairs," reads in part: "Six eager beavers of La Perla's San Miguel section have created a right-around-home repair shed designed to aid their community . . . "we built the shed last week because there are lots of houses that need repairs," Baretto said "Our job is to make temporary emergency repairs until the proper government authorities can get down here." The committee has also decided to help the aged, widows, and sick not only to repair homes, but to "make whatever building additions are necessary." . . A re-channelling of a sewer which was passing under one neighbor's home was done to eliminate possible infection. "We had called the government about this." Barreto said, "But nothing happened so we decided it was up to us." La Perla is the *arrabel* (favela) site of O. Lewis' *La Vida.*

6. In justice, it must be pointed out that one small part of the data in Pearse's article (1958) is based on an uncited source for 1948, another part on the census figures of 1950 (it being dubious that the criteria or field procedures for the two sets of figures, which are compared in the article, were comparable). The major part is based on a survey carried out by a nun in 1955, the methods of selection, the field procedures, and the questions for which, like the methods of selecting the nineteen families used for more intensive interviewing, are not given. In contrast, Leeds' earliest contact with favelas was only in 1961 when Jose Arthur Rios was implementing the earlier formulations of Gov. Lacerda's policies toward favelas, i.e. there had already been a year-and-a-half or more of a new kind of intervention which had not existed when Pearse was there. The greater part of our qualitative data is from 1965-66, a ten-year interval from Pearse's contact during which, conceivably, vast changes may have taken place. We attempted to control the changes which might have occurred by getting the best historical descriptions we could – especially of the political relations of favelas to their interests for the entire time period. We also made some effort to get a picture of changes in policy emanating from the public agencies because these set limits on the possibilities of integration at any given time (see below). Better historical material is available for the barriadas because Mangin, Turner, and Matos Mar have been in continual contact with them for at least a decade and the urban ecological development of the barriadas, which began much more recently than the favelas, is relatively well-known. From both cases, we conclude that there has been less an evolution of experience and ideology of favela and barriada residents than an evolution of their articulation with the contextual society (cf. Peattie, 1968, Ch. 1, 2). This articulation is governed by shifts of policy or political and other needs of that society's agencies and, increasingly, by the evolution of the internal social structure of the favelas themselves.

7. What follows would have been predictable from theory before the field study were social scientists accustomed to producing hypotheses by thinking theoretically about empirical materials.

8. In Rio, these consist of the types listed on the left below, while the equivalents for Lima are listed on the right. Approximate definitions are given below (cf. Harris and Hosse).

a.	conjunto	conjunto
b.	vila	urbanizacion popular
c.	corticos	callejones

d.	parques proletarios	villas de emergencia
e.	avenidas	viviendas continuas
f.	cabeca de porco, casas de comodo	casa de vecindad
g.	favelas de quintal	corralones
h.	favelas	barriadas
i.	(slums proper, no term we know of)	turgurios, barrios insalubres

a. In Brazil, a 'housing project,' regardless of income or stratification level; most are occupationally specialized, and it is, therefore, justified to speak of "working class" *conjuntos.* b. 'Working class "levittowns." c. 'Row apartments' – essentially a single building of one or two storeys divided into a string of apartments horizontally, surrounding a long courtyard containing one or more water faucets, sinks for washing clothes, and toilets. In Sao Paulo, the term has come to be applied to rooming houses. d. 'Temporary government working class housing' made of wood; in effect, permanent housing in Rio. We have not yet uncovered a similar term for Lima. e. 'Row houses.' f. 'Rooming or tenement houses.' g. 'Backyard favelas' – favela-type constructions permitted by the owner of the back yard or a street-front house in order to raise his income. j. 'Unauthorized squatter settlements.' i. We discovered no term for this in Rio – the extensive area of once-reasonable housing which has decayed, existing on official streets, and officially having such urban facilities as water, lights, and sewerage.

9. For bibliographies on various countries, see Mangin (1967, p. 90, fn 2) and Turner (1966c). In addition, for Colombia, see Reichel-Dolmatoff (1953). For Brazil: Cate (1961, 1962, 1967), Estado de Minas Gerais (1966), Goulart (1957), Magalhaes (1939), Medina (1964), Pendrell (1967) and Silva (1960). For El Salvador, manuscript materials by Mr. Alistair White of Cambridge University exist; for Guatemala, Roberts (1966, 1967). For Nicaragua, see O. Toness (1967); K. Toness, Mss.

10. Figures for this table have been calculated from data given in *Estudos Cariocas* (Estado de Guanabara, 1965), No. 5, section on "Populacao por Naturalidade e Grupos de Idade" in the tables for the favela population and for the state of Guanabara as a whole. There is no pagination.

11. There is also, of course, a sizable immigration into the city as a whole of middle-income and even wealthy persons, as well as foreigners of various

economic levels. Most of these do not go to favelas, except some poor foreigners, mostly Portuguese. The rest never enter into the discussion of cityward migration because, *by assumption,* being moneyed they cannot be rural, and because of the artifice of separating favelas from the rest of the city. We know little about these immigrants except, perhaps, for the foreigners. The percentage in favelas of Rio is about 0.9 percent, and for Rio as a whole, about six percent, surprisingly low.

12. We encountered *no* persons from the following areas of Brazil: Para, Piaui, Alagoas, Sergipe, in the Northeast; Mato Grosso, Goias, in the West; Santa Catarina in the South; nor from the national territories, Acre and Rio Branco. One or two each are from the following stages: Amazonas, Rio Grande do Norte, in the Northeast; Sao Paulo, Parana, Rio Grande do Sul in the South. A considerable number (but a small percentage) are from Bahia and Ceara, a much larger number from Paraiba and Pernambuco. The very great majority are from Espirito Santo, Minas Gerais, State of Rio de Janeiro, and Guanabara in the South Central area. A small but highly significant group are foreign-born, especially Portuguese. Almost the only genuine peasants we met in the favelas were Portuguese.

13. After some time of doing field work with favela residents, it dawns on one how many official papers they have: rent receipts, water receipts, light receipts, sewer payment receipts, identity cards, elector's cards, military service cards, health post inscriptions, social security cards, cards for memberships in clubs, churches, etc., warranty deeds, bills of sale for houses, birth certificates, marriage certificates, wills, testaments, land titles and other papers dealing with tenure, *Diaros Officiais* in which they have had official announcements printed, and so on, endlessly. Almost all houses have a drawer or box where such mountainous collections of papers are kept. Residents are fairly free about pulling them out and showing their legal status on any matter whatsoever to the researcher. This marked concern with the juridical, the official, is clearly a general cultural emphasis in Brazil, the "Cartorial State" as someone has called it, an emphasis intensified in the favela because of the illegal status of the favela as such. Presumably this is the residents' effort to protect themselves as much against all the forces which can (and do) use any technicality or irregularity against them, as they can. This "cartorial" emphasis is also clearly most urban.

14. See note 10 above.

15. Please note that we do not consider this undesirable. It is customary among so-called development economists and sociologists to think of this sort of labor market articulation as a Bad Thing, a true sign of Underdevelopment and Inefficiency (in turn, a true sign of Underdevelopment) and Undesirable because it is Unproductive (as compared with the Ideal Condition typified by the United States or by the theory of the market). Actually such an articulation – *note well, that it is a highly characteristic form of integration* (see Introduction to paper) *specific to a whole class of societies* – is in many ways highly adaptive. It is probable that a great many more people are "kept employed" by means of odd-jobbing, self-employment, working for companies (*biscate*), costermongering, and peddling, etc., in the city than could be employed in a more strictly curricularized and channelized labor market. Second, it also probably means a wider application of social welfare benefits, however exiguous these may be. Third, where management, credit systems, money transfer systems, accounting procedures, and the consumption market itself are all in constant flux, in ups and downs, and characteristically unchannelled and uncurricularized, it is plain that the employment situation is in constant flux (ultimately in response to national economic conditions and policies, and, in part, to international economic conditions such as fluctuations of prices of exports and imports in the world markets, over which Brazil, Peru, and similar countries which are dependent entities, have little control). One small example will suffice: the check. It is only in the last three or four years that a National Check-Use Law (a Lei do Cheque) has existed. This advanced the use of checks enormously so that one may now write checks on one's own bank and give them to other parties in payment. They must, however, go to my bank, usually even the specific branch that I do business with (the telephone service in Rio is so bad that it is hard to confer from branch to branch) in order to cash the check. Neither *their* banks, nor *any* other, will cash my check. There is no check clearing house. Again, to cash a traveller's check in a bank in Brazil, even at a branch of the American bank issuing the check, e.g., The National City Bank branch in Rio, a form must be made out with ten copies. Payment systems, then, must also be in flux and adaptable at all times, to circumvent rigidities of this sort.

16. The Rurality Myth has led observers into selective non-perception. D. Yaya's neighborhood provides a typical example. It is true that one sees a bunch of women chit-chatting, often washing clothes "together", often giving each other a hand in this or that, and one finds that some of them are relatives and from the same region (in this case several were born here). One tends to say, "Aha! the rural neighborhood in the city! A survival of rurality!"

– the self-proving assumption. In fact, however, as it turns out, some of these families in Yaya's neighborhood are paying rent to D. Yaya's aunt and mother, the former having control of the land and houses, while the latter depends on her. The aunt lives outside the favela in a smallish "middle class" house she acquired by using rents for the favela shacks. The washing is, in fact, not "together", but in parallel; it is not a cooperative endeavor, but an eminently individual one. Some of the users of D. Yaya's mother's water tap pay her for the water, and so on. In other words, the neighborliness occurs in certain contexts only, whereas quite urban behavior towards rents, charges, extortions, and the like, are to be found in other contexts. Brazilians are much better able to mix friendly neighborliness and "reasonable" extortion, especially in situations of duress, than are Americans, so that, generally, Americans are blocked from seeing both at once in the same set of people. In America, landlord and tenant so rarely hobnob! Also, Americans, including social scientists, tend to see the world in black-white dichotomies so that it is difficult for them to see multiple concurrent relationships or role sets displayed by one set of people with respect to another, let alone to several others.

17. Cf. Vayda, Leeds, and Smith, 1961. A series of complicated arrangements exist with respect to pigs in the favelas: raising pigs for slaughter, selling adult animals, buying shoats at the market for raising, raising for shares; ambulant buyers, specialized pig-killers who work for percentages of the meat or for pay, and so on. Pig-raising may be undertaken on commission for people living *la embaixo* who do not have access to land. The calculus of pig-raising is fairly complex but must be left for another time.

18. Built into discussions of stress is the implicit assumption that it is a bad thing. From the point of view of the cognizing individuals such as the people in our example, this is most probably so. A functional analysis of the feed-back of such stresses, their effects on the individuals, and the responses of the individuals or their impact on them (such as being shoved out of the labor market and off the welfare rolls) suggests that under varying conditions of the society and its economy, such stress is adaptive to the system, sad as we may feel this to be.

19. We know of no rural settlement patterns in Brazil which correspond to anything like a favela. We feel that a great deal of discussion should be given as to how purportedly scientific investigations can come to such conclusions. Several things seem involved, all relating to fundamental methodological

problems, most especially the choice of assumptions and the use of questionnaires. The question of assumptions is discussed throughout this paper.

No adequate questionnaire can be made up without prior extensive and intensive ethnographic participation and observation. One cannot know what categories are relevant; one cannot know the appropriate linguistic forms; one cannot know how to interpret the shreds of data that may be at hand; one cannot know how to interpret the responses, since the meaning contexts of the items have not been investigated. Furthermore, the method of applying questionnaires is itself totally foreign to the life experience of informants (especially outside the U.S.) so that unnatural, conventionalized, or misinterpreted responses – thought by the informant to be appropriate to the question asked – are elicited, but not the information about the reality situation that the questionnaire item is supposed to be looking for. This problem becomes particularly acute where cultural differences from the implicit concepts in the investigator's questions, frameworks, and even instruments are involved. Where the investigator is an American "middle class" academic, he faces a double cultural difference – first of understanding and translating into his Brazilian or Peruvian peers' language, then of understanding and translating into the language of the Brazilian or Peruvian proletariat. Bonilla completely, Pearse partially, and many others fail to make these translations – to understand the central meanings of behaviors, institutions, and ideas of the "lower classes," as they confront the other "classes," in their own terms and perspectives. CF. similar failures, in other contexts by Chaplin (1967), Goldrich (1965), Goldrich, Pratt, and Schuller (1966) Kahl (1965), Needler (1967), Rosen (1962, 1964) etc., etc.

All fail to recognize, in part or in full, that even the same words in the same language mean quite different things in different contexts even for the same people, and may have still more sharply varied meanings when major differences in "class," regional, situs, or other locations in the society are involved. One example: *Malandro*, for the Brazilian "classes" means a "deliquent," a "hood"; for the "masses" to whom the former apply, it means a "cool guy," a "clever fellow." For the "classes," it is strong condemnation; for the "masses," it is admiration of a cynosure. The non-participant observer who might use the term about a person in the favela might also end his investigation at that point, while the participant observer using it in the right way is one of the boys.

20. Cf. E. Leeds, 1966. It is most important to note that when an incautious or uninitiated outsider looks at the latter kind of relationship, he sees it

through the eyes of the agency or status level, though in a detached manner. Given its position, the agency operates in a paternalistic manner. The detached, but one-sided observer sees the relationship as paternalistic – a "perpetuation of ruralism." He fails to see the subtle and exploitative manoeuvers and countermoves made by the persons in the complementary position of the relationship, who quite sensibly and with great sophistication make use of the imposed paternalistic mode to their own advantage – until there is nothing more to be gained from it. Then they evanesce. The personnel of the agency or higher status level then tells the observer how "ungrateful" the favelados or the *operarios* or the what-have-you are, how undependable, how treacherous. Peasant cunning, no doubt, but when seen from their side, not paternalistic, just an opportunistic mode of making the best of a bad thing.

21. In a survey, COHAB (see p. 27) estimated (Estado da Guanabara, 1963) Jacarezinho as having 176,000 inhabitants. This would have meant an electorate of about 70,000. Adding Jacarezinho 7,000 C.E.E. houses consuming electricity to about 3,000 still on other private lines, a maximum of about 10,000 are to be found there. Favela households, in several surveys, have averaged between 4.6 and 4.8 persons. Today many of these houses have several households, perhaps averaging about 1.2+/house. Consequently a figure of about 60,000 is reasonable, with a range of from 50,000 to 90,000 (if one calculates at a maximum average of six per household, 1.4 households/house, and about 14,000 households).

22. The evidence for these statements has to be pieced together from data such as those presented in Naro (1966), and E. Leeds (1966), who show how discriminatory barriers are maintained today, and also from historical reconstructions, especially through interviews with residents in a number of favelas and with present and past personnel of administrative agencies. This is necessary because virtually all the published data are based on the Rurality Myth so that they a) repeat all the assertions of rurality, and, b) also fail to look at the context and structure in which favelas exist. It is particularly when one examines the political histories of favelas with a very careful eye to seeing how both (or more) sides play the game – with what strategies, tactics, rules, intentions, tricks, rhetorics, etc. – that one understands the essentially urban nature of both favelas and favela residents. One begins to understand how the allegedly rural characteristics – extended family, et. al. – are in fact highly adaptive institutions in an oppressive and repressive situation (cf. Leeds, 1964b).

23. Research was carried out in the summer of 1966 on the complex structure of Brazilian Afro-Catholic cults in relation to social stratification inside and outside the favelas and as economic enterprises. The work is continuing at present (1969). The work was done by Diana Brown, Department of Anthropology, Columbia University. We much appreciate her cooperation.

24. Cate (1962, 1963, 1967, and in personal communication) has pointed out that the illiterate, apparently truly rural migrants who come into Recife from the Pernambuco State hinterlands are inducted into urban life in the Recife favelas or *mucambos* through a number of schools financed and staffed by the extraordinary network of carnival groups, many of whose now-literate directing members were illiterate migrants of an earlier era.

25. Probably, Cristina Schroeter, a social worker from the School of Social Work of Rio's Catholic University, knows as much as anyone about crime in the favelas. She made contact with a number of gangs of different specialization and with their leaders, some of whom she got to know quite well. With several, she had repeated interviews, the basic content of which she imparted to us. We are most grateful for this information.

INFORMAL COMMENTS BY THE AUTHOR: *ANTHONY LEEDS*

The problem treated in our paper is really part of a much larger one, the understanding of the total society in Brazil. My first field study there was in a plantation, a latifundium area of the monocultural zone in Southern Bahia; my second study involved working in a series of cities, studying elites, and the third has been in urban working class areas. In other words, I worked in various sectors of the society trying to get different perspectives on the total institutional structure, choosing various points in the total system.

What I have tried to do in the comments which follow is say something about the general framework I have employed, which is also relevant to the question of the relationship of agriculture to urban areas. Underlying much of my thinking on this topic is my belief that the distinctions usually made between the urban and rural sectors of a society are misleading.

First of all, I suggest that the great, metropolitan city labor market is a national labor market, that is to say, it draws from the entire polity and sometimes from beyond it. Andrew Pearse's use of the term, "selling labor at a distance," very much reflects what I have in mind. I think it very characteristic of cities that, in fact, they are labor markets for at least an entire segment of a polity, or the entire polity itself; international migration is associated with their being labor markets for still larger areas.

My second point is that the greater the absolute mass of the city and the greater the relative mass of the city in the polity, the greater is the penetration of the city into the non-city areas as a locus of the labor market. In other words, the larger the cities, the more will be the penetration outward into the non-city areas that Pearse describes elsewhere in this volume in his two-fold analysis of penetration – institutional and economic-commerical.

Third, I suggest that the mass of the city or cities is proportional to the number of specializations in the technological, social, and economic operations of society as a whole. The greater the number of specializations, the greater the density and size of the cities. This is looked at in the general-evolutionary perspective that anthropologists are prone to. The increase in density and size of a city and of its specializations revolves around an evolutionary selection, in the long run, for effective communications and operations, or cost-minimizing in the broadest possible sense. What I am introducing here is an efficiency principle which includes effectiveness of communication among the various types of specializations – technical, social, and economic.

In terms of the effectiveness of tying these things together, the aggregate costs will decrease if the unit-specializations are concentrated in a single place. The city may be looked at, socially, as the densest point of interaction among specialists who must, by the nature of specialization, be in constant contact. The notion of a specialist entails the idea of other specialists and of interaction among them. The city is also, technologically, the densest point of coordination among specialized tools, tasks, and resources, which must be in immediate contiguity with each other. Economically, the city is the densest point of *transaction* among specialists. Actually, of course, the city involves the interrelation of all these specializations so that there are social, technological, and economic interactions all going on at once.

My thesis is that these are most effectively carried out in the least possible space; in general, this, then, is an argument concerning what we may call space-intensiveness of activity. The city, ecologically and locationally, is found at some point geographically most suited to certain sets or a preeminent set of specializations. For example, with the trans-shipment from sea-carriage to land-carriage, a port develops, with a set of specializations revolving around shipping and processing activities, and with related economic and social specializations attached to them, possibly with the servicing of the resources trans-shipped and all the other commercial activities connected with them.

Then, there is the point (more or less self-evident, but useful to say) that the physical apparatus of all these specializations – the buildings, transportation systems, and major tools – are the visually striking elements we most readily recognize as a city and sometimes even define as a city, mistakenly, I think, because they are just the physical properties and not the more essential characteristics that a city "is all about."

In sum, a major characteristic of society in general is that it is made up of specializations. Through evolutionary processes, more and more specializations develop and, consequently, there are more and more concentrations of specializations in a space-intensive way. The more of these there are, the larger the space-intensive concentrations will be, the greater the mass will be, and the greater the penetration into areas which are not space-intensive.

I turn now to those areas which are space-*extensive*. There are a few major specializations within the total range of cultural specializations which cannot, under any presently-known technology, be limited to small areas nor located with reference to the ecological determinants of urban location. They are primarily three – agriculture, mining and fishing. Under all known present conditions, they are necessarily space-extensive. Nevertheless, I would argue that the major transactions involving even these activities are not in the physical areas of specialization, the agrarian and rural areas, but in the cities. Most major policy decisions and the most important coordinating institutions of agriculture are concentrated in the cities; such institutions are urban (assuming for the moment that the rural-urban dichotomy has any real value) and not properly rural institutions at all.

It follows that the essential features – the controls, the decisions, the basic policies, the central monetary institutions, the systems of credits and markets for agricultural produce – are to be sought in the cities, not in the areas of space-extensive specialization. The latter cannot be understood without a thorough description of the former. That is, one will never fully understand any agricultural system unless one looks at what is going on with respect to that system in the coordinating areas, which are the cities. Even land tenure systems cannot be fully understood without reference to the fundamental and controlling transactions in the cities.

Through evolutionary time, it becomes "useful" to develop coordinating institutions which we call "government" and "administration." Even among these, there are higher levels of coordinating institutions which we call central governments and central administrations. Now, these central coordinating bodies are also reflected in the cities' structures so that one finds, for example, administrative cities which may or may not be tied to the total transaction system of the society. For example, Brasilia is a very peculiar city in that the administrative and coordinating specializations are more or less separated from the rest of the specializations of the society. No industry and virtually no commerce except small business and consumer-oriented shops exist there. Canberra is another example, and Washington, D.C., is a third. Again, without an understanding of where and how administrative functions are concentrated, it is impossible to give a coherent explanation of the situation in agriculture in any particular time and place.

Thus, instead of seeing agriculture as a separate sector, an idea which has been foisted on us most formally in the dichotomy between Rural Sociology and Urban Sociology (although they have changed considerably in recent years), I see a single structure in which agriculture is simply another element of the total system of specializations in the society. As the society becomes more urbanized, it follows that agriculture becomes more urbanized as well. I think it appropriate to speak of urbanized agriculture, for example, in reference to American agriculture, as such institutions as the Department of Agriculture and all the major agencies of the national government, the universities, the commodity markets, and other urban-centered institutions penetrate out into the countryside.

In short, I think that the whole notion of "urban" has been conceived historically primarily in terms of the physical apparatus of the city, rather than the total institutional structure of the society. It seems closer to the truth to say that the many specialized sub-systems of a society are neither urban nor rural, but societal, and as the society urbanizes, so do the sub-systems.

BIBLIOGRAPHY

Note: 37th ICA refers to a group of papers read in a symposium on urban anthropology at the 37th International Congress of Americanists, September, 1966, held at Mar del Plata, Argentina. These papers, plus that of Modesto, are to be published under the editorship of A. Leeds, by the Institute of Latin American Studies, University of Texas.

Abrams, Charles

1966 *Squatter Settlements – the Problem and the Opportunity.* Washington: Department of Housing and Urban Development, Div. of International Affairs.

Bierstedt, Robert

1967 "Power and Social Class," *In* A. Leeds, ed., *Social Structure, Stratification, and Mobility.* Washington: Pan American Union.

Bonilla, Frank

1961 "Rios Favelas: The Rural Slum Within The City," *Reports Service* 8(3): 1-15, Amer. Universities Field Staff.

1962 "The Favelas of Rio: The Rundown Rural Bairro in the City," *Dissent,* 9:383-386.

Briones, Guillermo

1963 "Movilidad Occupacional y Mercado de Trabajo en el Peru," *America Latina* 6(3):67-76.

Browning, Harley and Elizabeth and Jorge Balan

1967 *Movilidad Social, Migracion, y Fecundidad en Monterrey Metropolitano.* Monterrey and Austin: Centro de Investigaciones Economicas de la Universidad de Nuevo Leon, and Population Research Center, University of Texas.

Browning, Harley and Waltraut Feindt

1967 "Natives versus Migrants: A False Dichotomy?" Population Research Center, Department of Sociology, Univ. of Texas (mimeo).

Caplow, Theodore, Sheldon Stryker and Samuel Wallace

1964 *The Urban Ambience: A Study of San Juan, Puerto Rico.* New York: Bedminster Press.

Cate, Katherine R.

1962 Final report to the technical secretariat of the OAS Fellowship Program. July 15 (typescript).

1963 Letter to Dr. Vera Rubin, Director, Research Institute for the Study of Man, Sept. 11 (typescript).

1967 *O Folclore no Carnaval de Recife.* Rio de Janeiro: Ministerio de Educacao e Cultura. (Under the pen name of Catarina Real).

Chaplin, David

1966 "Industrial Labor Recruitment in Peru," *America Latina,* 9(4):22-40.

Clifton, James

1966 A Petition for a Grant-in-aid of Research to the Wenner-Gren Foundation for Anthropological Research, Project title: "A Study of Processes of Urbanization and Adaptation in a Chilean Callampa Community." Nov. (mimeo).

Comissao Coordinadora para a Alianca para o Progresso (COCAP)

1965 *Vila Proletaria da Penha: Levantamento Socio-Economico.* Rio de Janeiro' BEMDOC (Brazil-Estados Unidos Movimento de Desenvolvimento e Organizacao da Comunidade.

DESAL (Centro para el Desarrollo Economico y Social de America Latina)

1965 *Poblaciones Marginales y Desarrollo Urbano: El Caso Chileno.* Santiago (mimeo).

n.d. "Poblaciones Marginales, Un Ejemplo Latino-Americano: Chile." Santiago (mimeo).

Epstein, A. L.

1967 "Urbanization and Social Change in Africa," *Current Anthropology,* 8(4):275-296.

Estado da Guanabara

1967 "Favelas da Guanabara," Rio: COHAB (Companhia de Habitacao Popular da Guanabara, (xeroxed).

1965 Estudos Cariocas, 5 vol., No. 5: I. Mobilidade Populacional: II Condicoes Socio-Economicas, Rio: Secretaria do Governo, Coordenacao de Planos e Orcamentos.

1967 "Favelas da Guanabara por Regioes Administrativas," Rio de Janeiro: Secretaria de Servicos Sociais, Departamento da Recuperacao das Favelas (mimeo).

Estado de Minas Gerais

1966 *Levantamento da Populacao Favelada em Belo Horizonte: Dados Preliminares.* Belo Horizonte: Secretaria de Estado do Trabalho e Cultura Popular, Departamento de Habitacao Popular.

Frank, Andre Gunder

1967 *Capitalism and Underdevelopment in Latin America: Historical Studies and Brazil.* New York: Monthly Review Press.

Galjart, Benno

1964 "Class and Following in Rural Brazil," *America Latina, 7(3):3-24.*

Goldrich, Daniel

1965 "Toward the Comparative Study of Politicization in Latin America," *In* D. Heath and R. N. Adams, eds., *Contemporary Cultures and Societies of Latin America.* New York: Random House, pp. 361-378.

Goldrich, Daniel, Raymond Pratt and C. R. Schuller

1966 "The Political Integration of Lower Class Urban Settlements in Chile and Peru: A Provisional Study," Paper presented at the Annual Meeting of the Amer. Political Science Association, Sept.

Goulart, J. Alipio

1957 *Favelas do Distrito Federal.* Rio de Janeiro: Ministerio da Agricultura.

Guilherme, Benedito

n.d. *O Buraco da Lacraia* [Centipede Hole]. Ms., (typescript).

Harris, Marvin

1956 *Town and Country in Brazil.* New York: Columbia Univ. Press.

Harris, Walter and H. A. Hosse

1963 *La Vivienda en el Peru.* Washington: Pan American Union.

Hoenack, Judith

1966 "Resources and Sources: Marketing, Supply and the Social Ties in Rio Favelas." 37th ICA.

Hutchison, Bertram

1960 *Mobilidade e Trabalho; Um Estudo na Cidade de Sao Paulo.*

1963a "The Migrant Population of Urban Brazil," *America Latina,* 6(2):41-71.

1963b "Urban Social Mobility Rates in Brazil Related to Migration and Changing Occupational Structure," *America Latina,* 6(3):47-62.

Instituto Brasileiro de Geografia e Estatistica

1951 *Sinopse Preliminar do Censo Demografico.* Rio: Conselho Nacional de Estatistica.

1963 *Anuario Estatistico,* 1963. Rio: Conselho Nacional de Estatistica.

Jesus, Carolina Maria de

1962 *Child of the Dark,* [Quarto de Despejo.] Trans. (badly) by David St. Clair. New York: New American Library.

Kahl, Joseph

1966 "Social Stratification and Values in Metropolis and Provinces; Brazil and Mexico," *America Latina,* 8(1): 23-36.

1966 "Los Valores Modernos y los Ideales de Fecundidad en Brasil y Mexico," *America Latina,* 9(2).

Leeds, Anthony

1957 *Economic Cycles in Brazil: The Persistence of a Total Culture Pattern: Cacao and Other cases.* Ann Arbor: University Microfilms.

1964a "Brazilian Careers and Social Structure: An Evolutionary Model and Case History," *American Anthropologist,* 66(6): 1321-1347.

1964b "Locality Power in Relation to Supra-Local Power Institutions." Paper presented at symposium on urban anthropology, Wenner-Gren Foundation for Anthropological Research, Burg Wartenstein. August. In Press.

1965 "A General Systems and Transactional Study of Power in Brazil and Colombia." Research Proposal Submitted to the National Science Foundation, January (mimeo).

1966a "Evaluation of the Urban Community Development Project-Bemdoc." Report to U.S.-A.I.D.-Brazil (mimeo).

1966b "Future Orientation: The Investment Climate in Rio Favelas," 37th ICA.

1966c "Perspectives from Anthropology: The Subject I as Object." Paper read at symposium, "The Effects of Field Work on the Anthropologist as Humanist," Annual Meeting, American Assoc. for the Advancement of Science, Washington.

1967a (Editor), *Social structure, Stratification, and Social Mobility,* Washington, D.C.: Pan American Union.

1967b "Some Problems in the Analysis of Class and the Social Order," *In* A. Leeds, ed. (see 1967a):327-361.

Leeds, Anthony, Elizabeth Leeds and David Morocco

1966 "The Politico-Administrative Power in Relation to Electricity in Rio Favelas." Paper read at Annual Meeting, American Association for the Advancement of Science, Washington, D.C.

Leeds, Elizabeth R.

1966 "Political Complementarity of Favelas with the Larger Society of Rio de Janeiro," 37th ICA.

Lewis, Gordon K.

1967 "Culture of Poverty or Poverty of Culture?," *Monthly Review,* 19(4):444-53.

Lewis, Oscar

1952 "Urbanization without Breakdown: A Case Study," *Scientific American,* 75:31-41.

1960 *The Children of Sanchez.* New York: Random House.

1963 "The Culture of Poverty," Trans-Action, 1(1):17-19.

1966a *La Vida: A Puerto Rican Family in the Culture of Poverty.* New York: Random House.

1966b "The Culture of Poverty," *Scientific American,* 215(4):19-25.

Magalhaes, Agammenon

1939 *Observacoes Estatisticas Sobre os Mucambos do Recife.* Recife: Imprensa Oficial.

Mangin, William

1964 "Sociological, Cultural and Political Characteristics of Some Rural Indians and Urban Migrants in Peru." Paper read at Symposium cited in Leeds (1964b).

1965 "The Role of Regional Association in the Adaptation of Rural Migrants to the Cities in Peru." *In* Heath and Adams, ed., cited in Goldrich (1965).

1967a "Political Implications of the Barriadas in Peru." Paper read at the Latin American Colloquium, Department of Sociology, Brandeis University, May.

1967b "Latin American Squatter Settlements: A Problem and a Solution," *Latin American Research Review,* 2(3):65-98.

1967c "Squatter Settlements," *Scientific American,* 217(4):21-29.

Mangin, William and Jerome Cohen

1964 "Cultural and Psychological Characteristics of Mountain Migrants to Lima, Peru, *Sociologus,* 14(1):81-88.

Matos Mar, Jose

1962 "Migration and Urbanization: The Barriadas of Lima – An Example of Integration into Urban Life," *In* P. Hauser, ed., *Urbanization in Latin America.* New York: UNESCO, pp. 170-189.

1964 "Consideraciones Sobre La Situacion Social del Peru," *America Latina,* 7(1):57-70.

Mayntz, Renate

1967 "Methodological Problems in the Study of Stratification," *In* Leeds, ed. (1967a):8-26.

Medina, Carlos Alberto

1964 *A Favela e o Demagogo.* Sao Paulo: Martins.

Modesto, Helio

1966 "Favelas – Reflexoes Sobre o Problema," Ms. (mimeo).

Morocco, David

1966 "Carnival Groups – Maintainers and Intensifiers of the Favela Phenomenon in Rio de Janeiro," 37th ICA.

O'Neil, Charls

1966 "Problems of Urbanization in Rio Favelas." 37th ICA.

Patch, Richard

1961 "Life in a Callejon: A Study of Urban Disorganization," *Reports Service,* 8(6):1-24. American Universities Field Staff.

Pearse, Andrew

1958 "Notas Sobre a Organizacao Social de Uma Favela do Rio de Janeiro," *Educacao e Ciencias Socias,* III, 3(7)L9-32.

1962 "Some Characteristics of Urbanization in the City of Rio de Janeiro," *In* P. Hauser, Ed., see citation in Matos Mar (1962), pp. 192-200.

Peattie, Lisa Redfield

1968 *The View from the Barrio.* Ann Arbor: University of Michigan Press.

Pendrell, Nan

1967 "Urban Squatting: The Brazilian Case." Paper read at Annual Meeting, American Anthropological Association, Washington.

"Populacao Brasileira em 1960," Revista Brasileira dos Municipios, 14(55/56): 180-197.

Ray, Talton

1966 The Political Life of the Venezuelan Barrio. Ms (typescript).

Reichel-Dolmatoff, Gerardo

1953 *El Marco Cultural en el Estudio de la Vivienda.* Resumen de Clase No. 4, Bogota: CINVA (Centro Interamericano de la Vivienda).

Roberts, Bryan

1966 "Some Aspects of Urban Life in Guatemala City." Paper read at annual Meeting, Amer. Association for the Advancement of Science, Washington, December.

Rosen, Bernard C.

1962 "Socialization and Achievement Motivation in Brazil," American Sociological Review, 27(Oct.):612-624.

1964 "The Achievement Syndrome and Economic Growth in Brazil," *Social Forces*, 42(3):341-354.

Safa, Helen Icken

1964 "From Shantytown to Public Housing: A comparison of Family Structure in Two urban Neighborhoods in Puerto Rico," *Caribbean Studies*, 4:3-12.

1965 "The Female-based Household in Public Housing: A Case Study in Puerto Rico," *Human Organization* 24:135-39.

1966 "Comparative Study of the Assimilation of Urban Poor," Read at 133rd Annual Meeting, American Association for the Advancement of Science, Washington, D.C.

1967 *An Analysis of Upward Mobility in Low Income Families.* Syracuse: Syracuse University, Youth Development Center.

SAGMACS (Sociedade de Analises Graficas e Mecanograficas Aplicadas aos Complexos Sociais).

1960 "Aspectos Humanos da Favela Carioca," *Estado de Sao Paulo*, supl. especial, April 13, 15.

Silva, Luiz

ca. 1960 *Apontamentos Sociograficos sobre a "Favela dos Marmiteiros."* Belo Horizonte, Departamento Municipal de Habitacoes e Bairros Populares.

Smith, Nancy

1966 "Eviction! – Land Tenure, Law, Power, and the Favela." 37th ICA.

Tilgher, Adriano

1930 *Work: What it Has Meant to Men Through the Ages.* (Trans. Dorothy Canfield Fisher) New York: Harcourt, Brace.

Toness, Kay

n.d. "Women and Work in a Nicaraguan Slum" (typescript).

Toness, Odin

1967 "Power Relations of a Central American Slum," M.A. Thesis, University of Texas, Austin.

Turner, John F. C.

1963 "Dwelling Resources in South America," *Architectural Design,* August, pp. 360-393.

1966a "Barriers and Channels for Development: The Actual and the Potential Roles of Planning and Building Standards in the Urban Growth of Modernizing Cities" (mimeo).

1966b "Uncontrolled Urban Settlements: Problems and Policies." Paper for the United Nations Interregional Seminar on Development Policies and Planning in Relation to Urbanization, Pittsburgh.

1966c "Assentamientos Urbanos no Reglados," *Cuadernos de la Sociedad Venezolana de Planificacion,* No. 36.

1967 "Autonomous Urban Settlements: Problems or Solutions?" Paper read at Colloquium cited in Mangin (1967a).

Turner, John F.C. and Rolf Goetz

1966 "Environmental Security and Housing Input," *Carnegie Review,* October, pp. 13-20.

Vayda, Andrew P., A. Leeds and David B. Smith

1961 "The Place of Pigs in Melanesian Subsistence," Proc. *Annual Spring Meeting,* American Ethnological Society, pp. 69-77.

White, Alistair

n.d. Typescript report on field work in El Salvador.

Wilson, L. Albert

1965 *Voice of the Villas – Socio-Economic Analyses of the Residents of Villas in Parque Almirante Brown,* Buenos Aires, Argentina. Washington: Foundation for Cooperative Housing.

Wygand, James

1966 "Water Networks: Their Technology and Sociology in Rio Favelas." 37th ICA.

POLITICAL ASPECTS OF URBANIZATION IN MEXICO

Martin C. Needler

Like most of the developing countries, Mexico is going through an urban revolution of impressive magnitude. From 1950 to 1960 the proportion of the population living in urban areas, as these are defined by the Mexican census,[1] rose from 43 percent to 51 percent, while in absolute figures, the total population was growing from about 25 to about 35 million.[2] For 1968, a reasonable estimate would be a proportion of 55 percent urban in a population of 45 million. Rapid urbanization has brought with it the familiar problems of mushrooming shantytowns, unemployment and underemployment, and an overstress on the provision of municipal services even at the expense of some of the much needed economic growth.

Mexico is more fortunate than most developing countries, however, in the economic and political resources it can bring to bear on the solution of these problems. The gross national product has been growing fairly steadily at a long-term rate of something over six percent annually, which means that even after allowance is made for a rate of population growth between 3.0 and 3.5 percent per year, Mexico has been surpassing the Alliance for Progress target of a 2.5 percent annual increase in per capita income. The value of the peso has remained stable since 1954. The balance of international payments has been relatively untroubled, and the inflow of foreign currency is not unhealthily dependent on one or two major export items, as is the case with most other Latin American countries, although tourism is a key source of income and could prove volatile. At the same time, the rate of domestic savings and capital formation is high, and a pragmatic economic policy has made room for private and public enterprise and domestic and foreign initiative, in a fairly well-balanced combination.[3]

On the political side, a single dominant party provides stability and continuity, while an opposition exists and functions in a relatively free political environment.[4] This will probably continue to hold true despite the evidence of the street battles in Mexico City just prior to the 1968 Olympic Games there.

The present paper will examine three aspects of the process of urbanization in Mexico: 1) its relation to the unevenness of social development; 2) the political orientations of the new lower-class city-dwellers, and especially the extent of political alienation among them; and 3) the effects of urbanization on the generalized attitudes which make up the "political

TABLE I – TRENDS IN "MARGINAL" POPULATION IN MEXICO

Year	Rural	School-age children not in school	Not using shoes	Speaking primarily or exclusively an Indian language
1930	11,010,000	1,690,000	– – –	2,250,000
1940	12,760,000	2,550,000	9,850,000	2,490,000
1950	14,810,000	2,970,000	11,410,000	2,450,000
1960	17,220,000	3,120,000	12,740,000	3,030,000

SOURCE: Gonzalez Casanova, (1965, Chapter 5).

culture." In discussing Mexico, I shall also try to bring to bear insights growing out of work on other countries.

I

To speak of urbanization is, of course, only to abstract one aspect from a whole process of demographic change. More precisely stated, these changes consist of rural-urban migration proper, migration from smaller towns to larger cities,[5] and migration from the poorer to the more prosperous sections of the country, especially to areas along the United States border.[6] In the Mexican context, therefore, this whole set of demographic shifts signifies movement from the more traditional sector to the more modern. The gap bridged by such movement is especially great in Mexico, since the traditional sector is in many cultural respects, strongly Indian. The difference between the two sectors, accordingly, extends not only to questions of occupation, standard of living, and beliefs and attitudes, but also to types of food consumed, styles of life, and even language spoken. In recognition of this fact, the Mexican census tries to elicit information about cultural style by asking respondents if they habitually eat wheat bread or corn tortillas, wear shoes or go barefoot, sleep on the floor, on a hammock, or in a bed, and speak Spanish or an indigenous language.

Although the major streams of migration are from the traditional to the modern sector, such migration falls short of draining off numbers of people equal to the natural increase of population in the traditional sector. This has been pointed out in a careful analysis published recently by one of the most perceptive Mexican political scientists, Pablo Gonzalez Casanova (1965). Thus, as Gonzales Casanova points out, the number of people speaking indigenous languages has shown an *increase* over the period up to 1960, as have the numbers of people in other categories which define what he calls "marginal Mexico" (see Table 1). A disturbing picture is created if one combines these figures on the increase in the number of "marginal Mexicans" with figures indicating that the benefits of the country's economic growth are being channeled disproportionately into the modern sector.[7] It becomes clear that the gap between traditional and modern Mexico is growing while the number of people in the traditional sector is increasing. At the same time, the marginal Mexicans are not effectively organized for political action, either in pressure groups or in subsidiary organs of the governing party, and so lack the means to redress the social and economic imbalance that grows greater as time passes.

While this picture is a disquieting one, there are two mitigating factors which must be borne in mind. The more obvious point is that although "marginal Mexico" is growing in absolute size, its *rate* of growth is nevertheless much lower than the rate of growth of the total population. Accordingly, the marginal Mexicans represent a steadily decreasing *proportion* of the total population. This helps to place the problem in proper perspective.

More importantly, perhaps, it seems unwise to extrapolate the gap in standard of living between the two sectors into the indefinite future. By its nature, development does not occur evenly throughout the society in its early stages, but rather focuses in the most favorable zones, in the Mexican case the national capital, the largest cities, and the areas close to the United States border. As development proceeds, however, it spreads to zones whose comparative advantage in factors such as lower tax and wage rates exceeds the "external economies" available in the more developed areas, and differential rates of development shift as a certain amount of "catching up" takes place. Some of these effects have been observed, for example, in the American South in recent years, and appear to be beginning in the Brazilian Northeast, long regarded as an area hopelessly doomed to perpetual backwardness. One should nevertheless not overlook the fact that even in a developed society areas of hard-core underdevelopment can persist, on the model of Appalachia.

II

There has been much speculation about the political role of new migrants to the cities of Latin America. Drawing on impressionistic eye-witness experience, most observers have stressed the explosive possibilities of direct political action by the disaffected residents of the highly visible shantytowns built on marginal lands sometimes within, but usually adjoining, the city – the *favelas* (Brazil), *callampas* (Chile), *barriadas* (Peru), *ranchos* (Venezuela), *barrios brujos* (Panama), or *villas miserias* (Argentina), as they are variously known.

Now, this impressionistic picture is misleading in several ways. In the first place, not all the lower-class migrants to the cities settle in the marginal shantytowns; many go to stay with relatives in older parts of the city, or move into the centrally located older slums known as *conventillos* or *vecindades* (Mexico), or *callejones* (Peru), (Patch, 1961). Those who do so make an adjustment, good or bad, to an already structured situation as individuals; they do not confront society collectively.

Thus, the move to a shantytown is commonly a step up for recent migrants who have spent some time in a central-city slum. Frequently, dwellers in shantytowns express themselves as satisfied with their new situation, which represents an improvement in their condition. That this situation appears unsatisfactory to a North American observer is no reason to assume that residents in shantytowns are inevitably disaffected and alienated. In several of his analyses of the *favelas*, Anthony Leeds (1967a, b) has shown that many of their inhabitants move rapidly into entrepreneurial roles and manage to get along rather well. In other words, it is subjective consciousness of deprivation that is the significant factor in shaping behavior, not any absolute condition.

But in any case, it does not follow that even those dwellers in the shantytowns who are disaffected will express their resentment of the situation in which they find themselves in political terms. They usually have a low awareness of the political system;[8] their time and energies are likely to be absorbed in the daily struggle for existence leaving little surplus for political involvement; and the settlements are normally physically removed from the center of the city where symbolic political acts take place and protest demonstrations might have some effect.

At the same time, it would be foolish to argue that there is never any revolutionary potential in the new settlements. An adverse change in the general level of economic conditions can frustrate the rising aspirations of even the most vigorous shantytown entrepreneur, thus creating the classic revolutionary situation. And the initial outbreak of revolutionary violence can occur elsewhere in society, penetrating the consciousness of even the normally least-political shantytown dweller and making possible his mobilization into revolutionary activity. José Moreno (1967) has shown, for example, that, although they did not participate in politics before the fighting broke out, it was young residents of the *barrios altos,* the shantytowns of Santo Domingo's *Ciudad Nueva,* who came to play the major role on the Constitutionalist side during the Dominican civil war of 1965.

There are thus many factors which militate against the newly urbanized poor's forming a focus of mass revolutionary activity. But in the Mexican context there is an additional force working to integrate the newly urbanized into the political system in supportive roles, and that is the government party, the *Partido Revolucionario Institucional.* One should bear in mind that the reason for the organization of the "official party" in the first place was precisely to limit violence in the political system by providing a mechanism for the representation of interests and the satisfaction of demands (Needler, 1961).

The PRI plays somewhat the same role with respect to the newly urbanized that was played by the urban political machines in the northern United States with respect to new immigrants in the late 19th century; party politicians make the cause of the poor their own, intervening with the bureaucracy on such matters as securing jobs and licenses, arranging bail, and clarifying titles to plots of land. This traditional machine-politics approach of the PRI to integrating the newly urbanized lower classes by a policy of favors and handouts is particularly well-suited to the situation. As Daniel Goldrich has pointed out, political attitudes among the urban poor are oriented especially to immediate gratification, rather than to questions of ideology or program (Goldrich, 1965, p. 369). Thus the poor relate to politics as individuals petitioning powerful figures for special favors, not as a class using the weapons of mass action. Accordingly, their political behavior becomes patterned on the basis of the patron-client arrangement with which they were familiar in the rural or small town areas from which they came. And the expression of their demands becomes a mechanism for tying them in to the government party, rather than a vehicle of opposition sentiment. The PRI, always on the lookout for unaffiliated groups of potential supporters, has recognized the urban poor in its characteristic fashion by establishing an organization affiliated with one of the sectors of the party to represent their interests: the *Ligas para la Defensa del Consumidor,* which are now included in the federation of organizations that comprises the "popular" sector of the party.

That this strategy seems to be successful is indicated by the voting records of the cities. It is true that the opposition to the PRI is stronger in the cities and the more developed areas of the country; for example, in the legislative elections of 1961 the opposition parties won thirty-five percent of the vote in the Federal District and thirty-three percent in Lower California North, but less than one percent in the states of Chiapas and Tlaxcala (Gonzalez Casanova, p. 106). However, the growth in the opposition vote has been almost entirely on the part of the *Partido de Acción Nacional,* which represents middle-class elements and opposes the PRI from a more conservative position. The comparable party to the left of the PRI, the Popular Socialists, on the other hand, has had virtually no success in recruiting urban voters. This suggests that the PRI has thus far managed to channel the demands of the newly-urbanized lower classes in ways that can be contained without difficulty within the operating political system. There has, in fact, been violent direct action recently on the part of the poor, led by politicians to the left of the governing party, but this has been confined to the rural areas, where it has taken the form of land occupations, or *paracaidismo.*

Political violence has, of course, been taking place in many of the urban areas of Latin America in the forms of demonstrations, riots, and even organized terrorism, but, as in the gubernatorial nomination in Sonora in 1967, the instigators have frequently not been the poor at all, but rather, the students. It is worth noting in this connection that students differ from the urban poor in almost all of the characteristics adduced above to explain the lack of political violence on the part of the poor. Students have an excess of both time and energy, the university is usually located close to the city center,[9] and they are highly conscious of what goes on about them. The outbreaks of fighting in Mexico City in 1968, for example, were led by students, (or, rather, by the police against students).

III

Another set of relations between the processes of urbanization and the political system lies at a different level. Viewed in developmental perspective, Mexico is a country which is trying to progress from a political system operating on the basis of the use of force, favoritism and personal connections, and an obedient population, to one based on honest government, responsiveness to popular needs, and civic participation. At present in a transitional stage, Mexico clearly has a long way to go to reach the second pole of the continuum.

Change in this dimension presupposes the modification of institutions, behavior, and popular attitudes.[10] However, the most widely accepted generalizations about Mexican character and behavior posit characteristics especially appropriate to the traditional authoritarian pole of the development continuum.[11] Observers have stressed the common image of authority as essentially arbitrary and self-interested, which means not only that the population is unlikely to play the role of democratic citizen required of it in a politically developed Mexico, but also that those placed in authority, through election or appointment, are likely to fall into a pattern of abuse of power.[12]

Unfortunately, it may be the case that urbanization reinforces these inappropriate attitudes rather than modifying them.[13] Statistics indicate that for Mexico, as for other countries, lower-class urbanization is accompanied by social disorganization, the weakening of family ties, the absence of a male head of household or a succession of temporary occupants of this role, higher rates of juvenile delinquency, and so on (Iturriaga, 1951). In other words, the lack of stability in the family and continuity in the father's role is likely to reinforce the tendency of the growing child to conceive of authority as unstable, arbitrary, and self-interested. Accordingly, to the extent that the urban lower classes constitute a key population element, it may well be that

Mexico will continue to find its greatest obstacle to the achievement of full and stable political development in the problem of developing and strengthening democratic civic attitudes.

Under this set of circumstances, it is noteworthy that it is the opposition party of middle-class orientation, the *Partido de Acción Nacional*, which has made the achievement of the norms of good citizenship part of its programs.[14] Originally a party of fairly violent and principled opposition in the Mexican tradition, glorifying pre-modern values and the Hispanic tradition and condoning the use of violence, the PAN has now evolved to the position of a loyal opposition party.[15] The PAN presidential candidate in the 1964 election, José Gonzales Torres, acknowledged that he had been defeated fairly and sent his congratulations to the winner – something new in Mexican politics. The party has abandoned its stance of total rejection of the goals of the Mexican Revolution, and has instead expressed agreement with the PRI on overall goals, focusing its opposition on questions of honesty and responsibility in the public administration and the electoral process. Clearly these elements in the PAN's program contain political objectives, and not just disinterested advocacy of good government: PAN urges the purity of the electoral process, meaning that the votes it receives should *all* be counted, and implying that it does better at the polls than the official figures show; it urges that municipal autonomy be respected, since the party controls some municipal governments but not the central government; PAN attacks corruption by federal office-holders, none of whom come from its ranks. It is nevertheless significant that this more modern civic-minded approach to the role of opposition has been taken, rather than that of a traditional revolutionary opposition. In this respect, the new orientation of the PAN is indicative of the character of the new urban middle classes it represents.

At the same time, similar tendencies affect the PRI. A body of "reform" opinion has been growing within the official party demanding greater rank-and-file participation and an end to bossism, and the ferment was quieted only temporarily by the removal of the spokesman for this tendency, Carlos Madrazo, after only a year as party president. The desertion of large numbers of PRI voters to the PAN over the "bossism" issue, which gave PAN the mayoralty of Hermosillo in 1967, has made clear to the leadership of PRI that concessions must be made to middle-class reform sentiment if the party wants to maintain its near-monopoly of power.

IV

The conclusions suggested by this analysis may be summarized as follows:

1. Mexico is experiencing a rapid rate of population growth especially in its urban areas, and this has created or intensified the set of social problems associated with this phenomenon throughout the underdeveloped world.

2. The elements of the national population outside the modern sector in both the economic and cultural senses have increased in numbers but decreased as a percentage of total population. The gap in living standards between the marginal population and the modern sector has remained constant or increased. It should not be assumed that this situation will continue indefinitely, however; it is more likely that eventually the gap will begin to close.

3. Demographic pressures have been clearly responsible for some instances of illegal direct political action in the countryside, but direct action in the cities continues to be undertaken by students rather than the newly urbanized poor. Disaffection among the urban poor may under some conditions take the form of political violence, but so far the dominant political party has been able to channel popular demands in non-violent ways.

4. Although the newly urbanized lower classes do not threaten the stability of the political system, neither do they provide a citizenry whose attitudes support the political modernization desired by the country's leadership. It is likely that attitudes engendered by the life-style of the urban poor are dysfunctional for political modernization. However, the development of the urban areas is also providing the country with a more modern middle class, valuable especially in the transformation of political opposition in the direction of loyalty to constitutional procedures.

5. It appears probable that the PRI will attempt increasingly to modify its internal organization and practices to make them more acceptable to this growing middle class by making provision for greater rank-and-file participation, and reducing arbitrariness and corruption in government.

Thus, although the high rates of population growth and urbanization it has experienced are sources of stress for Mexican society, thus far the economic and political systems have proved able to manage these new stresses without serious damage to the country's stability or to its movement in the direction of modernization.

NOTES

1. The Mexican census considers "urban" any settlement containing more people than the rather low figure of 2,500, but the United States, as it happens, uses the same figure.

2. Howard F. Cline (1962, p.82). Urquidi (1966) estimates that the 1960 census under-enumerated the population by about one million.

3. A survey of the recent performance of the economy is given in Dwight S. Brothers (1966). For a comparison with the other Latin American countries, see Pan American Union (1966).

4. The best descriptions of Mexican politics are Vincent Padgett (1966), and Robert E. Scott (1965).

5. A recent study of migration to Santiago, Chile, has indicated that the overwhelming majority of the migrants come from the smaller towns. Since the population of these towns is growing faster, and the rural population slower, than the overall national rate, this indicates that those leaving rural areas go predominantly to the smaller towns. This parallels the experience of nineteenth-century England, and is probably the typical pattern. See Bruce H. Herrick, (1965, p. 51). See, also, the useful analysis of the components of cityward migration in the essay by Anthony Leeds elsewhere in this volume.

6. The magnitude of this third type of migration is indicated by the fact that the two greatest rates of population growth during the 1950–60 decade were shown by the states of Lower California North (232 percent) and Tamaulipas (61 percent) on the Texas border. Both rates were greater than that for the Federal District (49 percent), which includes Mexico City. (Cline p. 86).

7. For data supporting the latter conclusion, see Oscar Lewis (1960). It should be noted, however, that the maldistribution of income cited by Lewis derived partly from the inflation that was still a factor in the early '50's. Since the devaluation of the peso in 1954, inequality deriving from this effect has been substantially reduced.

8. This factor and several related ones are discussed in Daniel Goldrich (1965, p. 363 ff.).

9. The writer suspects, but has not tested, the hypothesis, that student political activity has dropped where new campuses have been built out of town, and in fact that that has been the purpose of governments that have constructed "university cities."

10. The best discussion of the attitudes appropriate to a developed polity can be found in Gabriel Almond and Sidney Verba (1965).

11. For a survey of research on Mexican national character, see Gordon Hewes (1954).

12. This is reflected in the findings by Almond and Verba (1965, p. 70) that over half their Mexican sample expected that they would *not* receive equal (i.e., fair) treatment by the bureaucracy and the police. This group was several times as large as the corresponding groups in the other countries surveyed (the United States, Britain, Germany, and Italy). The authors regard this response as a function of culturally-determined attitudes on the part of their Mexican respondents. The present writer would regard this as partly the case, but believes it also reflects quite correct perceptions of reality.

13. Michael Maccoby (1967) found in his study of a Mexican village that only a minority (although a large one) show the *machista* syndrome, and only about thirty percent of his respondents could be called authoritarian personalities. Although he goes on to argue that Mexican character structure could support more democratic attitudes if society and government practices changed so as to warrant them, he does not discuss the possibility that authoritarian characteristics may be strengthened by urbanization.

14. A good example is "Los Problemas Mayores de Mexico y de Nuestro Tiempo," the platform adopted by the party's national convention in 1961.

15. The story of how the party's evolution came about is told in Padgett (1966, pp. 68-73).

BIBLIOGRAPHY

Almond, Gabriel and Sidney Verba

1965 *The Civic Culture,* (abridged edition) Boston: Little, Brown.

Brothers, Dwight S.

1966 "Mexico Economy: A New Stage," *Current History.*

Cline, Howard F.

Mexico: From Revolution to Evolution. New York: Oxford U. Press. 1962.

Cott, Kennett

"Trends in Mexican Migration," University of New Mexico.

Goldrich, Daniel

1965 "Toward a Comparative Study of Politicization," *In* Dwight B. Heath and Richard N. Adams, ed., *Contemporary Cultures and Societies of Latin America.* New York: Random House.

Gonzales Casanova, Pablo

1965 *La Democracia en Mexico,* Mexico: Ediciones Era.

Herrick, Bruce H.

1965 *Urban Migration and Economic Development in Chile.* Cambridge: Massachusetts Institute of Technology Press.

Hewes, Gordon

1954 "Mexicans in Search of 'the Mexican': Notes on Mexican National Character Studies," *American Journal of Economics and Sociology.*

Iturriaga, Jose E.

1951 *La Estructura Social y Cultural de Mexico.* Mexico: Fondo de Cultura Economica.

Leeds, Anthony

1967a "The Investment Climate in the *Favelas,*" talk at the University of New Mexico.

1967b Discussion in A.J. Field, ed., *Urbanization and Work in Modernizing Societies,* Detroit: Glengary Press.

Lewis, Oscar

1960 "Mexico Since Cardenas," *In* Richard N. Adams *et al.,* eds., *Social Change in Latin America Today.* New York: Harper, pp. 320-26.

Maccoby, Michael

1967 "On Mexican National Character," *The Annals.*

Moreno, Jose A.

1967 *Sociological Aspects of the Dominican Revolution,* Ithaca, New York: Cornell University Latin American Studies Program dissertation series.

Needler, Martin

1961 "The Political Development of Mexico," *American Political Science Review.*

Padgett, Vincent

1966 *The Political System of Mexico,* Boston: Houghton Mifflin.

Pan American Union, Department of Economic Affairs

1966 *Latin America: Problems and Perspectives of Economic Development, 1963-64,* Baltimore: John Hopkins University Press.

Patch, Richard

1961 "Life in a *Callejon:* A Study of Urban Disorganization," *American Universities Field Staff Reports.*

Scott, Robert E.

1965 *Mexican Government in Transition.* Urbana: University of Illinois Press (second edition).

Urquidi, Victor L.

1966 "Mexico's Economic Development Prospects and Population Growth," *Mexico This Month.*

ABOUT THE AUTHORS

Solon L. Barraclough is Professor of Agricultural Economics at Cornell University. At the time of the Conference, he was Project Manager with the Institute for Training and Research on Agrarian Reform, Santiago, Chile. He has directed a series of studies of land tenure conditions and socio-economic development of the agricultural sector in Argentina, Brazil, Chile, Colombia, Guatemala, Ecuador, and Peru, and co-authored (with A. L. Domike) several publications on these topics.

James M. Blaut is Professor of Geography at Clark University. He was founder and director of the Caribbean Research Institute, College of the Virgin Islands, and has taught both Geography and Cultural Anthropology and conducted research in Latin America and the Far East.

David Chaplin is Associate Professor of Sociology at the University of Wisconsin, and author of *The Peruvian Industrial Labor Force.*

Arthur L. Domike is currently with the Inter-American Development Bank. At the time of the Conference, he was Regional Colonization and Land Tenure Officer for Latin America, Food and Agriculture Organization, United Nations, Santiago, Chile. His teaching field is Agricultural Economics.

Arthur J. Field is Associate Professor of Sociology at Rensselaer Polytechnic Institute and Acting Research Director of R.P.I.'s Urban-Environmental Studies Program. In 1967, he edited *Urbanization and Work in Modernizing Societies.* His most recent book is *Urban Power Structures* (Cambridge: Schenkman, 1970).

Irving Louis Horowitz is Professor of Sociology at Rutgers University and Chairman of the Department at its Livingston College. He is also the Director of *Studies in Comparative International Development.* Dr. Horowitz is the author of numerous works on social change and social theory, among which are: *Latin American Radicalism* (Random House, 1969), *The Rise and Fall of Project Camelot* (M. I. T. Press, 1967), *Three Worlds of Development* (Oxford University Press, 1966), *Revolution in Brazil: Politics and Society in a Developing Nation* (E. P. Dutton, 1964). He has also contributed major papers to all leading journals in the area of development.

Gerrit Huizer, Doctorandus in Political and Social Sciences, University of Amsterdam, Netherlands, is International Labor Office Advisor for Latin America on Agrarian Problems. He is also the author of several articles on peasant organization and community development in Latin America and Southern Italy.

Anthony Leeds is Professor of Anthropology and Research Associate in the Institute of Latin American Studies, University of Texas. He has written extensively on Brazil and conducted field work with the Taruro Indians of Venezuela. He was chief of the Urban Development Program, Social Affairs Department, Pan American Union (1961-63), and is the editor of *Social Structure, Stratification, and Mobility*.

Elizabeth Leeds is doing graduate work in Political Science at the University of Texas, and has had extensive field work experience in the *favelas* of Rio de Janeiro.

Martin C. Needler is Associate Professor of Political Science and Director of the Division of Inter-American Affairs, University of New Mexico. Author and editor of several books on Latin American politics and American foreign policy, his latest book is *Political Development in Latin America: Instability, Violence, and Evolutionary Change,* (Random House, 1968).

Andrew C. Pearse, Fellow at St. Anthony's College, Oxford, is presently completing a book on the Latin American peasant. He has worked as sociologist and United Nations consultant in Brazil, Ecuador, Colombia, and Chile in recent years, and earlier at the University College of the West Indies.

Andrew Hunter Whiteford is George L. Collie Professor and Chairman of the Department of Anthropology, and Director of the Logan Museum of Anthropology, Beloit College. His most recent book is *Two Cities of Latin America: A Comparative Description of Social Classes.*

Conference participants also included:

C. J. Austermiller (Economics), Oakland Community College, Michigan

Stanford N. Gerber (Anthropology), Clark University

Richard Laskin (Sociology), Illinois Institute of Technology

Juarez R. B. Lopes (Sociology), University of Sao Paolo, Brazil

Robert Marans (Urban Planning), Survey Research Center, University of Michigan

Edward E. McClure (Urban and Regional Planning), Florida State University

Peter I. Rose (Sociology), Smith College

Howard Stanton (Sociology), University of Puerto Rico and Clark University

Franklin M. Zweig (Community Social Work), Dean, School of Social Work, State University of New York at Buffalo